D1497826

Agents of Change

Agents of Change

Crossing the
Post-Industrial Divide

CHARLES HECKSCHER, MICHAEL MACCOBY,
RAFAEL RAMIREZ, AND
PIERRE-ERIC TIXIER

OXFORD
UNIVERSITY PRESS

OXFORD
UNIVERSITY PRESS

Great Clarendon Street, Oxford OX2 6DP

Oxford University Press is a department of the University of Oxford.
It furthers the University's objective of excellence in research, scholarship,
and education by publishing worldwide in

Oxford New York

Auckland Bangkok Buenos Aires Cape Town Chennai
Dar es Salaam Delhi Hong Kong Istanbul Karachi Kolkata
Kuala Lumpur Madrid Melbourne Mexico City Mumbai Nairobi
São Paulo Shanghai Taipei Tokyo Toronto

Oxford is a registered trade mark of Oxford University Press
in the UK and in certain other countries

Published in the United States
by Oxford University Press Inc., New York

© Oxford University Press, 2003

The moral rights of the authors have been asserted
Database right Oxford University Press (maker)

First published 2003

British Library Cataloguing in Publication Data

Data available

Library of Congress Cataloging in Publication Data

Agents of change : crossing the post-industrial divide / by Charles
Heckscher . . . [et al.].
    p. cm.
    Includes bibliographical references.
    1. Organizational change.   2. Pressure groups.   3. Industrial relations.
    4. Organizational change—Case studies.   1. Heckscher, Charles C., 1949–
    HD58.8 .W6775 2003   658.4'06–dc21   2002035589
ISBN 0-19-926174-1 (hbk.)
ISBN 0-19-926175-X (pbk.)

1 3 5 7 9 10 8 6 4 2

Typeset by Newgen Imaging Systems (P) Ltd., Chennai, India
Printed in Great Britain
on acid-free paper by
Biddles Ltd., Guildford & King's Lynn

CONTENTS

ACKNOWLEDGMENTS

The authors gratefully acknowledge the very generous contributions of many friends and colleagues, both to the original stories and to this reflection on them. The four authors are equally responsible for the final text.

In particular we would like to thank Paolo Celentani, Richard Normann, Pietro Spirito, Ralph Craviso, Lorraine Fauconnier, John Petrillo, Morty Bahr, Paul Adler, Lavinia Hall, Hal Burlingame, and Wally Olins for their comments on drafts of this manuscript. Maria Stroffolino provided invaluable support throughout.

LIST OF FIGURES

INTRODUCTION

1

INTRODUCTION

1

Introduction

In the last 30 years the established system of industrial democracy and stakeholder representation has been disrupted throughout the industrialized world. The roles of unions and of government regulation, central to the post-Second World War order, have everywhere been weakened or have come under attack, as management presses the need for flexiblility to confront increased market turbulence.

Though some, now, argue that there is simply no longer a need for outside stakeholders or regulation, this pure market view has not advanced very far in practice. In real life economic actors have become not less but more interdependent and reliant on relationships of trust and cooperation. Companies rely ever more on allies and partners outside their walls, and they need increasingly to "co-produce" with others.[1] In real life new market conditions lead even "free-market" CEOs to seek government protection; indeed, the growth of international trade has given government a renewed role in setting the conditions for market definition. Despite conservative ideology and the delegitimation of state regulation, governments have continued to grow. Though managers may dream of unfettered flexibility, in real life they face increasingly assertive internal stakeholders as they struggle to maintain the commitment and involvement of their knowledge employees; and they encounter every day emboldened new external pressure groups. At the international level free-market policies, far from spreading triumphantly, have encountered violent protests and growing resistance.

Such developments suggest that, although the familiar structures of unions, governments, and business may need changing, *some* form of organized stakeholder relations is needed to bring together differing values and to avoid a spiral into disorder. The real problem is the need for stakeholders to work better together, and for the stakeholder system as a whole to be better structured to encourage change and flexibility as well as justice and human values.

Over the last 25 years the four authors have been consultants in many conflictual situations in companies emerging from semi-monopolistic national status and struggling to deal with global competitiveness. This book is a reflection on those experiences and on intervention in general. Our work, as we have come to understand it over time, has essentially been about trying to ease the transition from industrial to post-industrial systems: first, by helping the stakeholders of the old order understand the passage and to work through it in as peaceful a manner as possible; and second, by helping them to develop the new capacities needed for operating in an economy dominated increasingly by knowledge and services.[2]

We have learned through practice about both the potential and the limits of cooperative change. We have concluded, in comparing our experiences on both sides of the Atlantic, that the basic shift toward greater competitiveness is creating similarly intense turbulence throughout the industrialized world; that a great deal can be done to help unions and companies, as well as other stakeholders, work through the change process together; but that in the end a more fundamental reconstruction of the system of stakeholder relations may be needed to achieve stability.

Four cases in which we have been particularly deeply involved will form the basis of our reflections: the telecommunications giants AT&T and Lucent in the US; EDF, France's former electricity monopoly; and Ferrovie dello Stato, the Italian state railway. All of these have gone through highly tumultuous transitions, none of which is yet complete. Though in one sense they represent a narrow economic sector—infra-structural monopoly companies with strong ties to the State, thrown into the fray of the open market—their experience is also *typical* of the industrial economies as a whole: in country after country, and industry after industry, stable nation-based oligopolies have been broken apart by the forces of globalization and technological change. The story of telecommunications or railways is not fundamentally different from that of automobiles or steel.

Our record has successes and limits. We have had considerable success in building more trust in the labor–management relation and in helping the parties discover ways to adapt together in difficult economic transitions. We contributed to understanding how to bring together independent stakeholders in a genuine dialogue. We have created new forums, turned conflictual discussions toward problem-definition and problem-solving, developed shared understanding of business strategy, catalyzed emotional discussions of values and ideals, helped unions and other groups with their internal planning and development, and initiated "mutual gains" analyses of fundamental interests. Along the way we have learned a good deal about the power and the limitations of these techniques.

Yet we have gradually become aware of a deeper issue: every agreement we have helped to build has been challenged and undermined by the continuing and relentless pressure of an economic transformation whose scope we are still only beginning to grasp. And as this pressure has grown in our own interventions and on the wider scene, economic values have come more and more frequently to dominate human ones. Sometimes, as in the case of AT&T described below, the relationship has finally deteriorated into near-warfare.

In the end, the old framework of stakeholder dialogue, even in its best forms, has proved no longer adequate to the social challenges. Thus we have a new problem: not to improve the dialogue but to create new ones; not to build trust among already-defined actors, but to build a new framework to bring in actors who have not been effectively included in the past.

ACTION AND ANALYSIS

Our focus on action—what to *do* about change—is somewhat unusual for scholars grounded in traditional disciplines. Social science has always been uncomfortable in making the passage to action. The classical view, carried into modern sociology by Max Weber, is that scientists should be detached and objective, above the battle. Activism from this perspective distorts science by injecting motives other than the pure desire for truth. Scientists might venture to suggest what others should do—deducing the suggestions from their analysis; they shy away from thinking about what *they* might do.[3]

The separation between the two realms, however, creates problems for both. First, social analysis does not help as much as it should in planning actions, because one cannot move directly from analysis of a system to recommendations for action. This is mainly because the objects of the analysis—human beings—also act. Physical objects do not develop personal feelings toward the scientists studying them, or at least do not let it affect how they respond; but consultants constantly find that their own relation to their clients and other stakeholders determines the consequences of their advice. There is no such thing as "right" analysis if, as often happens, the client does not want to hear it.[4]

Social scientists regularly commit the elementary error of assuming that analysis can pass directly to action, and those who follow their advice suffer for it. Many studies have shown, for example, that participative work systems produce statistically significant improvements in productivity. But even if that relation is true scientifically, it often *becomes* untrue in action: if the person trying to *implement* this proposal is viewed with suspicion by middle management fearful of losing their power, or by unions concerned about management manipulation, the idea can lead to open or covert resistance—and all the studies suddenly mean nothing.[5]

The ability to act, in other words, does not depend solely on the ability to understand the system on which one acts; it also depends on the ability to *connect* with actors in the system and to interact with them in a positive way. That complicated alchemy of knowledge, technique, empathy, distance, and patience is the focus of Chapters 7–9.

The second problem with the separation of action from knowledge in the social sciences is that one of the best ways to gain knowledge is to try to change things. Those who study societies are hampered by serious obstacles: patterns are seldom repeated; they cannot do controlled experiments; human beings continually insist on acting in unexpected and unprecedented ways; and at the level of nations or large systems there are usually too few cases to be able to draw sound conclusions.

So it is for many purposes impossible to apply objective methods or statistical tests of truth. Social scientists since Weber have therefore found it necessary to apply *Verstehen*—"understanding," their own human ability to *make sense* of social situations—as a way of getting at "truth." We extend this proposition to suggest that the best way to make sense of social situations is often not to watch them but to act in them, and then reflect on our experiences.[6]

In the case of the issues we focus on here, there have been many efforts to understand the evolution of corporate strategy, organization, and relations to stakeholders. Observation of past and present cases tells a very ambiguous story: efforts to generate new levels of value from the organization of knowledge, or to effectively mobilize employees across levels and divisions, are promising but have run into consistent problems. By reflecting on our interventions we can see these limits, as it were, dynamically. It is not just a matter of theorizing that something should be done: because we have actually *tried* doing many things, we can see directly what works and what does not, and we can sketch the shape and power of the resistances.

Thus many authors have suggested that unions and managements should engage in mutual-gains problem-solving; we can say that we have tried it, and we have seen both what it can accomplish and some of the repeated obstacles. Others have said that worker participation is key; we have tried that and found that it meets some but not all the needs. Some have suggested forms of "co-determination"—direct union or stakeholder involvement in operational planning beyond the usual level of collective bargaining; again, we have tried it and found it only gets part way to a stabilization of relations. Finally, some have suggested thorough strategic partnerships; here our efforts are more preliminary and the assessment more tentative, but we have experienced the problems.

If scientists can learn from action, it is of course also true that activists must learn from science. Lacking rigorous attention to evidence, prior research, and existing theories, most consultant accounts of change fall victim to subjectivism, special pleading, defensiveness, and overgeneralization. We attempt here to find the narrow path through these dangers lying between the two realms by examining experience with an analytic eye.[7]

Our experience base as data

Our experiences are the evidence on which this book is built. It is therefore worth reviewing their scope and limitations. For the most part we four have worked separately and developed our approaches independently, on different projects on both sides of the Atlantic, even in different languages, coming together only since 1995. Two of the authors are American.

(1) Charles Heckscher started with a degree in sociology and an interest in industrial democracy. His first job was with the Communications Workers

of America, a union that will figure heavily in these pages. He then taught Human Resources Management at the Harvard Business School, followed by a move to the Labor Studies Department at Rutgers University. He has written about the future of unions, the changing forms of corporate organization, and the emergent role of middle management. His consulting work has centered on mutual-gains negotiation and organizational development in many industries and unions; AT&T, Lucent, and the Communications Workers have been his longest-running clients.

(2) Michael Maccoby trained as a psychoanalyst with Erich Fromm after receiving a BA and PhD at Harvard in social relations; together they developed the concept of "social character" and conducted an anthropologically-oriented study of a Mexican village. He carried on this work with managers; *The Gamesman*, published in 1977, generated great interest among companies who wanted to understand the changing demands on management. From 1978–90 he directed a program on work and technology at Harvard's Kennedy School of Government. He began an engagement with AT&T in 1977 which lasted until 2000; he also worked for many other companies and unions in the US, Canada and in Europe, guiding strategic planning processes and efforts at improving relationships. His research has continued to explore the development of social character and leadership in the new economy.

The other two authors are French nationals who have worked primarily in Europe.

(3) Rafael Ramirez has lived in 5 countries (Mexico, Canada, the US, the UK, and France). He holds degrees in geography and environmental studies, for which he studied with Eric Trist and Gareth Morgan, and a doctorate in Social Systems Science from Wharton. After suffering an industrial accident in 1976 he focused these trans-disciplinary interests on organization design. The relations between organization and value creation became the central theme of his work in 1985, when he joined SMG, a Swedish research and consulting firm. He has consulted with public and private organizations in over 20 countries, and is Professor of Management at HEC, one of France's leading business schools.

(4) Pierre-Eric Tixier was trained as a lawyer before moving into sociology.[8] He worked first on self-management and conducted his first major research project on and with the CFDT union. For the last 10 years he has been a professor at the Institut d'Etudes Politiques de Paris (Sciences-Po) and director of a research group. He began consulting to EDF in 1989. His current work focuses on the way in which European countries, especially France, are dealing with the pressures of globalization. He has written on industrial relations, on companies' responses to globalization, on the human effects of corporate restructuring, and on the move from monopoly to competition among public enterprises.

Though we have worked on many interventions, the four that we will use as the primary basis for our reflections are ones that have lasted a long time and gone through many permutations.

- Maccoby's work at AT&T, beginning in 1977 on management strategy, moving to workplace restructuring and worker participation, and finally to an effort to involve unions in operational planning for the business.
- Ramirez' involvement in an effort to redefine the strategic direction of Ferrovie dello Stato—the Italian State Railroad.
- Heckscher's efforts to facilitate strategic dialogue between unions and management at Lucent Technologies.
- Tixier's engagement with EDF, the French electric monopoly, and its unions as they struggled to deal with the pressures of opening markets.

Systematic reflection on experience: the learning network

The use of experience as a source of data is full of dangers because it is difficult to get an objective check on perception. In these cases, where we have also been active agents, there is a particularly high danger of distortion from a desire to look good or to avoid angering clients. On the other hand, it is hard to imagine a better way to get information about the "real" dynamics of the intervention process. Standard social science methods of surveys and interviews have crucial limitations: they lack "privileged access" based on trusted relationships; they usually focus on a narrow time slice in what is a very long process; they cannot ordinarily get at the "micro-dynamics" of meetings and conversations. In an ideal world one could conceive of a method that would combine reflection by the interveners with interviews by an independent team. The complexity and scope of such an undertaking, however, would be so massive that we decided to take another avenue: to reflect systematically on our experience in order to maximize its power.

Thus we have explored our experiences through a long process of discussion among the four authors and beyond. In the mid 1990s, all of us separately began to think about the accelerating forces of deregulation, internationalization, and restructuring and how they affected our work. Although we had interacted in various combinations over the years, our conversations in that period took a more reflective turn. In 1995–96 we held two meetings of about a dozen consultants with similar experiences. This diverse group agreed on two points. First, we saw a need to take a broad and complex approach to intervention; we saw weaknesses in the traditional consulting approaches linked to firms like McKinsey or Accenture, which often center on offering technical solutions and tend to underplay the longer-term structural bases of relations among and within organizations. Second, we shared a sense of increasing frustration and difficulty in our work: as we said in a 1996 memo, "participative and joint efforts keep running into the same obstacles and remain marginal to the overall organizational trend."

Over the course of the next 6 years the four authors crystallized as a working group, meeting at least twice a year on different sides of the Atlantic. We spent a great deal of time getting to know each other's work and way of framing interventions. We began by writing detailed descriptions of major cases we had worked on, which we then analyzed and critiqued in detail. We interviewed each others' clients to deepen our understanding of each other's work, and to provide some independent check on the perceptions of the intervener himself.[9] Through this process we began to develop some frameworks that we tested against the data in the different interventions, by discussing them with each other and with the client organizations. We tried to do better than the common way of using experiential data, which is to think of a proposition and find a story to illustrate it; instead we checked our ideas systematically against the four cases, as well as any other trustworthy knowledge we could find, to make sure they held up beyond a single story.

In our discussions we found substantial differences in approach, but also important similarities: all of us had come to see the importance of combining many dimensions of strategy and relationships into a coherent approach in order to even have a hope of meeting the challenges of the current transformation. Each of us added particular skills—psychoanalytic training, sociological theory, and strategic analysis—to this increasingly complex mix. In the end we wrote the bulk of the book, aside from the case studies, in a joint manner, circulating partial drafts, critiquing, and gradually putting together a collective product. This "8 hands writing" effort is rare in itself—there are few books indeed in which 4 authors have managed to write as one, sorting out all of the disagreements not by reaching a least common denominator, but through listening to the rationale of different, initially unreconciled, points of view, and convincing each other of a view we can in the end all adhere to.

Over this long process we broadened and changed our focus. What had begun as a study of intervention in labor–management relations in deregulating monopolies expanded to the problem of the transition from monopolies employing an industrial mode of production to international competitive markets in the knowledge-solutions age. Finally we recognized that the interventions we had done so far were only the beginning of a road that we could dimly see, involving the transformation of an entire stakeholder system grounded in law and practice throughout the world. The increasing pressure of this enormous shift accounts for the frustration, felt by ourselves and the rest of our colleagues, about the fact that nothing we do seems to obtain a stable end-point—agreements and restructurings keep coming unraveled, and every step of progress soon seems insufficient.

We all started from different points: helping with union–management relations, or with worker participation efforts, or with strategic reorientations. We have converged on the notion that at the core of all of these is the *reconstruction of systems of relationships*. Each of the organizations we have worked with is facing changes so massive that they cannot be dealt with by simply "implementing" previously designed plans through existing functions and roles; they need to reconfigure. That means that each part—both internal, management levels and functions within management, and stakeholder groups like unions or environmental activists—has to establish a position anew in a system of dynamic relations.

CORE LEARNINGS

The argument as finally developed in this book consists of two rather different reflections: on the methods we have used as interveners, and on our emerging understanding of the essential problem that we face.

A "full engagement" approach to relational interventions

Our "activism," in retrospect, is centrally about helping different stakeholders work together through difficult changes in as constructive and discursive a manner as possible. How does one do this? Our experience is that it is a long and complex process, in which the intervener's role is often hard to define. Most consultants take a quicker route, offering expert analysis and packaged solutions; but that, in our experience, tends only to lock in defenses and established patterns. Major changes in relationships, by contrast, require an approach that works through deep patterns of identity at all levels of organizations and across traditional barriers—an approach of *full engagement* with many players in many dimensions.

Such an intervention is first of all not expert but *interactive*. It focuses on building dialogue among groups that normally remain separate or relate in purely formal ways. The union–management connection is one important one; other important interactions are also put under strain—between top management and middle management; between business leadership and "people functions" like Human Resources and Labor Relations; between national union leaders and their locals and members. Though we understand the value of conflict, we seek to work through that conflict by helping the parties understand each other rather than merely threatening fearsome consequences.

Interactivity also requires that the consultants themselves engage the parties and win credibility and influence. In order to do this they must avoid being "slotted" into defined roles as experts on some topic, serving particular organizational leaders. Whatever effectiveness interveners of this type have comes from the fact that they stand outside existing relationships, not beholden to any one party, and not fitting into a predefined function. This frees them up to cross-organizational lines and also to move through time—to bring back the past, or take thinking into the future, with greater ease than the system's stakeholders often can.

Full engagement is, second, *systemic*, in the sense that it seeks to touch every aspect of systems of relationships—from corporate strategy to operations to blue-collar work identities, from management to unions to the shifting and indistinct array of other claimants on company resources. Ramirez, starting as a strategy consultant to top management, found that insufficient focus on the operational and stakeholder environment severely limited what the project could achieve; the other three of us, when addressing problems of union–management or worker–management relations, found that ignoring rapid changes in the strategic landscape was equally dangerous. We all converged, therefore, on an approach that combines strategic and relational logics. An important conclusion is that it is no longer possible to separate analysis and prescription, on the one hand, from implementation and revision, on the other.

Finally, full engagement deals not only with rational interests, but with deep emotional patterns often traceable to events long past. This is the realm of *socio-dynamics*, where the effort of individuals and groups to maintain their identities and sense of pride can be as important as their current interests—and much harder to deal with. If these aspects are swept under the rug by purely analytic processes, they reappear as resistances and manipulations that obstruct change. One aspect of intervention, therefore, is to ensure that the actors' sense of identity is respected and that they feel they have a place in the visions of the future.

Our approach to intervention thus stands in contrast to purely cognitive and analytic approaches to consultancy. Though we are often hired as experts, we quickly disavow the role. What we bring is largely two simple abilities, which can only be provided by someone standing "outside" the system: the ability to make new connections among actors and to encourage understanding and systematic reflection. This approach creates particular problems in the role of the interveners as they try to position themselves to be trusted by many parties but taking the side of none. We explore the dynamics of this role and the elements of the intervention process in Chapters 7–9.

The development of "post-industrial relations"

We began by trying to change aspects of the large companies with which we worked—more participation, improved strategy, and deeper cooperation. Over time, however, we have come to see that the challenges they face require not incremental improvements but a fundamentally new system of stakeholder relations and involvement to replace one which is in decline. We reached this point because narrower definitions of the problem have not *worked*. Time after time plans and agreements achieved with great difficulty have been swept away by unexpected pressures—managers with new strategic missions, governments changing the regulatory framework, competitors moving in on formerly safe markets. We began to feel collectively that the problem we were facing was larger than it appeared—that the resolution to the growing challenges is not just a matter of improving the relation between these immediate actors, but might involve a larger reconfiguration.

The familiar system of collective bargaining and government regulation is one particular solution to the stabilization of economic relations. It grew out of periods of bitter and often violent conflicts which took somewhat different forms in different countries over the last century and a half—though the broad outlines of the system turned out to be surprisingly consistent. It is characterized by relatively centralized bargaining, strongly rule-based contracts, public policies aimed at stabilizing employment, and strong corporate communities providing long-term security in exchange for loyalty. We see this system as one particular "stakeholder regime"—a crystallization of fluid forces and movements into a stable web of relations with rules accepted by all the parties.

What is happening now is the dissolution of the existing stakeholder regime under the pressures of new actors and economic forces. The familiar pattern of periodic negotiations among large organizations is losing favor everywhere as economies move toward a focus on knowledge and complex services, requiring a high level of "co-production" among many actors rather than vertically-integrated mass production. So the intervention problem shifts from how to shore up and stabilize an existing regime, to how to catalyze the transition to a new set of relations.

Clearly this involves more than working with management or with the union–management connection within a single firm, however large. To make a difference, interveners would need (in the long run) to take up three tasks. One is to help "old" stakeholders like corporations, unions, and government agencies to examine the changes under way and to rethink their place in the emerging system. A second may be to help "new" stakeholders—associations that do not have a stable place in the neo-corporatist order—to define themselves and develop the organizational strength to become a part of the larger dialogue. The third may be to try to design new mechanisms for working out the conflicts among these groups—something beyond the existing mechanisms of collective bargaining and government regulation. The authors have in different ways been exploring such frontiers; the book concludes in Chapter 12 with reflection on this work and possible directions for the future. Here it is system governance, rather than bi-lateral agreements, which is the focus.

The core question of this book, bringing together the two themes, is: Can we (as consultants) help with a transition to an effective form of stakeholder relations for the current economy, reducing the mistrust which otherwise threatens to disrupt the change process? Our hope is modest: that we can contribute to making this deep shift in relationships somewhat less conflictual, somewhat less painful, somewhat more orderly than it would otherwise have been. The development of new forms of relations with stakeholders is necessarily a matter of conflict, as various actors fight to get into the game. The aspiration is, however, that the process can be smoothed a bit through deliberate collective learning and reflection, and through dialogues that prevent conflicts from spinning into self-sustaining destructive spirals.

In the end the lessons are twofold. Our experience shows that it is possible to make a difference in stakeholder relations, helping to increase trust and the ability to manage differences through dialogue. On the other hand, the efforts so far have only begun to explore the borders of a large-scale social change whose size and scope have yet to be mapped in detail.

2

Overview of the Cases

The four cases that ground our analysis differ greatly from each other in many respects. To help in navigating these complex stories, this chapter provides a rough "map" of the relations among them.

(1) At AT&T, Michael Maccoby began working with management in 1977, and soon after with its principal union. At that time, AT&T was the largest company in the world with one million employees. The initial effort was to focus management on the demands of business customers. Then, he was asked to develop worker participation in decision-making on the job. After that had progressed quite far, with thousands of teams operating around the country, the company was split up in the initial divestiture of 1984. After some years of turbulence and confusion Maccoby helped to catalyze an ambitious attempt to move union involvement beyond the shopfloor level to engagement in business unit planning. Groundbreaking progress was made in several business units. But then in the 1990s there were further divestitures, a new CEO from outside the Bell family, and a shift in strategy away from basic phone service toward high-technology cable and wireless transmissions. In this move the management became more resistant to the union and the joint efforts went into deep freeze.

(2) Ferrovie dello Stato (FS)—the Italian Railroad—took the first step toward deregulation when it was severed from the Ministry of Transportation in the early 1990s. Normann and Ramirez were brought in to help transform what had been part of a ministry into a business. They attempted to define a business logic that would enable FS to deal with radically new challenges. Efforts were undertaken to rethink the business logic, to implement a new logic organizationally and inter-organizationally, and to share this understanding with key stakeholders. The redefinition of the business ran into many conflicting pressures from multiple stakeholders: regulators, suppliers, employees, unions, NGOs, competitors, customers, and multiple arms of government. In the short run these resistances from both inside and outside the organization grounded the effort; in the longer run the business logic identified by the consultants has continued to develop.

(3) Lucent was spun off from AT&T in 1995. Initially the unions and management simply wanted to continue and develop the joint efforts from AT&T.
But when the company, in a dramatically changing marketplace, decided to
outsource its manufacturing work, it put into question the very foundations
of the relationship. The parties entered into a process of strategic dialogue
with an almost unprecedented level of union involvement in decision-
making about sales and divestitures, in order to preserve the company's
strategic flexibility while also addressing the security needs of the unions
and their members. The process was partially successful but was continuously undermined by the growing troubles of the company as well as by the
traditional regulatory approach of the government's labor relations agency.

(4) EDF, the French state-owned electricity company that is today the world's
biggest electrical utility firm, was created in 1946 as a result of the postwar
market by uniting approximately 2000 independent producers. This enterprise is currently experiencing a major transition from monopoly to market
and is entering the international stage through acquisitions, notably of
London Electricity in the UK and Montedison in Italy. Its objective is to
become the largest operator on the world scale; with that intent it aims to
get 50 percent of its revenues from abroad by 2005. These major changes
have been accompanied by strong internal tensions. It has taken 10 years to
persuade managers and unions to sit around a single table to develop a
new system of industrial relations. The CGT, the most powerful union, historically communist, was particularly resistant. But can these efforts continue in the face of increasing market pressure? Tixier's role has been to
help managers understand the effects of their policies toward workers and
unions and to help with the negotiation of social agreements. More
recently he has played a role in the development of corporate strategy.

One distinction in particular stands out. Three of these—EDF, AT&T, and
Lucent—were initially *relational* interventions: we were first brought in primarily to improve union–management or worker–management relations. The
fourth, Ferrovie dello Stato, was by contrast a deliberately *strategic* intervention:
the consultants were asked by a new leader to help him reconceptualize the railroad in its move from public toward private enterprise. Normann and Ramirez
focused on analysis, including writing a book with their client on the future of
Italy; the others focused on building trust and understanding among managers,
employees, and their union representatives.

The four cases come together, however, because, as we gradually realized, they
all require both of these dimensions. All of the organizations in these cases
faced—and continue to face today—enormous strategic challenges: they were
having to fundamentally redefine themselves as they moved from quasi-monopoly
to more competitive environments. In the course of that redefinition they put
into question agreements and social contracts—implicit and explicit—that had
been in place for generations. The Ferrovie dello Stato case faced the strategic

challenge head on but came later to a realization that not fully involving *internal* stakeholders earlier was a costly choice, while the other three began with the problem of internal discord and only gradually began to recognize that they failed to fully and sufficiently deeply address the scope of the strategic shift that was involved. All four ran into obstacles (explored in detail in Chapter 10): the strategic intervention was largely thwarted by internal resistances and "politics" that were not directly addressed by the consultants; while the other cases ran into barriers as the strategic challenges to the organizations grew and put continual strain on the internal relations on which they were focused.

THE STRATEGIC PROBLEMS

All our cases involve large companies with unions that until the 1980s enjoyed relatively protected market positions. This picture characterized most of the industrial sector of the economy after the Second World War throughout Europe and the US, and was particularly evident in "public utility" activities, as in our four cases. It was undermined by the familiar forces of global competition and technological change.

The core strategic problems have been remarkably similar, at least at a high level of abstraction, across the cases and beyond to much of the industrial economy. The issue for all of them is how to face increasingly competitive, more international, markets by becoming more responsive to customers and more disciplined about costs in light of tighter fiscal policy, enhanced transparency, and demand for greater accountability.

There are of course some important distinctions. In the US, the pressure for liberalization on the whole began earlier than in Europe, and the decline in political support for government intervention was sharper than in either France or Italy. Further increasing the pressure on the US companies was the fact that telecommunications underwent a technological revolution earlier and more broadly (with the advent of the microprocessor) than electric production and distribution or rail transport.

AT&T and EDF started their move toward competitiveness rather gradually, pushed by government and competition but well-shielded by past market power, and therefore taking years to make the shift. Ferrovie's external challenge was a move from being a Ministry to a legally private-sector, but still state-owned, firm. In these three cases the initial impetus for change was muted enough that, despite the concerns of top leadership, there was little sense of urgency in the middle and worker levels of the organizations. The AT&T case has run long enough to experience a severe rise in the level of "crisis"—and the resulting turmoil has put into question the work that had gone before. Lucent is distinct in that it was thrown straight into a maelstrom, an industry among the most turbulent and unpredictable in the world. It found itself very quickly in a fight for survival.

The two American firms, AT&T and Lucent, moved rather rapidly toward reducing their scope and "focusing" on a core business of providing complex services and solutions, rather than manufacturing goods. Though some of the Normann–Ramirez proposals went in this "American" direction, the two European firms in practice stayed much closer to a model of vertical integration, which is less disruptive to internal and external stakeholders. EDF has even gone on a buying spree with the intention of becoming the largest producer of electricity in the world.

But for the purposes of this book the distinctions among the strategic trajectories is less central than those among the relational interventions.

THE RELATIONAL CHALLENGES

The presenting problem in three of the cases was around union–management relations. We gradually came to see the problem, however, in terms of a wider array of stakeholder relations—including the difficulties of developing relations between top and middle management, between national and local unions, between companies and their customers. Increasingly other stakeholders, such as environmentalists and consumer groups, have begun to force their way onto the scene and to demand some of the attention formerly focused exclusively on unions.

Our experience has spanned four very different types of relational challenges, though often in complex combinations as follows.

Institutional cooperation: improving relations among stakeholder organizations

One task we have worked on involves a move by unions and managements from a divided, adversarial game to one where the parties see themselves as interdependent and needing to solve problems by discussion.

There have always been instances of cooperative labor–management relations. In the US, in fact, after labor largely gave up the idea of social revolution early in the century, most labor leaders have been eager to establish stable and cooperative relations; it has been management that has been more often resistant. In France the situation is different because some unions—particularly the CGT—have continued to oppose the idea of capitalism and to hope that it could be overthrown. The CGT, as we see in the EDF case, refused to sign contracts until 1999 because it did not recognize the legitimacy of the overall legal and economic framework. (The Italian situation is more varied and decentralized than either of the others.)

The backgrounds of our cases are shaped by these forces. The Communications Workers' union at AT&T has always seen its success as closely tied to that of the business. Its leaders have consistently supported technological innovation and sought positive relationships with management. This has not always been reciprocated: management has consistently sought to prevent the union's spread into any unorganized sectors, and it has frequently shown hostility. At EDF the hostility was more mutual. While the CFDT's attitude is relatively close to that of the American CWA, the CGT continued its policy of refusing to engage in dialogue or cooperation with management. The company, conversely, pursued a policy of trying to weaken and destabilize the CGT.

In both cases, therefore, a first step of the intervention was to establish the fact that the parties were inescapably interdependent. Then the challenge became to build enough trust that the parties could solve problems together. This involved discussions in which the parties came to understand each others' interests more deeply and problem-solving efforts where they tried to find solutions that they could both live with. At EDF the centerpiece of the intervention was the attempt to find a negotiated compromise around job creation and employment security, exchanged against flexibility of hours of work. At AT&T the issues of security and involvement were the core of most of the discussions in the business units and worksites. At FS a significant downsizing was worked out through the use of a government-financed early retirement plan. This, however, was kept separate from the strategy redefinition mandate of the consultants.

A great deal of the intervener role on this dimension is one of plus-sum or "win–win" mediation, broadly conceived. Like all mediation, this involves helping the parties determine what needs are realistic; but unlike traditional mediation, it also involves encouraging them to think of new ways to meet their basic interests. This can lead, as it has in the EDF case, to substantial work with the parties independently to help them reach an accurate diagnosis of the situation and to explore alternatives to their familiar demands.

Shopfloor involvement and organizational change

A second intervention problem we have faced involves "opening up" shopfloor decision-making to parties that have not had a direct role before—especially to union members through direct participation in shopfloor teams, and also to frontline supervisors and other managers. This requires managers and unions to take first steps toward understanding each others' issues, as workers begin to take responsibility for productivity and quality and managers involve workers in discussions about the quality of working life. The key issue is for the most part how to achieve both sets of goals by "working smarter, not harder."

The attempt to involve workers directly in decision-making is related to the leadership discussions, but it has its own dynamics. It is quite possible to build leadership cooperation without significant shopfloor involvement; this was common at least until the 1950s. The EDF case, whose core is the attempt to respond to deregulation, is mostly focused on leadership rather than the shopfloor dimension.

At AT&T the change process started largely from the bottom and preceded the deregulation of the industry. The initial driver was a series of protests by operators caused by extreme Taylorism combined with computerization; these led the union to demand ways of reducing job pressures. This in turn led in 1980 to the creation of jointly-sponsored workforce discussion groups seeking ways to improve the job environment.

This modest-seeming reform turned out to be surprisingly difficult for both management and unions. The task of the intervener was not merely to find an acceptable compromise by which the parties could live together, but to help both parties reconceive who they were: to help management see that it could lead without directing in a bureaucratic manner; to help the union see that it could encourage member involvement on the job without weakening its ability to fight when necessary.

Stakeholder dialogue about operational policies

A third type of intervention moves to the level of operational systems—the "middle level" of management processes between the shopfloor and the strategic, aiming at making the existing business work better. On the union side the key challenge is to get unions (and other stakeholders) to accept responsibility for the effectiveness of the company; the problem may be symbolized by the struggle over the word "productivity," which for many unions is a dirty word but which becomes a shared objective when operations are treated as part of the partnership. On the management side the tradeoff is taking on responsibility for maximizing employment security.

Much of the consultants' approach in FS was directed at trying to engage line managers to identify with, adapt, and adopt the strategic vision that the top management had derived with the help of the strategy team and the consultants. At AT&T the notion of higher-level dialogue between the unions and management did not develop until the 1992 contract. Again the problems were large: the union had to come to terms with participating as a partner, rather than an adversary, in discussions about potential layoffs and other workplace disruptions; and management had to accept the risk of opening up information and plans far earlier than they were used to. A new layer of management leaders was brought into the process and had to go through the same painful redefinition of their roles as had the front-line supervisors in the QWL effort. Both sides had to gain considerably more understanding of the other's needs and interests.

Strategic dialogue: the end of the line?

The most difficult and unresolved type of intervention we have experienced involves rebuilding relationships in a context of strategic turmoil—in particular, helping to think through how a relation could work in a world requiring radically more flexibility and speed than in the past.

This type brings together the two dimensions of our work which otherwise have remained separate. The FS intervention focused on the strategic issues from the start, and only later began to work with stakeholders outside top management.[1] It came to a premature end in part because political forces, internal and external, conspired against it. AT&T started with a focus on stakeholder relations, but progress made in that arena has been largely undermined by strategic shifts.

The question is whether an intervention can bring independent stakeholders together for discussion of the strategic direction of the company, rather than having stakeholders react after that direction is set. This is the effort currently under way at EDF and Lucent, though neither has gone far enough yet to assess its ultimate prospects.

The concern is that the fundamental challenges faced by these companies may make collaboration impossible within the traditional framework. The privatization of the state-owned power sector and the reconfiguration of the telecommunications industry are so rapid and deep that there is no "deal" to be had without reworking long-held traditions of the labor movement—and, in all likelihood, managerial decision-making practices as well.

In the cases that follow the consulting role has included strategic *analysis*— that is, helping the parties on each side think through their own strategies and fundamental orientations and the consequences of their choices. Ferrovie started with such an intervention, and the other three moved more and more toward including it. Both approaches however remain a step short of a more fully participatory strategic *dialogue*, in which different internal as well as stakeholders would actually discuss and negotiate these fundamental orientations.

The cases do not show—yet?—that strategic dialogue is possible and productive, but they certainly show it is called for. They show a great deal of struggle and confusion and experimentation that has not yet been resolved into a unifying, normative, and replicable approach. They bring out dramatically how fundamental the challenge is, especially to the traditions and structures of unions. As we discuss at length in Chapter 10, they raise in the end the question of whether these stakeholders, organized as they are today, can work out their differences through dialogue, or whether the strategic shift is so great that it will require a period of turmoil and reconstruction.

INTERVENTION TRAJECTORIES

These four categories of intervention are not meant to mark out a single path along which organizations must travel. The movement is not a linear one from one type to another, but has rather been a gradual "complexification," adding more and more elements, as we and our clients gradually became more aware of the scope of the changes we were facing. There is nothing so simple as a sequence from institutional to participatory or vice-versa: the various types emerged in different orders. Nor do they move from relational *to* strategic: rather, they have moved toward a synthesis of the two, starting from opposite ends of the spectrum. The essential trajectory seems to be one that, starting from various different places, converges toward a model that *combines* all four of the intervention levels, and combines both relational and strategic logics.

The first three of the types above—institutional cooperation, worker involvement, and operational dialogue—represent complementary efforts to manage increasingly rapid change. The establishment of a cooperative relationship at the leadership level is often a first step, but it is not a matter of "solving" this problem once and moving on: rather, the problem of sustaining collaboration keeps popping up in new forms as more complex problems develop. The first part of the French (EDF) case concerns moving management away from a deliberate strategy of avoiding and undermining the CGT, and the CGT from its tradition of refusing to recognize the legitimacy of employers. In the AT&T and Lucent cases the hostility was less overt and ideologically fixed, but still needed to be confronted strongly at the start. It also kept reappearing every time a new crisis developed.

The second type, focused on worker participation, was the core of the initial AT&T intervention during the 1980s. Involving workers directly in problem-solving turned out to be a separate, and equally difficult problem, from the initial improvement of leadership relations. But this was not the end of the story: shopfloor involvement then led further, to a perceived need to get a deeper agreement on the direction of a fast-changing business among operational business leaders, top level HR leaders, and unions. This was the core of the "WPoF" phase during the 1990s. At Lucent, however, strategic discussions among the leadership has preceded wider involvement by members or operational managers.

Each level of change requires changes both within groups and between groups. Within groups, management has to engage in deep reexamination of its systems and behaviors, and unions must go through agonizing internal reorientations toward some cherished traditions. Between groups, there is the problem of getting them to talk to each other and develop a code that both can accept for their new relationship. This double aspect is also to be found with other stakeholders, such as workers or middle managers: in one sense they form a separate interest group which needs to understand its own identity, and in another sense they are part of the larger system.

In the fourth, "strategic," type we have done more work within groups rather than working toward consensus among different stakeholders. Normann and Ramirez worked primarily on this aspect with the management leadership; they analyzed the relationship to many stakeholders, including unions, but did not involve them directly in discussions. Tixier has begun working with the CEO of EDF as a strategic counselor around "sustainable" development, and to manage the consequences at the internal level of internationalization of the firm—as well as helping one of the unions to grapple with the implications for *its* organization.

Table 2.1. The basic distinctions

	AT&T	FS	Lucent	EDF
Urgency of strategic/ competitive reconfiguration	Initially low (1980), growing steadily towards crisis (2000+)	Medium, with prospects for more change not yet realized	Extremely high—direct threat to survival within four years of its creation	Medium, moving towards higher level in future
Main types of relational intervention	Institutional (labor–management steering committees) Participatory (workplace participation—"QWL") Operational partnership (WPoF)	External stakeholder consultation Participatory management dialogues	Strategic negotiations around divestitures Sharing of business information Top-level dialogues about the future	Research on policy consequences of new economic pressures Institutional relations (labor–management mutual-gains) Joint strategic analysis Consultant as personal sounding-board for CEO
Intervention trajectory	Initially relational, adding some strategic Labor–management committees Workplace participation teams Union involvement in division-level business planning Internal strategic reviews by unions and management	Initially strategic, adding some relational Strategic analysis Planning process with chief executive Middle management forums	Initially relational, moving quickly to strategic focus Initial effort at labor–management participation Joint review of strategic drivers of manufacturing subcontracting Coordinated negotiations with third parties	Initially relational, strategic gradually becoming central Labor–management dialogue around dealing with privatization New contractual approach (35-hour week) Increasing strategic focus with CEO

At AT&T, Maccoby has also done considerable strategic work with management and has worked closely with one union to help it rethink its future in the light of the business developments. At Lucent, because of the acuteness of the crisis and the constructiveness of the unions and of a powerful labor relations manager, the two parties have actually approached the possibility of negotiating their strategic futures—entering into a deep shared understanding of the challenges, with management accepting in part that it cannot make strategic decisions without first understanding the unions' views.

These basic distinctions can be summarized in Table 2.1.

CASES

3

AT&T: Cooperation is not Enough

The AT&T story is one of developing union–management cooperation over a period of 20 years, starting in 1980 with designing frontline teams throughout the Bell System to improve the quality of working life (QWL) and the quality of service. After the break-up of the Bell System in 1984, union and management were in conflict until workplace of the future (WPoF) was created in 1992. This resulted in union involvement in process change at the business unit level as well as frontline participation in adapting the company to a fiercely competitive marketplace. The results were positive in terms of both productivity and employee satisfaction. Management style began to become more participative. However, the unions were never significantly involved at the strategic level, and in the late 1990s, AT&T bought non-union companies and brought in a new CEO who did not continue the strong support for WPoF. New managers resisted union organizing and some of the most active managerial leaders left the company. The union finally withdrew from WPoF, and labor relations reverted to adversarial bargaining as the company struggled to survive in the new marketplace.

The story passes through five main stages.

- Maccoby started working with the management of AT&T Long Lines, which was sensing that the days of its monopoly position were limited and it must become more responsive to its customers and more cooperative with its unions.
- The Communication Workers of America (CWA) invited Maccoby to help them deal with job pressures. He designed the QWL process which was signed into contract by AT&T, CWA, the International Brotherhood of Electrical Workers (IBEW).
- The break-up of the Bell System led to down-sizing of employees and union–management conflict. There were strikes and some union participants in QWL cross picket lines, angering the unions and suggesting that QWL undermined union solidarity. The company started to institute a quality improvement program without union participation.
- Maccoby helped develop a new, systemic model of union participation, WPoF, which was very successful.

- Finally, new managers bringing non-union companies to AT&T resisted union organizing and the result was to destroy cooperation.

INITIAL ENGAGEMENT WITH MANAGEMENT: BUILDING UNDERSTANDING AND CREDIBILITY

Corporate staff of AT&T first invited Maccoby to talk about his book *The Gamesman*, a study of high tech managers, soon after it was published in January 1977. A month later, Hal Burlingame, who was running the corporate policy seminar under Rex Reed, vice president of Labor Relations, asked him to speak at 15 of the seminars which would be held for director level and above managers from all parts of the company. He wanted Maccoby to describe the Bolivar Project, the first American joint labor–management initiative to create worker participation in an auto parts factory.

Work on that project grew out of research starting in 1970 on the relation between technology, work, and human development. Maccoby approached the workplace as an anthropologist and psychoanalyst. He could see the value of Taylorism to productivity, but the human cost of repetitive, formatted tasks seemed high. He asked the question of whether there was a way to make factory work more satisfying and less stressful. This was a time when workers at GM's Lordstown, Ohio factory rebelled by sabotaging a speeded up assembly line. Managers as well as union leaders were beginning to recognize a problem brought about by continued efforts to increase productivity by using Tayloristic methods.

Maccoby's views and values were also influenced by the 1960s and the movement for greater democracy in the workplace. He believed that the product of work was not only things and services, but also people. Workers allowed to use their brains and make decisions at work were more likely to become better citizens. They would be less angry, less resistant to the civil rights and anti-war movements. Or so he and others reasoned. It also seemed reasonable that greater worker participation in decisions directly affecting them could improve productivity. A number of studies, starting with those at the Western Electric Hawthorne factory in the 1930s, showed this to be true.

Maccoby also believed that unions had to be engaged in changing work. Managers might use participative programs to manipulate workers if they were not protected by unions. Also, unless unions saw their role as furthering worker democracy and development, the unions might resist or undermine change, seeing it as a way for management to pacify workers and weaken unions. Maccoby's vision was that the industrial union agenda would expand from worker protection and wage bargaining to taking the lead in promoting industrial democracy and the continual education of workers. Furthermore, a more empowered and productive workforce would be less likely to follow destructive demagogues and more supportive of human rights for others.

In 1971, Maccoby helped organize a day-long seminar at the annual meeting in Philadelphia of the American Association for the Advancement of Science on "Technology and the Humanization of Work." Representatives came from companies which were experimenting with increased worker participation. Eric Trist, then at the Wharton School, described the socio-technical approach to redesigning work in a coal mine. Due to the considerable interest generated by the meeting, Neil Herrick of the US Labor Department organized seminars with managers, union leaders and academics to discuss initiatives to improve both productivity and the quality of working life. Among the participants were Sidney Harman, CEO of Harman International and Irving Bluestone, vice president of the United Auto Workers in charge of relations with General Motors. Harman had been a social activist for civil rights in the 1960s and felt guilty about exploiting workers in factories run on Tayloristic principles. He wanted to bring his business practice in line with his social ideals and he was motivated by the vision of leading a movement to humanize the workplace. Bluestone was a social democrat whose goal was a more democratic workplace. He saw a project in one of the Harman auto parts factories, in Bolivar, Tennessee as a laboratory for the UAW to learn how to change work at General Motors. Maccoby had met independently with both of them and brought them together at a US Senate hearing on worker alienation presided over by Senator Edward Kennedy. They asked him to direct the project.

At that time, Maccoby's research was supported by the Harvard University Program on Technology and Society. He gained funding for travel to Bolivar and salaries for two on-site "researchers–educators", Bob Duckles and Margaret Molinari, from the short-lived US Productivity Commission set up in the Ford Administration, and the Ford and Sloan Foundations. Duckles and Molinari facilitated worker teams which set standards and determined how work would be done. They also kept a running commentary on work improvement activities. And Maccoby looked for guidance from Einar Thorsrud, Director of the Work Research Institute in Oslo and the Norwegian Participation program. The Norwegian approach to participation was straightforward and effective. It had support from companies, unions and government.

Before beginning the project, Maccoby directed a team of psychologists and anthropologists to study the culture of Bolivar. They also surveyed workers on their attitudes to work and found differences between people who only worked at the factory to make money (their vocations were farming, and craft work) and those interested in industrial careers. The former group did not mind repetitive work if they were able to socialize with friends at work. The careerists wanted challenging work that allowed them to develop their skills.

The Bolivar Project results were positive and widely publicized. But it was a small factory, fewer than 1,500 workers, and AT&T, the Bell System, was the largest corporation in the world with one million employees in 21 operating companies, the Bell Labs, and Western Electric Manufacturing (now Lucent Technologies).

In 1913 Theodore Vail had persuaded President Woodrow Wilson to declare AT&T a regulated monopoly for telephone service. AT&T's position as a regulated monopoly began in 1913, after the company had aggressively conquered most of the telecom market. The Telecommunications Act of 1934 established universal service. In return, AT&T dedicated itself to provide service for all Americans, charging businesses higher rates to keep the cost to households and rural areas affordable. The theory that sustained this arrangement until 1984 was one of "natural monopolies." This theory was challenged when MCI offered long distance service at considerably lower cost to business customers over the heavily used St. Louis to Chicago route. The Bell System was broken up into 7 regional Bell Operating Companies (RBOCs) and AT&T which held onto Long Lines, the long distance company, Western Electric and the Bell Labs.[1] This was the result of an agreement negotiated by AT&T with the Justice Department and modified by Judge Harold Greene in 1982.

But in 1977, there was still one large system dominated by corporate AT&T. Work in the Bell System was designed according to the principles of Taylor's scientific management. Bell System practices described exactly how office workers should sit, place a pencil, respond to customers. The bureaucratic hierarchy was controlled by process and outcome measurements. For example, based on wage rates and capital costs, algorithms calculated that one minute of a telephone operator's average work time (AWT) for the system was considered to be worth one million dollars over a year's time.

Although AT&T was known for experiments in worker participation (Elton Mayo and researchers at the Western Electric Hawthorne plant in the early 1930s) and job enrichment (Robert Ford's experiments in the 1960s), these had become encapsulated and short-lived. Managers were rewarded by getting the right numbers. In the mid-seventies, AT&T employee surveys showed increasing dissatisfaction with work and deteriorating morale.

In general, managers considered the unions as a reproach to their own bad management and a negative influence which dampened productivity. Jim Olson who became CEO for a few years after the break-up once told Maccoby that the only problem was that some supervisors did not know how to listen to and communicate with workers. Olson's view was that paternalism softened Taylorism and increased productivity. This was essentially the message of Elton Mayo in the early 1930s. According to this theory, effective paternalism should also block union organizing. However some 700,000 AT&T employees were unionized, about 650,000 were members of the CWA, and the rest, mostly in Western Electric factories, were members of the IBEW.

When Maccoby described the Bolivar Project at the corporate policy seminar, AT&T executives were not interested. After all, the company was regulated by public utility commissions as a cost plus operation. As long as managers convinced the commission that they were doing their best to improve productivity, they could raise prices to maintain a profit of about 10 percent. They had no competition, and they saw little need to get involved with the unions any more than they were forced to do. After three seminars where participants gave him very low evaluations, Burlingame suggested that Maccoby change his talk and describe the personality types of managers in technology companies which he had studied for *The Gamesman.*

Once he started talking about people who were similar to themselves and to the people they admired in companies like IBM and Hewlett-Packard, the evaluations jumped ahead of all the other speakers. However, the CWA vice-president for Bell System bargaining, John Carroll, had attended one of his seminars on Bolivar, and he liked what he heard; that became important later in developing Maccoby's relationship with the union.

Reed was still determined to educate the system about the value of participative management to improve morale and productivity. Some of his staff had brought in consultants who proposed forms of "managerialism," better human resource management and participation without unions. But Reed saw this approach as a dead end in a highly unionized company. He believed it would provoke union resistance, and according to labor law, it might be illegal to go around the unions. On the positive side, he was persuaded by the Bolivar Project and a subsequent similar program Bluestone had developed at the General Motors Plant in Tarrytown, NY that with union cooperation, it was possible to improve both productivity and the quality of working life. He found examples of successful outcomes of participation that involved the unions by innovative Bell System managers in Ohio and Washington and with the help of his aide Gene Kofke, organized a presentation to a meeting of Bell System presidents in January 1978 in New York City at the St. Regis Hotel. Maccoby was invited to give a keynote talk. As a result of this meeting, he received invitations to speak at a meeting of managers at Pacific Bell in San Francisco and Long Lines regional headquarters in Kansas City.

His talk in San Francisco bombed. It was after supper and managers had been drinking after a long day's meeting where they had been harangued by consultants about their autocratic management style. They were restless and angry, and they did not want to hear about cooperating with the union. After Maccoby's talk, one manager screamed at him about the union leadership. During a recent strike in California, workers had become violent. He said, "The top management here knows nothing about unions, and they bring in a consultant like you who knows even less." He went on, "These people even threw a bomb on my lawn. Can you understand that?" "I'm beginning to," Maccoby said.

After that experience, Maccoby sent a message to Bob Gaynor, the Long Lines vice president, that he wanted to interview first level managers before coming out to speak in Kansas City. He reasoned that these supervisors who faced both the workers and upper management could give him an objective view of problems at work.

He interviewed about 20 supervisors who described the rigid bureaucracy in which they were pressured to increase productivity and were not backed up by upper management when the union raised unjust grievances. They felt like parts of a machine that ran by itself. No one had any real authority to change anything. Maccoby asked what value their bosses added. The answer: the good ones support you for promotion. Nothing more.

Maccoby also met with middle managers. One filled him in on the three rules for managerial success in the Bell System:

- If you can't measure it, it doesn't exist.
- You get what you measure.
- The bearer of bad news will be shot.

He explained that successful managers got results even if this meant sometimes using a sharp pencil to make the numbers look good. Who would know the difference?

Maccoby's talk in Kansas City was a hit, and, on the spot, Gaynor hired him as consultant to a project to create a more competitive organization for a future he believed, prophetically, was fast approaching. This project involved interviewing all the district level managers (third level) and above in the region about their values. These turned out to be dominated by a spirit of service and a paternalistic sense of caring for employees. While productivity was a value, few managers mentioned profitability which for them was a given. In this regard, when AT&T first had to face competition in the mid and late 1980s, many managers objected to giving special service to key business customers. The prevailing value was a spirit of service, including equal treatment, even for those who paid less than the cost of service. Managers saw AT&T as a "public trust."

One manager said, "The core problem revolves around the Bell System's attachment to a rate-base oriented financial approach to nearly all management decisions. Such management decisions have emphasized the length of service for, and quality of equipment, long depreciation schedules and, finally, controlled obsolescence of equipment through protracted market windows. These decisions are dictated by the Bell System's rate base needs and not by competition or customer needs.

"The external environment has changed—at the FTC and at the Justice Department—and with respect to competitors and customers. Technology has been accelerating rapidly, and the Bell System has been slow to respond. Meanwhile, customers and competitors have begun moving much more rapidly, particularly in computer-related segments.

"Elements found lacking in the Bell Marketing System include sales personnel, integration of product R&D (Bell Laboratories), production (Western Electric), installation by local OTC's, and interconnection relationships (Long Lines). These elements have not reacted responsively, or in some cases, responsibly, to consumer requests, especially for large business customers."

Maccoby wrote a report based on the survey and interviews. From 1979 to 1980, he facilitated Gaynor's leadership team's exploration of the issues raised in the report, focusing on customer needs and AT&T's lack of responsiveness. One of Gaynor's directors, Bill Ketchum, was in charge of the mid-west long distance network. He asked Maccoby to help him bring the CWA into a partnership to improve the relationship between management and labor. About 12 local presidents from the region were invited to a meeting to discuss what to do about the latest survey results. The union leaders were enthusiastic about being consulted. One of the most militant took Maccoby aside to warn him that he was too pro-union and would not last long at AT&T.

UNION INVOLVEMENT AND THE BIRTH OF QWL

Soon after this, there was a visit to Maccoby's office in Washington by Ronnie Straw, CWA director of research, who reported directly to Glenn Watts, the union president. Straw asked if he would be interested in helping CWA deal with job pressures caused by new technologies. Filing grievances did not help to solve the problem. Computers were forcing an increased pace of work and Tayloristic job design split the work into smaller and smaller repetitive and meaningless segments. Could Maccoby help them to study the problem and propose solutions?

This was exactly the offer Maccoby had hoped for. He was very excited and enthusiastic about the opportunity. He had been trying without success to find someone to introduce him to the national union. It seemed to him like divine providence. Here was a chance to wrestle with Taylorism in the largest company in the world. He believed that if there was progress here, it could influence managements and unions everywhere. However, Maccoby was a consultant to AT&T management, and told Straw that he could not help the union unless AT&T agreed. What did he think of that? He said he would have to ask Watts.

Reed met with Watts. They decided it was OK for Maccoby to work with the union. Reed said: "You know us, and if they don't hire you, they might get a consultant who was anti-management." Reed in fact believed that the union could be a lever to push management into better practice that would raise the morale of the workforce, and he was in charge of morale.

Maccoby then put together a research team including Richard Balzer who had written a book about work in a Western Electric factory, and Charles Heckscher, then a graduate student in sociology at Harvard and a fellow of the Program on Technology, Public Policy and Human Development (The Harman Program) which Maccoby directed together with Harvey Brooks (a physicist and former dean of the school of Engineering and Applied Sciences) at the John F. Kennedy School of Government. Sidney Harman had endowed the program in 1977 as thanks for the Bolivar Project which had not only succeeded economically, but had also given him a national platform leading to his appointment as Undersecretary of Commerce in the Carter administration.

The team's strategy was to interview union leaders and managers to find good examples of union–management cooperation that improved the quality of working life. This reasoning came partly from Maccoby's psychoanalytic experience of seeking positive or creative activity and building on it. In that way, he believed they could tap into creative energy as opposed to directing people to attempt what the expert considers to be positive activity. Maccoby also reasoned that if the team could refer to positive examples within AT&T, this would be more compelling than showing good cases from other companies (like the Bolivar case). People always argue that their company culture is unique. AT&T managers often said, "we are not like auto companies." This was true, to some degree, since there was more service work and union–management relationships were, in many parts of the system, less adversarial. However, the similarities of Taylorism overshadowed cultural differences and there was much AT&T could learn from Bolivar and Volvo (where Maccoby had also become a consultant working with both management and the metal workers' union on designing a new factory at Uddevalla where teams of workers would build a whole car).

The team also sought to understand the variations of union–management relationships in AT&T throughout the country. The research team first interviewed the members of the union executive board and then at the CWA's convention in Los Angeles in June, 1980, they interviewed over 100 local union officers.

They found that union officials had little power to influence work practices. They interacted with lower level labor relations managers who were themselves powerless to effect change.

The Bell System had become the epitome of the industrial-bureaucratic system, designed by engineers in the Bell Labs with the goal of eliminating the human element by making individuals, in effect, parts of the machine. Authority had become anonymous. The system was designed to eliminate the need for decision-making by managers as well as workers. This sometimes produced ludicrous results, as in Cleveland where, on the basis of traffic flows, the computer decided that telephone operators should have a break between 8:00 and 8:15 a.m. The operators who regularly came to work at 8:00 a.m. asked to be allowed to arrive at 8:15 a.m. This request was rejected. Operators had to clock in at 8:00 a.m. and then take their break.

The team found three examples of union–management relationships that showed a promising direction. One was at Ohio Bell where Larry Lemasters, a young manager of outside plant services, brought together the unionized service technicians to brainstorm ways to improve work practices. A second was a garage in Bloomfield Hills, Michigan where union and management had cooperated to improve worker satisfaction by allowing workers to participate in decisions about scheduling. The third was South Central Bell where the company president and union vice president in charge of that region had developed a cooperative relationship for solving grievances.

Both the Ohio and Michigan cooperation resulted in improved productivity. In both cases, the workers had service jobs that could not be fully controlled by management. Taylorism did not fit knowledge-solutions work. A service technician in a truck can lengthen the time he takes to do a job. Management cannot predict traffic delays or difficulties encountered at the work site. Particularly, if a worker resents an autocratic manager, there are ways to translate resentment into slowdowns. Service technicians in telecommunication and electrical utilities have ways of improving the processes given them by industrial engineers. If they are treated with respect and encouraged to share their ideas, both produc-tivity and the QWL improve.[2]

In 1980, before the Japanese competitive challenge was fully recognized, the auto workers considered productivity to be a dirty word that meant "speed-up." QWL programs were careful not to talk about increasing productivity as opposed to improving both the quality of work and working life. However, CWA leader-ship was open to the idea that productivity could be improved together with the quality of service and working life. Unlike the auto industry where management and workers were profoundly hostile to each other, except at the highest levels, many managers and workers at lower levels in the telephone companies respected each other. The Pacific Bell hostility was not repeated everywhere. Many union officials had relatives in management, rare in the auto industry. There was a sense in which AT&T was a large extended family. This sense was strengthened by paternalistic management and a monopolistic culture that promised a job for life to those who performed up to standard.

Maccoby presented a report on the team's findings to President Watts who asked him to explain it to the CWA executive board. He asked Maccoby what they should do next. Since the three year collective bargaining cycle was up and they were cur-rently bargaining a new contract, Maccoby suggested they use the next three years to further study what would work best with a joint union–management team. "No," said Watts. "We should start now. I'd like you to write a draft of contract language. Why don't you do it right now."

Maccoby went into another room and drafted a clause for the agreement that set up a national union–management committee to improve the quality of ser-vice and QWL. The committee would hire a consultant to be paid half and half by company and union who would advise on education and strategy. Obviously, Maccoby wanted this job. The AT&T managers chosen for the committee wanted to hire a management consultant who had worked with AT&T senior managers, but not with the union. The CWA members said it would either be Maccoby or no one, and finally the company agreed, although Reed recognized that making him the consultant would strengthen the union. Reed, unlike most other managers, believed a stronger union would be better able to cooperate with management to improve productivity and morale.

Maccoby was contracted for 10 days a month, paid 50–50 by union and man-agement, an arrangement that lasted eight years. Maccoby reported to the national QWL committee composed of three Bell System executives and three CWA vice presidents.

To begin the QWL process, Maccoby recruited Richard Walton, a distinguished professor of organization development at the Harvard Business School and a pioneer as a researcher and consultant in transforming the workplace. Walton and Maccoby designed a two day workshop, first held at the Kennedy School, for the union leadership and corresponding Bell System executives, chief operating officers and vice presidents of human resources. Case histories of improving work at other companies were presented including the case of GM and the UAW where despite a positive example of improved productivity and quality of working life in the Tarrytown, NY factory, the company provoked union hostility by being insensitive to worker concerns. Management were given large raises right before workers were asked to make wage concessions. Participants discussed this and what it said about management arrogance. They also discussed union intransigence due to lack of business knowledge and the need for management to educate the union.

This was the first time that most regional CWA vice presidents had contact with Bell System COOs and HR VPs. Usually, they dealt with directors of labor relations. In the extremely hierarchical Bell System, forming these relationships was essential to getting the QWL process started.

Most of the companies followed the suggestion of setting up QWL councils composed of union and management leaders to sponsor education and workplace projects. Rather than trying to bring his own team into the project, Maccoby worked closely with Straw and Kofke who used their staff to set up meetings with managers and union counterparts throughout the system. His reasoning was to increase the ownership of the project by the actors. He asked Straw to hire Heckscher as a member of his research department in order to have an associate within the project who could help educate the union.

At first, Western Electric refused to cooperate with the union. The head of labor relations told Maccoby that his union counterpart was totally uncooperative, a habitual naysayer. There was no chance of a positive partnership. Maccoby met the union vice president who admitted to having been adversarial in the past but promised to cooperate if the company was sincere about increasing worker participation. The Western Electric vice president was unmoved, still unwilling to cooperate.

Maccoby called Reed and made the case that failure to respond to the union when the vice president had promised cooperation would be a breach of the agreement. Given this, Maccoby would have to resign. Looking back, Maccoby was amazed that he made such a threat and took the chance of the company's accepting his resignation. However, he felt that it was not only a case of maintaining his integrity, but that this program was gaining national recognition, and he had involved Harvard. He had a sense that Reed would not want the publicity of AT&T failing to follow up on its agreement, and that he risked the union withdrawing also. The gamble paid off. Soon after this call, the Western Electric Vice president called and demanded that Maccoby show up at LaGuardia airport a few days later at 10:00 a.m. He was there to meet Maccoby, and they were driven to Western Electric headquarters where Maccoby was introduced to the company president and general managers. The Labor Relations VP told them that "Dr. Maccoby has vouched for the cooperation of a union VP who has never helped us with anything. We are going to try this QWL program and Dr. Maccoby will now tell us what we are going to do."

Eventually, this Labor Relations VP became a helpful leader of the process and was always available to give advice. The only brush with conflict was when the union asked Maccoby to speak about the QWL program to a group of Western Electric engineers they were trying to organize. He called the VP to ask what he thought about this, His answer was brief: "If you do that, you'll never work for this company again." Western Electric did not want an expanded union with greater power.

In 1981, Gaynor became vice president of personnel for Long Lines and after divestiture, for AT&T Communications, Gaynor brought Maccoby in to facilitate officer meetings to determine the strategic direction of the company and to develop teamwork among officers. Some of the younger officers wanted to develop marketing efforts. They predicted, accurately, that competition would soon eat into their market share. Others objected because they wanted to avoid being seen as a predatory monopoly; AT&T needed to accept a certain loss of market share. They prevailed.

After Maccoby had helped the president of AT&T Communications, Morris Tannenbaum, to develop his team of vice presidents, Tannenbaum felt Maccoby was not being paid enough. Maccoby responded that as long as he was still working as the consultant to both union and management, if he received more money from the company, the union might question his neutrality. However, he suggested that AT&T make a grant of $50,000 to the Harman Program, which was done. Maccoby's work with Tannenbaum in fact proved useful to the QWL effort since he was willing to support the program and speak together with Glenn Watts, the CWA president, at a company-wide meeting. Without top level support, the program would have disintegrated.

Maccoby also served as a consultant to Larry Lemasters who was developing the division of the company serving the millions of holders of AT&T stocks and bonds. Working with Dick Walton, they designed American Transtech which became a fully owned subsidiary of AT&T located in Jacksonville, FL. This was an innovative organizational design which empowered frontline teams with information technology to serve clients. It expanded its market and took on the stock and bond services for other large companies. However, in the early 1990s, it became a problem for union–management relations when CWA attempted to organize the employees and management resisted the organizing drive.

During the early 1980s, Maccoby was also called by some of the CWA's regional vice presidents to facilitate meetings with their staffs in order to increase communication and teamwork. Glenn Watts asked him to do this for the executive board. A discussion brought out that the main obstacle to better cooperation was lack of trust. Some participants called it paranoia, but in fact there were reasons for distrust and suspicion about coalitions that could influence elections for national office. Also some assistants ran against their vice presidents.

THE DECLINE OF QWL AND THE BIRTH OF WPoF: INVOLVEMENT AT A MORE AMBITIOUS LEVEL

In 1984, the break-up of the Bell system and increasing competition resulted in downsizing at AT&T. Although the top levels of the unions and management continued to meet periodically in Common Interest Forums with Maccoby present, the relationship became more adversarial. QWL did not survive the adversarial climate that followed strikes in 1986 and 1989. Some union QWL coordinators and facilitators crossed picket lines. Because of union negativism, management had unilaterally initiated quality improvement programs which the union rightly viewed as attempts to undermine its influence. The problem was complex. The solution, including a more flexible union and more participative management, would require not only a transformation of the union–management relationship, but also in the roles of managers and union leaders and the culture of the workplace.

Even in this increasingly hostile situation there were continuing efforts to maintain and extend the achievements of QWL. One positive note was the negotiation by Bahr and Ray Williams, AT&T VP of Labor Relations of "The Alliance," a joint program to provide training for union employees so they could maintain their marketability if downsized. This program has been a significant success and a continuing model for other CWA negotiations down to the present.

By 1991, AT&T management was puzzled about how to approach upcoming bargaining with the unions. Managers recognized the need to transform the company to be more productive and customer focused. Increasingly, they saw the unions as vestiges of the bureaucratic era when AT&T was a monopoly, rather than a contender within a fiercely competitive industry. In particular, attempts to improve efficiency were sometimes resisted by the unions which insisted on following work rules bargained in the past. Seniority rules kept more technically competent younger workers from key technical roles.

Although over 90 percent of the occupational workforce of 126,000 employees were unionized, new units acquired by AT&T were non-union, and some newly recruited managers expressed a strong anti-union ideology. They argued for an aggressive adversarial policy which appealed to some managers who had struggled with the union. Most managers with large numbers of union represented employees were more cautious and favored compromise. Company surveys showed that the corporate downsizing of over 100,000 employees had caused employees to feel insecure and resentful, and they trusted the union more than management. However, all business unit managers wanted the company negotiators to achieve greater union flexibility.

Since some of the managers persisted in the view that the company should attempt to decertify the union, Maccoby proposed that they take seriously what this would cost in terms of money, time and disruptions of work. When they considered this, it became immediately clear that it would be a disastrous mistake to try to destroy the union. The choices then were either to accept and muddle along with an adversarial relationship or take a chance to raise the level and achieve cooperation. Once put this way, the decision to attempt cooperation became a no-brainer.

The new vice-president of labor relations was Bill Ketchum, whom Maccoby had worked with in Kansas City in 1977 and again as HR Director of AT&T

Communications in 1984. In fact, Maccoby had recommended him for this job to Hal Burlingame, now Senior Vice President for Human Resources. He saw his task as crafting a corporate policy that could gain the support of all these operational managers, and he asked Maccoby to help.

On the union side, CWA had surveyed their members and found they wanted their leaders to be both tough bargainers and partners with management in developing worker participation. They wanted the union to gain for them not only better pay and working conditions, but also a direct say in how their work was organized.

With approval from Ketchum and Jim Irvine, CWA Vice President for AT&T members, Maccoby began by interviewing both key managers and union leaders about what they would support. Both sides, while skeptical about the other's good faith, agreed that a higher level of cooperation could benefit them. From these discussions, Maccoby drew the following conclusions.

- The solution had to be systemic. QWL had failed because it was not integrated within the management system. This system had to be understood not only in terms of technical and financial aspects, but also social and cultural factors, including shared values, management style, measurements and incentives, as well as organizational structure. Maccoby also believed that AT&T had to change its work culture from an overcontrolling bureaucracy to one that empowered workers to solve customer problems and that learned from frontline experience.
- The solution should encompass all levels of the company. The decision-making structure of the company could be conceived in terms of strategic, operating and doing levels, represented as follows (Figure 3.1): The strategic level included top management. The operating level included the middle managers and supervisors that ran the plant, sales, billing, and technology development. The doing level included operators, technicians, sales and service personnel. The solid lines described the current flow of information and decision-making. The dotted lines needed to be strengthened with worker participation at the doing level and participation by union leaders at the strategic and operating levels. For these levels to change together, it would be necessary to develop an ongoing dialogue so that, for example, teams of doers in the front line could interpret operational directives without causing problems for other parts of the organization. AT&T was a huge company with many locations across the country, connected by a complex network.
- The roles and responsibilities of management and union had to be clarified. In the QWL program, there was often confusion about these roles. In the QWL process, union leaders selected non-elected members to be trained as facilitators. Some of these people lost their union identification and began to identify with their managerial counterparts. During the strikes of 1986 and 1989, when they crossed the picket lines, union hostility to QWL grew, and Maccoby considered it essential that for WPoF to succeed elected union

Strategic level

HR board

Operational level

BPCs —
Process teams

Doing level
Workplace teams

Fig. 3.1. Workplace of the Future structure.

leaders should see their role as representing their members in the continual change process that was taking place.

While managers should still be responsible for strategic and operational decisions, these decisions would be improved and better implemented if elected union representatives participated in the process. This would require full access to relevant information and the meaning of that information.

For the union to gain real influence rather than formal power, management had to respect union leaders as democratically elected legitimate representatives of the occupational workforce. This meant that the union should have the authority to select the workers who would participate on joint committees.

- The solution would require education for the participants. Union leaders and workers needed to understand the business, its relation to customers, competitors, and owners. Correspondingly, managers needed to understand the union as a combination of service organization and democratic movement for social justice. Management and union had different logics or belief systems, different values and identities. When they discussed issues, managers tended to focus on the future, the changing markets and technology and the pressure to adapt. Union leaders tended to focus on the past, the struggles to gain rights and benefits and the need to protect these gains. Managers valued financial results; they were rewarded for meeting budgets. Union leaders valued the well-being of their members. They were elected for their ability to increase wages and benefits, defend dignity, and voice the feelings of workers. To work together, unionists and managers needed to understand and respect each other's roles and identities. Only then could the needs of customers and owners be balanced with those of employees.

These conclusions were supported by Ketchum and Burlingame and by Morton Bahr, now President of CWA, and Irvine. In drafting language for the 1992 contract, Maccoby worked with the union and management bargainers to include the above considerations, and the contract language reflected the understanding that change required holistic understanding and "radical transformation in the roles of managers, occupational employees and union leaders."

The agreement instituted an "innovative model" called WPoF. Planning Councils were to be formed at the operational (business unit or divisional) level composed of management and union representatives and led by an operational vice president. Also created was a Constructive Relationship Council of union and management negotiators who were empowered to approve initiatives from Planning Councils that modified the contract. The Planning Councils had a key role in organizing education and stimulating workplace teams. The contract stipulated that they would design "ideal futures", which meant a holistic description of a customer focused, participative workplace.[3] At the strategic level, a Human Resources Board was established, to engage union leadership in human resource planning and to support activities at the other levels.

There was discussion about union participation in strategy formulation, but this did not happen. In fact, top level strategy at AT&T was held close to the chest by the CEO and one or two advisers (legal and financial). What seemed possible was involving the union in planning for future jobs, including retraining workers and participating in operational decision-making.

It is one thing to gain agreement about an innovation and quite another to make it happen. To bring to life the elements described in the contract, innovative managers and union officials had to take the lead. Part of Maccoby's function was to recruit these leaders and facilitate the first meetings of the planning councils and the design of ideal futures. Two operational vice presidents, Stan Kabala and Jim Carroll, together with Irvine initiated the first planning councils. (Maccoby helped to get nine councils started. Typically they met every month or six weeks for two days.) Maccoby facilitated the design of ideal futures and using gap questionnaires developed knowledge of how far the group was from their ideal future and agreement as to the steps needed to close the gaps. It became clear that due to new technology and market pressures, the company was continually changing its management processes. For the union to participate in these changes, which affected members' jobs, union members had to join process design teams which would then evaluate change according to the ideal future.

Maccoby had significant help from Heckscher and Sue Schurman, then professors at Rutgers University, who developed an educational program and trained management and union educators to be the teachers. The education included understanding different values and the need to base an ideal future design on a balance of stakeholder interests: customers, employees, and owners.

In 1993, some CWA officials, especially those with no direct experience of WPoF, were questioning the wisdom of participation, concerned about its weakening the union's ability to aggressively represent its members. Bahr asked Maccoby to facilitate a study and evaluation by members of the CWA executive board of WPoF and other examples of CWA participation with telecommunication companies. What was the benefit for the union and its members? What should be union policy? The study, based on interviews with union and management representatives in six companies led to a report and policy recommendations which were approved by the executive board. The report affirmed that union participation in management decision-making was a necessary expansion of collective bargaining. Because of continual change, the union could not wait to negotiate every three years. But the CWA executives also believed that participation was politically risky; the union could be blamed for decisions that negatively affected members. To participate effectively, both leaders and members needed education, and the union should participate only with a management that respected the union's role and the institution of collective bargaining.

Results and evaluation of WPoF

In the 1995 contract, WPoF was affirmed and expanded. The bargainers reported that those issues which had been analyzed by planning councils were easily approved, in contrast to those which were not. Since most union bargainers had served on planning councils, they had gained a much better understanding of the business and its needs and were better able to present union positions. From the adversarial bargaining of the past, they had moved to a joint planning process on most issues. Management respect for the union increased.

Although there was no way to measure this, one executive estimated that WPoF had saved the company hundreds of millions of dollars due to improved productivity. In one instance, union representatives had participated in a large cost cutting exercise that saved $300 million. In the past, the union might have objected to the loss of jobs and at the least, slowed down the process. Another senior executive put the figure at two billion dollars including money saved from preparing for and operating during strikes.

In the 1995 bargaining, union organizing became a major issue. The union believed it deserved credit for its cooperation and that management should remain neutral when attempts were made to organize non-union acquisitions. Management wanted to follow a policy of cooperation, including card check recognition in already unionized entities but resistance to organizing in non-union entities. Card check called for recognition of a unit if a majority of employees signed cards designating the union as their sole bargaining representatives. The company wanted to be able to present its position before having a secret ballot election. But this meant in practice that managers in non-union entities would hire union busting consultants who would try to make the union appear an unneeded third party who would cost employees dues money and ruin relations with management. This became a heated issue; the union saw its strength being progressively eroded.

Maccoby had always stayed out of the bargaining when wages were involved. This was a game in which he had no special expertise, and it was by nature adversarial. However, he saw the conflict over organizing threatening the cooperative relationship underlying WPoF and at the request of both parties, especially Larry Cohen of CWA, he mediated the negotiation. He suggested that organizing campaigns in the new units be governed by the values that AT&T's CEO, Robert Allen, had articulated: respect for individuals, dedication to helping customers, highest standards of integrity, innovation and teamwork. Disputes about these agreements would be sent to a mutually agreed to third party. In fact, neither company nor union was able to keep to the principles; the company in particular kept resisting union organizing which eventually did undermine cooperation.

In 1996, AT&T was again split. The manufacturing part became Lucent Technologies, leaving telecommunications and information services in the parent company where WPoF was most firmly established. In September 1997, there were about 130,000 employees at AT&T of whom about 50,000 were represented by unions, 48,000 by CWA.

A report by AT&T labor relations quoted union leaders and managers testifying to improvements in their relationship and operating results. They noted that adaptation to new market conditions was now managed more rapidly. People close to a problem had become empowered to act. There was less resistance to change, because people understood the reasons for it.

The AT&T Opinion Survey in 1996 showed that those employees who participated in WPoF teams scored higher than those not yet participating in 14 out of 15 categories, such as teamwork, understanding goals and objectives, workplace spirit and interactive empowerment. Furthermore, managers involved in WPoF reported that their style had become more participative; they were learning how to be coaches and facilitators.

In recognition of the project's success, union and management representatives were invited to describe WPoF at conferences in the US and Canada, and the AFL-CIO Center for Workplace Democracy selected it as a model for unions to study.

After 5 years, WPoF was still a work in progress. Despite significant achievements, there were also gaps and challenges.

- Less than one-third of the workforce was involved.
- Measurements and rewards for managers were not yet fully aligned with WPoF. However, in some business units, management bonuses depended on WPoF participation.
- The HR board did not meet regularly, and the union did not participate in decision-making at the strategic level.
- Some new units remained non-union, and CWA attempts to organize were met by local managerial resistance, causing distrust that limited a fuller partnership. However, the union recognized that they were gaining management support. Those managers who have participated directly in WPoF

argued that with participative management the union added value to management and there was no reason to oppose its organizing efforts.

A report by the Rutgers group based on interviews with 10 workplace teams indicated both the success of WPoF in facilitating innovation by the frontline and the need in some cases for better education and support for worker initiatives.

THE UNRAVELING OF THE RELATIONSHIP

In 1998, Mary Anne Walk, a new vice president of labor relations, took over. At her request, Maccoby had supported her for the job with Hal Burlingame who was her boss. And Maccoby also gained support for her from union leadership which had been mistrustful of her because of her dealings with them in the past. Burlingame considered this support crucial for her ability to do the job. Although she remained cordial and outwardly collegial in her relations with Maccoby, she told company managers that they no longer needed to work with him. He remained as a consultant, but increasingly kept out of the action, except for the meetings of the HR board where he remained a member. Some union and management leaders continued to seek his advice, but Walk kept him out of the 1998 bargaining.

In both 1992 and 1995 bargaining Maccoby worked with both union and management to clarify as much as possible the expectations of what each organization would gain from the agreement. The goals as the parties saw them were as follows. Management would gain the union's help in adapting to change, becoming more effective and efficient. There would be a living contract, allowing experiments and modifications between bargaining periods. The union would gain the ability to represent its members' interests before decisions were made that affected jobs. They could also expect the company eventually not to resist their organizing efforts in new units, but to maintain neutrality, refraining from criticizing the union during organizing campaigns.

In 1998 with a new CEO, Mike Armstrong, and many new managers who had never dealt with unions, Maccoby recognized that the whole relationship was seriously at risk. He proposed that top management study the true costs of union–management conflict and learn from Southwest Airlines, a unionized company that was the most profitable in its industry. Maccoby's view was that line management should take the lead in working with the union and labor relations should be a support. Union and management leaders should together determine the ideal future of their relationship. Irvine supported this idea, but Walk squashed it. She had a different view. She believed she could force the two growing parts of the company, cable and wireless telephony, to stop resisting union attempts to organize them.

In 1992, AT&T had become the first major US company to grant neutrality and card checks for units that were already organized. Unlike a secret ballot election, card check may subject workers to pressure by fellow workers who are unionists since they know who has signed and who has not. With card check, the union may win, even though this might not be the case with a secret ballot. In the 1998 negotiations, Walk told the union that the new management that had come in from McCaw wireless and the cable companies (TCI and MediaOne) could not accept card check. However, she believed she could get them to agree to neutrality in secret ballot elections. The union accepted a speedy election process but negotiated an agreed-to umpire who would monitor the parties' conduct. But the managers who had always been "union free" felt betrayed by labor relations. Walk and her closest deputy lost credibility with management and by January 2000, both had left the company. Burlingame had moved on to another role, and there was a new vice president of human resources without experience with labor relations.

Walk's error was to try to return to a vision of labor relations from a previous era, when it could dictate to the operations units. That had been her experience as a labor relations manager in the 1980s. She ignored the lessons learned during Ketchum's tenure, that operational VPs needed to be educated and persuaded to manage the union-management relationship with a more participative style.

In November 1999, CWA, citing aggressive tactics by cable and wireless managers, withdrew from WPoF. The union–management relationship became increasingly adversarial. However, Bahr, the CWA president, still cited WPoF as the ideal union–management relationship.

REFLECTION: INTERVENTION AND PSYCHOANALYTIC UNDERSTANDING

Maccoby's relationships with union and management developed over a 12-year period before WPoF was established. Like a long psychoanalysis, there were stages in the relationship.

The first stage began with his being hired. He had been a consultant to AT&T management for three years before the union asked him to help them respond to job pressures caused by new technology and rigid work rules. He said he would take the job only if the company agreed. They did so, reasoning that if another consultant were engaged by the union, they would be taking a risk of facing someone who was adversarial. They knew and trusted him.

One reason the CWA first approached him in the late 1970s was that John Carroll, their executive vice president, had heard Maccoby describe the work improvement project of Harman Industries and the UAW to a group of Bell System executives. This CWA vice president later testified: "Maccoby talks the same way to union and management. We can trust him."

Was this trust on both sides "transferential" in the psychoanalytic sense? To some degree, we think the answer is yes, particularly in relation to their expectations about what he could accomplish (see Chapter 8). In analysis, the patient's relationship to the analyst may undergo a change from an initial positive transference to one in which unconscious childhood conflicts with parents are transferred onto the analyst. The positive transference causes the patient to overestimate the analyst's ability to help, but this infantile trust, combined with early analytic results, holds the therapeutic relationship together when the transference hits rough water. The analyst's role then becomes one of transforming the acting-out of these unconscious conflicts with the analyst (negative transference) into conscious memories. This is done by exploring when the patient first had the feelings he/she is experiencing with the analyst. In the process, the patient should recognize that his/her feelings toward the analyst are inappropriate. Rather than transferring these attitudes, the patient remembers early experiences that have been repressed. Then the patient begins to respond to the analyst more objectively. As the transference dissolves, the patient becomes more independent, no longer seeking a magic helper.

While AT&T and CWA were not individual patients, but large groups of people, they had tried unsuccessfully to resolve conflicts by themselves, and they were seeking an "expert" who would provide the solution and in a sense, change their lives. To call in such an expert requires trust and hope that is only partly based on evidence of such expertise. When Maccoby began working with AT&T and CWA in the early 1980s, he had achieved some success, including cooperative beginnings at AT&T in Kansas City, but he had never attempted such a huge project. Probably, no one had. At that time, there were one million employees in the Bell System. The leaders who hired him began to believe that he could provide a solution, and this belief, like the childlike belief in an all-powerful parent, had a strong transferential component. Maccoby's attempt to facilitate a design process to get them to do it themselves, was firmly rejected. "We want you to give us the model," he was told. (One can also interpret this as avoiding responsibility in the event of failure.)

In the second stage, the model Maccoby proposed was modified and distorted by the participants who acted (or acted out) their own beliefs and values. An example: from the start of QWL, Maccoby believed union participation should be integrated into operating processes and that management should lead change teams. This would have required the kind of participative management that only developed in the 1990s, with WPoF. The union and management staff charged with developing training insisted on a model of a parallel organization of union–management representatives. That way union representatives would have equal status and authority with management. Also, they designed leaderless teams which made suggestions to this parallel council, but the suggestions were not always adopted by line management which still had the real authority. That these teams tended to propose hygienic changes, such as flexibility in working hours or recognition programs, was to be expected. The workers and union leaders lacked the knowledge and clout to influence process changes or job design. Many teams ran out of ideas. Union and management facilitators took over the program, and some union representatives became confused about their role and began to identify with management.

In the third stage, when QWL failed with the break-up of the Bell System and subsequent downsizing, the negative transference was expressed toward Maccoby by some participants. It was only because of a strong relationship with both union and management leadership, Bahr and Irvine and Burlingame and Ketchum, that Maccoby could analyze the causes of failure with them and show that a sustainable co-evolution of union and management required the holistic approach adopted by WPoF.

Maccoby's intervention combined the roles of anthropologist, organizational architect and facilitator, strengthened with psychoanalytic understanding.

In the fourth stage, he became more active as the architect of WPoF and facilitator of the first planning councils. Could he have done this during the second stage and avoided the failure of QWL? Perhaps, to some degree, but we think that the culture of the organization, like the character of the analytic patient, would have resisted. AT&T was still a monopoly and was not yet forced to adapt to a competitive market. Intervention, like analysis, takes place within a cultural framework and the nature of transference is social as well as individual. We place other people and ourselves in culturally determined roles. To transform the role requires transforming organizational culture. In the case of analysis, the doctor–patient relationship must be transformed into one of co-investigators, co-learners. In the most profound of analyses, the analysand may change his/her mode of relatedness in love and work. In the most profound of organizational change, a better adaptation also results in more creative work and more cooperative relationships.

And the fifth stage showed how important were the personal relationships with leaders in sustaining WPoF. Once key leaders like Burlingame, Ketchum, and Carroll left the company, Maccoby had no partners and he was kept from trying to recruit and educate new leaders.

4

Ferrovie Dello Stato (The Italian State Railways): A Vision without Agreement

INTRODUCTION

The intervention at Ferrovie dello Stato—henceforth "FS"—focused on the creation of a new strategic vision. The customer was top management, and in particular, the CEO. The actual intervention took place with the strategy team of FS, which co-produced the intervention's findings together with the consultants for both the CEO and the COO.

The intervention began with a deliberately "detached" visioning process, in which the consultants tried to stay out of the political dynamics of the organization in order to build a fact-based model of choices for the future. Over time they sought to engage more heavily with a wide range of stakeholders, starting with divisions within the top management team; then broadening to the relationship between top management and senior line management.

Many external stakeholders were also key to enacting the strategic vision:

(1) its customers—in the sense of who pays for services: the State (more specifically the Ministry of Finance and the Ministry of Transportation, who financed much of its activity and under-wrote its capital expenditure); the country's regions, cities, corporations, and individual travelers,

(2) its owner (the State, and more specifically, the Ministry of the Treasury),

(3) its regulators (the State—more specifically the Ministry of Labor and the Ministry of Transportation; the European Union),

(4) its workers and their representatives (unions),

(5) its suppliers and competitors (e.g. Fiat, who plays both roles; Alitalia, construction firms, car users, truck and bus and ship companies),

(6) its partners (including other European rail operators, but also private companies in many joint ventures, port authorities, real estate firms, and so on),

(7) political parties, whose arrangements within Italy's democracy mean that there has been a new government virtually every year since the Second World War,

(8) and other stakeholders (owners of rights of way, environmentalists, other interest groups—such as archeologists hindering the extension of stations into Roman ruin sites, the Church, other actors in Italy's transport industries ...).

The intervention did not directly engage most of these groups in collectively redefining the mandate of FS. Some relations were engaged by the FS strategy team and the top management, who often saw the counterparts not as allies but as obstacles to the vision they advocated—in particular the State, the political parties, parts of middle management, and the unions.

Thus, this is a story about approaching the problem of change from the strategy end. Compared to other cases our colleagues in FAIG have been addressing, the consultants in this case focused more on shaping the vision of how the company should relate to its stakeholders, and less on directly working on those relationships. Though the strategic vision has been largely validated by events in the intervening years, a core aspect of this story is the ability of internal and external stakeholder groups to frustrate the enactment of elegant and creative images of the future—though perhaps only in the short term, since the vision as such is slowly but surely becoming operational and meeting with success.

THE SETTING

Railways existed in Italy before Italy existed.

In effect, Italy as a country came to be when, in 1896, Garibaldi united various political entities to create a new country. Unification and integration required strong mechanisms—including a language: Venetians and Sicilians did not have a single common one. The rail concessions that had existed before could not be joined into one private company that could undertake the financing required for national unification. And thus, due to "market failure," the Railways came to be, as a national State entity, Ferrovie dello Stato in 1905 (Spirito, 1997: 5). Together with 3 other strong integrative mechanisms (a national schooling system, the telegraph, and the army),[1] the railroad came to have a political role, uniting a country that had not been one, enacting it as it were one.

In volume of passengers transported, Ferrovie dello Stato grew ten-fold from 1905 to 1997,[2] almost without interruption (the exception is the Second World War period), having sold 49 billion passenger-kilometers in 1997. In freight, it grew six-fold, having sold 25 billion ton-kilometers in 1997.

But after the Second World War, the country had not only been built, but also confirmed. A new era started, and the old mission of Ferrovie dello Stato, political unification, gave way to one of connection and transportation—to one of mobility enabler.

Beyond the *political* discontinuity, two more significant discontinuities intervened.

One was *economic*: The buying power of Italians, which was 33 percent that of Americans in 1950, became 70 percent that of Americans by 1990.[3]

The other was *technological*: car production became efficient, and car ownership and highways exploded.[4] Ferrovie dello Stato's new mobility mission was taken over by the car, the bus, the truck, and—later—the airplane. Fiat became not only the Ferrovie's major supplier, but also—with Italian drivers—its major competitor.

Because of this situation, by 1990 the railways had lost their way. Their two successive "raisons d'être," nation builder and mobility enabler, had been surpassed.

Institutionally, FS was part of the Ministry of Transportation. Different political parties, which allegedly had made deals with each other in the numerous— almost yearly—post-war governments, apparently had obtained jobs in this or that sector for their members. No other rational reason can account for the fact that at least at one time over 250,000 employees were employed by a railway system that benchmark studies found could be run by less than 90,000. This applies in the same way, even if slightly more elegantly, to the argument that this was a political act to "create jobs" for the South of Italy to prevent it from imploding.

Many of the members of the political parties were also affiliated with trade unions that were more closely aligned with party interests than with the interests of a given profession. Yet, many of the trade unions representing FS workers had in fact emerged through struggles to genuinely defend the working conditions of different professions. At the time of our intervention, some unions were considered to be more "political," some more "technical," and some combined both aspects. In addition, the unions operated in different ways in different regions, and local, regional, and national levels were not always aligned. The result was of nightmarish complexity: according to one estimate, at the beginning of our intervention, well over 300 unions represented FS workers.

One result of this is that for many things in the railways, party politics and/or union membership apparently came to be more important than business, State policy, or economic considerations. Opacity thus took "market share" over transparency and accountability. The substantial amounts of money which important investments entail in this business opened up considerable opportunities for outright corruption. Ferrovie's administrator, Ludovico Liggato, arrested in November 1988 on charges of mishandling public contract awards without following appropriate procedures, was murdered after leaving prison in early 1989.

In May 1989, the government brought in a private sector manager from Montedison, who understood his appointment as a mandate to bring business policy to guide the company, instead of allowing political forces—"external" and/or "internal"—to shape decisions. Several managers told us that his disagreements with key politicians on this assumption led to his resigning at the end of May 1990.

Lorenzo Necci was then hired as "extraordinary administrator," coming in from ENI (the State energy company) on June 19, 1990. In other words, upon entering Ferrovie, Necci was, in Anglo-Saxon terms, an "acting CEO." He became the key customer of the intervention this case describes.

Necci immediately took three major initiatives. He utilized a law which allowed the State to take on retirement expenses, to reduce headcount from 220,000 to 150,000 people. Second, he converted FS from being a part of the Ministry of Transportation, into a State-owned, but legally a private-sector, firm (becoming Ferrovie dello Stato Spa, "Spa" meaning Società per actione, or a "joint stock," company). Third, Necci started Treni alta velocità (TAV), a public–private consortium to build high-speed rail lines and coaches. TAV, which was legally a different entity than FS, accounted for an estimated 25 percent of Necci's time between fall 1990 and end of 1992. FS would be TAV's operator, but did not have a controlling interest in it. TAV later attracted the interest of the legal system.

THE INTERVENTION

First steps

Richard Normann is the lead consultant in this story. His ideas have been extremely popular in Italy, where his books have sold well over 100,000 copies. Normann, a Swede, is the founder and chairman of SMG, a Stockholm-based strategy consulting firm, which he started in 1980, and which Ramirez joined in 1985. At various points he allied himself with Professor Lucio Sicca, then Dean of the STOA business school in Naples, who had created a small but very professional consulting firm called Resi Management Group (RMG).

In early 1992, Normann was asked to attend a meeting in Milan, at FS's offices in that city. Normann says he had expected a small informal meeting, but instead found a room with perhaps 20 people expecting him to give some sort of a "performance." It was supposed to be about quality, which was a buzzword much used at that time in both Italy and FS. Normann gave an extemporaneous performance, which led to obtain funds for a Normann–Sicca (SMG/RMG) project on service quality in FS. This project was basically performed by RMG, but Normann was used as what he calls the "hit person" and was remunerated for about one week's worth of invoicing for his help. But this led in turn to a conference with Necci and the fifty or so top people of FS. In the meantime, Normann had met DeCesaris, the Chairman (or "president") of FS. They built a rapport between them, although they had to use translators to communicate.

Normann got the impression that FS intended to institutionalize a measurement system and a quality function—an initiative that he thought would inevitably fail. He thought this would have been a way to avoid facing other, larger issues, and said so. He believes Necci was impressed with this argument. Normann said something like "quality cannot be achieved by some cosmetics, but has to come through a tough training camp and steeple chase," which Necci then quoted on television. Necci came to see the quality project, and Normann, as a means to "upframe" the process of changing FS.

In any case, some time after this Normann got the message through his Italian friends that FS planned two major projects: a "diversification" project, and a "core business" project. Normann and his colleagues were asked if they could run the second, core business, project. It was clear that the request came to him personally, but he would not have gotten it without the ground support and local presence of Italian colleagues, and the existence of sufficient professional consulting resources in Italy that could take on and deliver the project. In effect, Normann was asked to put a team full time on the project, and complied with this—manning it with SMG as well as RMG professionals. The project was scheduled for five months, and he dedicated half his time to it.

The core business analysis

The operational project leader in Rome had to be from SMG, according to the request. SMG had just acquired a company in France, and was busy merging its existing French operations—which had been headed by Ramirez—with the acquired company's. Normann and his SMG colleagues thought the FS project would give the merger a helpful impetus. And so, they decided to put one of the acquired company's consultants as SMG's lead man in Rome.

This consultant had never before worked with Normann, and did not know SMG's methods, values, or history. Furthermore, as he would be located in Rome, he would not share the "acculturation" process that his ex-colleagues would experience by having both firms move to new common premises in Paris. A senior, experienced SMG consultant who had been very involved in helping write the "core business analysis" consulting proposal, was added to the project team to assist the (from SMG's perspective) untried lead man.

The project began formally in October 1992 and finished five months later. Ramirez was brought in toward the end of this first "core business analysis" project, to help the joint team methodologically with a limited scenario initiative that supported the analyses that had been made.

Normann and his colleagues divided the "core business" analyses into three areas: passengers, local transportation, and freight. They quickly learnt that basic facts and economic figures were not known—by anyone! It seemed to Normann that this had probably been a more or less conscious strategy on the part of key actors, as lack of facts and the resulting opacity allowed—even demanded—politicizing and individual interest positioning. FS was running trains and performing services, but appeared to be unconcerned with economics and focused mainly on political games.

For the core business analysis, it was explicitly agreed that there would not be a great deal of interaction with the FS organization, since this was to be an analysis, not—at this stage—an interactive intervention. The unions, as well as most of the line management in FS, were excluded from the core business analysis as part of this general intervention strategy. Paradoxically perhaps, Normann and his colleagues liked their lack of contact with FS. They believed that the more a company is infected by politics, the more important it is for a consultant who wants to preserve his potential as a change agent to create an impeccable rational, factual analysis. Without a solid business logic and accounting data as starting-points for discussion, they feared, debates on policy among stakeholders would degenerate into the worst form of politics.

Yet there was a price to be paid for this choice: it prevented the problem from being articulated in terms of internal relationships. If maladaptive internal relations can be transformed to enable the system to become more developmental, then the cost of the choice can be substantial. Delaying it for "later," as in the strategy that was undertaken, is defensible—but may not be the only available option. Engaging interaction "internally" as well as between the organization and its "external" stakeholders earlier rather than later can thus be seen as a "both/and," rather than as an "either/or" intervention strategy choice. In fact, the "external/internal" distinction can even be argued to be an unhelpful distinction in the interactive approach to intervention.

The consultants' intention, as had been agreed with their customer, the new CEO, was to start the analysis from the organization's relations with customers, move onto offerings, then to operations and structures, and then to the bottom line—using a service management system "formula" for each business.[5] The project was in this sense interactive—it focused on the "moments of truth" in the interaction between customers and Ferrovie. These interactions would then be studied in terms of internal ("operational" and "structural") ones. However, the consultants soon found out that they had to back-track and create a model of the cost and revenue structure from the ground up, as no such model had ever existed before.

The progress in the project was regularly reported in meetings which included Necci, some of his direct reports, and a few strategic unit persons. Necci's late arrivals made these meetings frustrating. His lack of punctuality became a recurrent aspect of the interaction.

A big initiative—taking place in parallel to the intervention here described—involved reducing the number of employees in FS—again—from some 150,000 persons to about 120,000. Any attempt to include the unions in changing FS's strategy would at that time have been completely dominated by this issue. Necci and his colleagues wanted them separate.

In retrospect, another reason for the lack of contact can be advanced. At the time of the intervention, roughly half of the budget of FS involved employees, and another half went to suppliers. A sort of implicit pact evolved, where Necci dealt with suppliers and Vaciago, the HR director, with unions. Two more actors balanced this apparent—but as far as we know implicit—pact: Rizzoti, a bright, competent, experienced and respected railways engineer, held sway over the line managers of FS, which were obviously an important stakeholder. The second, Pantile, had been promoted step by step from the position of station manager to overall head of corporate strategy and policy—thereby holding the critical relationship with the State's Treasury—which funded much of FS. The four men (Necci, Vaciago, Rizzoti, and Pantile) with this implicit balance of power, worked effectively, perhaps more in parallel to each other than as a single coherent team, until mid-1994. Things then changed, as we will see below.

But the point is that as the interveners worked for Necci, the intervention here described could not be extended to the domains of the other three *without fundamentally re-defining its nature*. Had it extended into internal relations (with unions and line management) and with the critical lifeline to the Treasury—as the interactive full engagement approach would want it to—it would have *de facto* included reworking the top management team's inter-relations as well. This was not the mandate of the intervention.

"Reinventing Italy"

Upon the delivery of the core business analysis in early 1993, the consulting intervention got involved primarily in the strategic planning process and function. Normann—and those working with him—would have liked to become more involved in translating the results of their analyses into actual business development projects. Necci as well as other senior managers prevented this. Two reasons can be advanced for this. First, as shown above, this would have impinged upon the balance of power among the top four people. This balance of power resolved not only actual or potential internal conflicts, but also reflected a balance of power they had managed to obtain from different stakeholders. These included: the ministry of transportation, the ministry of labor, the treasury, political parties, trade unions, foreign banks, suppliers, other national railway operators, EC regulators, line managers, and different departments. In hindsight, it appears that Necci's predecessors' legacies, and even the very history of Italy, limited the freedom to bring business logics into a highly complex political setting.

So the interveners did not immediately center on getting the senior management, middle management, and unions aligned to get the businesses to become effective, because they felt this could not be done—at least not immediately. This is very different from—perhaps even the exact opposite of—the trajectory of the other interventions in this book. Had the interveners started out by involving key stakeholders in the business definition—and perhaps in data gathering and modeling—it might have been more successful in overcoming the stakeholder obstacles. Corrado Pasera's interactive strategy development upon his taking the CEO role in the Italian post office several years later shows that such a path is not only possible in Italy, but also viable and sustainable.

So, the relationship instead took two different directions: a "systemic" one and a "planning" one. The first initiative was manifested in the initiation of a joint book project, in which Normann and Necci would be co-authors. FS, as well as other institutions, contributed manpower and brain power, both in terms of research and in terms of working meetings in which many different individuals participated. The book initiative at the time appeared to reflect a move to a "systemic" logic: changing FS "internally" was seen as requiring changing the context—which in this case meant reinventing Italy! And "*Reinventing Italy*" became the telling title of the book. As we shall see below, collaboration on the book was carried out in parallel to a series of actual interventions in FS. In some ways, this was helpful to the interventions. The scenarios for Italy, which had been done as part of the core business analysis, were developed into a more robust form in the book, as part of the "business logics." This described how revenues would at least match costs, and laid out a strategy for the roles of the different businesses in relation to customers, the State, and other actors. An issue to consider in interactive intervention is co-writing between intervener and intervened—and the timing of such joint efforts in relation to ongoing interactive intervention. However, the work by Normann and Ramirez for the book was not financed by FS.

Hindsight, of course, can cast the book initiative in an entirely different light: the book initiative can be thought of as a political project. Was Necci following a Schimberni-inspired project of re-conquering a political game with business logics—or was he playing a political game? The consultants believed the former, as did many others: by 1993, Necci was universally admired across Italy as a visionary leader who could modernize colossal elephants and get them to dance. But later events would put this in question.

Much of 1993 saw the consultants focused on the "book effort." As the book appeared in 1995,[6] the attention to it would continue for almost 2 years. One of the conclusions after many meetings and workshops was that in Italy, much of the future would be centered on cities, or city-regions. For FS this was an important proposition: the "S" for (national) "State" in FS was in peril not only from the EEC—whereby significant parts of the market—freight in particular—would become continental and international, rather than peninsular and national; but also from "below." Regionalization meant that the considerable sums coming to FS from public sources would increasingly come from cities and regions, and less from the national level. This changed who FS' "competitors" (for funds) would be.

Building internal support for the strategy process

In March of 1994, SMG made the first moves toward engaging the wider organization in the strategic planning process. Over the next year, the core of the effort was trying to enlist support, and to bring about the organizational changes, needed to implement the visions sketched to this point.

Normann and Ramirez[7] began with a document to FS's planning staff criticizing the purely rational and analytic approach to strategy used by other consultants FS had hired, and urging that it be supplemented by a more "visionary" and interactive approach. They proposed to help FS' strategic planning unit in its role of

guardian of the synthetic values required to interconnect experiments institutionally, making sure that substance issues in the business are put on the agenda and addressed, helping communication between the center and the units, adding quality to the resolution of the strategic issues, and continuously co-invent events and processes to add quality to the strategic thinking capacity of the organization.

In April 1994, the strategic planning director asked SMG to take on the development of the "visionary/interactive" part of a planning process, while the more analytic parts would be done by them directly. The strategic planner had in addition hired in, to assist him as a member of his staff, the lead consultant of the original RMG team, which facilitated contacts further. SMG agreed to do this through workshops, called "forums" internally.

From this point in time onwards, SMG's client became FS's strategy unit, whose most important customer, in turn, was FS's top management—and most particularly, Necci, the CEO. SMG was thus working with the strategists for the future of FS—for a *possible, potential* FS that the strategy team helps top management to shape, rather than for the *current*, "every-day" FS. In this context, the *current*, "every-day" FS became in effect a resource to be used to develop the *possible, potential* FS.

Normann first conducted some interviews with management leaders. Necci told him that in his view what blocked business development for FS at that time was the lack of a common vision and management capacity among the top people. He felt he had to do a lot of their work—particularly dealing with outside counterparts—for them. An opportunity to engage in this interactively—treating it as a symptom of a shared problem that they could look at together was thus made available. But Necci did not wish SMG to act on this basis or in this role. An opportunity interactively to link becoming and being was thus missed.

The first internal forum
Based on the interviews, SMG articulated what it thought the visionary planning required to start becoming reality. It included the holding of a series of 3 workshops to be attended by an extended group of over 30 FS top managers. They would be exposed to outside speakers having faced similar business issues, and

to the internally developed factual analyses each business had undertaken with the guidance of the corporate strategy and planning team. This would enable the top managers—including the CEO—to develop, through extensive debate, a common understanding of the business issues and challenges they faced.

The idea was to make each of these forums a "transitional space" in Winnicott's sense.[8] This entails designing an opportunity, away from the present, in which one can explore possible futures in a context of relative safety—that is, not (yet) fully being "in" or committing "to" these futures; but instead being able to explore them and prepare for them. To this effect, SMG staged these events away from the company's headquarters. Although a direct train ride from Rome, many of the attendees arrived by . . . chauffeur-driven car!

Of course, an underlying assumption of proceeding in this way was that the managers attending such workshops could *learn*—learn how to individually and collectively become the bridge between the current operations of FS and the future ones. Recall that these managers had already been living a revolution, from Ministry administrators (in some cases as political appointees), to become actual managers having to deliver certain service quality, increased productivity, lower cost, or grow revenue growth targets. A further assumption was that top management (via at least these workshops) would support such learning.

In the first forum, participants were exposed to the different scenarios for Italy which had been elaborated for the Necci–Normann book. In his presentation, Necci said that in the past and today, Ferrovie had been and still was in the simple railway transporting business, but in the future, it had to become an "integrated service operator." In this capacity, he said, it would have to serve metropolitan areas, offer integrated mobility, and negotiate joint ventures with clients. Competitors in the new mode would include companies offering transport (spedizionieri), services (e.g. Italgaz, Telecom Italia, Enel), "vector" links (e.g. bus companies, truck companies, other railway companies in Europe), terminal systems (e.g. Fintecna), engineering firms, other networks (e.g. roads, canals) and financial services.

This led to a very complex discussion, in which no agreement was reached. The forum succeeded in setting the level of ambition which the CEO considered FS required to address its strategic challenges. But it did not deliver a common, explicitly agreed to, vision of the positions FS sought to obtain in the new contexts.

The second forum
At the end of June, SMG received a document authored by Necci, called "*Guidelines for the definition of the 1995–2004 strategic operational plan.*" In it, Necci stated,

We are now ending the first stage of recovery. In the last four years we have worked with what tools were available and those we could activate in order to obtain:

- a substantial productivity gain in the labor factor,
- economies in management and operational costs,

- improved punctuality in the railway service,
- an organizational structure more adherent to the principles of efficiency and economy,
- actions related to commercial policy...

But above all, thanks to the financial availability made possible by the shareholder and (...) activating mechanisms from private investors, in the first half of the 1990s, the Railways produced an investment plan with the following objectives:

- to upgrade the main infrastructural access of the country (particularly Alpine tunnels) in order to gain competitiveness over other modes of transport,
- to act on the main nodes of the network to improve traffic capacity in train operations (80 per cent of traffic was on 20 per cent of the tracks),
- to acquire quality rolling stock,
- to continue the programs of technological updating and renewal of the network.

He added that the plan's strategic core was centered on increasing revenues, not only on improving cost efficiency.[9]

Necci was by then focusing increasingly on how to secure the implementation of his strategic vision. He reminded forum participants that during the implementation phase of the 1993–95-business plan, FS had changed its mission from being a mono-modal operator specialized in railway movement to a service company in the field of transportation. He pointed out that the discontinuity had not been absorbed in operational management; this needed to happen.

As noted above, the gap between Necci's evolving understanding of the changing and challenging strategic situation on the one hand, and the reality of everyday operations for the vast majority of employees in FS on the other, was something which—despite many attempts—the intervention failed to bridge. It became apparent that the drivers for the change process that had been mobilized were insufficient. Many outside consultants, especially the local Italians who had worked with SMG, were hired into the company. Without Italian consultants in place, SMG was ill-equipped to assist FS management in the transformation of the company on an ongoing basis, as "every-day" meetings became too expensive. Language issues, the cost of travel and accommodation, as well as the reduced size of the team (two outside consultants) rendered this unduly difficult.

A lesson is that bringing so many of the outside consultants into the company actually weakened the intervention. It strengthened some aspects of FS's strategic capabilities; but this is not at the core of the interactivity which the process required. Had key players stayed as consultants, their accompanying the transformation of FS interactively on a longer term might have been possible.

Within FS, too, there was a lack of a clear change leader. The head of strategic planning, although a superb planner, was also structurally in a position preventing him from effectively intervening to change the interactions which blocked transformation.

And the split in power among the top players prevented thinkers and implementers from coming together as motors of an effective interactive change process.

The FS strategy team pushed ahead with the development of a sophisticated economic model. This model divided FS into five "strategic business areas," which came to be known as ASAs (*area strategici d'affari*).

The second forum was opened by DeCesaris, the Chairman of FS, in mid-July. Necci arrived very late. There were a number of presentations, and then group work. Normann's presentation followed the group work—with Necci still absent. Normann underlined that economic activity in general had been moving from a focus on industrial production to one on customers. He talked about what he called the "twenty plus twenty minus twenty minus twenty equal five hundred formula." As he recalls it, the idea was that if one invests 20 percent more in the 20 percent most profitable, high potential customers, taking away 20 percent away from serving the 20 percent most non-core customers, one obtains profit gains of 500 percent. Of course, with few exceptions, European railway-men thought of "users"—all of which had to be catered to in equal, standard, and rather anonymous ways—more than "customers." This was the same in AT&T and EDF, customers with choice did not exist, subscribers were considered as lucky, standardized, anonymous hostages. So, Normann was considered to be quite radical.

After a quick briefing, Necci said he was satisfied with the work that had been done by the groups. He commented that in his view there was more homogeneity among them than what the different reports allowed one to see at first glance. He said he believed that FS was on the right course and that the next step would be about investments. But Necci's own behavior (arriving almost an hour late, without explanation or apology) did not contribute to get the message that "the talk would really be walked" in terms of having one united "team around the theme," which had been something all had agreed was required.

Each ASA responsible manager then presented his view on the future of the ASA within the context of the challenges Necci had outlined, using the economic method which the planning staff had derived.

Necci's conclusions from the workshop were:

We have a choice: We can go back to be[ing] a monolith. Or we can have "diversification to retain a core business," as we have learnt.

This statement contained an unexpected land-mine: the use of the word "diversification." Though Necci meant the word to refer to a necessary adaptation to three key business challenges, it was taken as an attack on the core identity of FS as a company. His opponents interpreted Necci not as updating the core mission, but as spreading out into unrelated areas and building a personal empire. A lesson to be drawn here is that continuity and change depend on each other—leadership thinking must find a way to balance them. In large public administrations, however, change is not considered essential to enhance the viability of their identity, as can be the case in large private firms.

The three challenges identified by Necci were:

1. The move to a European scale. Much of the business (like freight and some inter-city passenger services) would in the near future be conducted at this level, as per Brussels-set policies and directives. Thinking in terms of "national" scales did not make sense. Instead, an international, "continental" perspective (with new opportunities, challenges, competitors, etc.) was required.

2. Adaptation to regional differences. Much of the business (in particular stations and metropolitan region passenger services) would now be conducted at a regional level. Thinking in terms of "national" scales did not make sense here either. Instead, a highly differentiated perspective (also with new opportunities, challenges, competitors, etc.) was required. In this game, very important actors in highly decentralized Italy were its cities. Traffic congestion in Milan and Rome—which had been forced to close down-towns to cars during working hours; or Naples where triple row parking was common—were also interpreted as substantial pockets of untapped demand for FS offerings. (One of the original RMG consultants would later rise to manage this Division.)

3. Unbundling of the railroad business activities. Because of both of the factors above, as well as the Brussels directive to separate the network from services using it, many of the cross-subsidies enjoyed by integrated national railway companies would disappear. The opacity of established railway ("Ferrovie") bundled activities would give way to transparency, in which cross-subsidies would become visible and open to question. Market-like mechanisms in which transfer costs could be established, monitored, and improved upon were to be brought in.

The struggles of the ASAs

The next step in the planning process was for the new five ASAs to produce a first draft of the strategic plan, which they were then meant to feed into the operational planning process 1995–97 and the budget process for '95. The documents from the ASAs, revised to take into account the learnings of the 2nd forum, were of an extremely high standard; "like top quality consulting reports."[10] However, each of the ASAs relied too much on "happy" forecasts which defended their own turf. There was very little said about what each of these ASAs would do if their forecasts did not materialize. And most seriously, the ensemble lacked a single, over-arching link allowing the diversity of economic logics among the ASAs to live together within the coherence that a common corporate logic required. The ASAs were not interacting with each other systemically; FS could not be unified as a single strategic actor through such an exercise.

At the end of August, SMG, reviewing the two first forums, proposed a new focus on organizational structures and processes, on management roles, and on how the strategic units of analyses were to be taken into account. It also proposed a process for integrating the visions of the different groups through further interviews and workshops.

SMG suggested it was important to decide whether supporting assets were meant to be profitable on their own right, or whether they should just act as cost centers supporting operations. In other words, SMG attempted to address key internal interactions that had so far been under-emphasized. They also discussed external interactions—what kind of alliances and joint ventures needed to be built, what kind of privatization processes should be undertaken, how to split the network from the rest of the company were issues that needed addressing together with outside counterparts. Most fundamentally, SMG proposed that FS must determine whether it would be a holding company or a mother company.

In the middle of September 1994, SMG and the FS planners interviewed top managers. They found that attention by the top on the ASAs and their plans, which were the most important way of operationalizing the vision, had been moved onto the back burner. Was this a political first step toward breaking up the company? In any case, Necci made it clear—without laying out details—that structural changes were politically risky at this time, and were he to proceed with these, his future could be on the line. And so, Necci requested what he called "a soft landing" in terms of the changes that had been discussed—that is, he wanted to avoid a radical break from the *status quo*. He sought a new bridge between strategy and operations—one that would not be seen as disturbing power relations in the company. He began to move people around rather than modifying the structure in order to reduce the political consequences.

SMG participants privately discussed the limitations of this approach. After these discussions, they met Necci again and suggested that the agreed strategy must move to operational planning and implementation more aggressively. While Necci stated that "yes, there have to be actions on organizational issues and people," he moved the discussion back to the book.

It became apparent to SMG in the following months that Necci was under increasing political attack, although he kept the particulars to himself. He shifted his attention from long-term visioning to an urgent effort to develop a three-year plan with clear deliverable targets for the State.

The difficulty of connecting the vision to stakeholders
The planning staff and SMG met again with the ASAs in October and early November, 1994. They sought to develop a "language" allowing issues to be clarified and commitments to be contractualized. On October 19, Ramirez went over the possibility of doing a "responsibility and accountability" charting of key strategy-relevant issues with the planning staff in Rome. SMG had had to accept that the existing planning process in place was neither credible nor trusted as a way of delivering the strategic vision: an alternative process was clearly required. In other words, SMG was seeking to enhance the effectiveness of interactions within FS so that the organization could function the way the strategy demanded it must.

But vested interests live off opacity, and, for reasons overviewed earlier, the CEO and his top management team did not—perhaps could not—offer the backing which the clarification that the "responsibility and accountability" charting method obtains.

In November, Normann wrote to Ramirez: "The strategic planning cycle has produced five ASA documents, and is moving into the operative plans. Cost cutting pressure is expected to continue, and it risks becoming the overall focus for next year." Normann suggested that strategic criteria—not only cost-cutting requirements—needed to be taken into account if FS was to enact the strategies which had been developed. Interdependencies had to be found between ASAs, the strategy needed to be contractualized not only with the top, but also among them, and with their subordinates—no performance objectives had been built into actual staff evaluation procedures.

Again, the lack of internal leadership came to the fore. The strategy function was being asked de facto to drive an internal transformation that was beyond its mandate. In effect, it needed to simultaneously improve operational management, act as a projects office for the CEO, carry out strategic programming and control, support enacting the CEO's strategic initiatives without his full explicit support, and improve internal communications with line management. This was clearly too much. And shifts in top management altered the power equation.

It appears in retrospect that a clearer distinction between the strategic and operational levels, and a more effective interaction or engagement of both with each other, was necessary for success. In later writings, Ramirez suggested that cost consciousness and cost improvement have become a must, and that strategy must treat these as a given and build from there on.[11] If cost reduction is not so treated, and becomes a priority on its own, strategy will not happen. To some extent, this unfortunate condition is what later took place in FS for far too many years, driven in part by the lira's entry into the euro.

Other obstacles to the implementation of the strategy began to emerge more strongly. It had not escaped the consultants that railway-men have historically had a very strong identity. This entails both strengths and weaknesses. SMG suggested that a change of identity for FS, from railway to something else, would have to be driven by a customer point of view. Yet, as we have learned later, trade unions in the French railways have, through industrial action, reversed customer-centric strategy initiatives. The customer-focused argument proved less persuasive than SMG had hoped as a reason for redefining the business, in face of vested interests, contractual advantages acquired through years of unionized struggle, and deeply held identities.

Increasingly the role of middle management and of organizational structure came to the fore. SMG argued that change would happen only if interactions throughout the organization were redesigned from the customer-end inwards. Structure needed to reflect the real interactions needed to enact the strategy. They therefore suggested the need for a matrix organization in which both levels—strategic and operational—could meet.[12] SMG noted that many strategic issues showed that borders among existing units in FS were unclear. These included borders between operations and maintenance, between development and investment, between production and sales, and between ownership and operations.

With this in mind, SMG sent FS a proposal entitled "assistance to the development of an organizational structure in FS, coherent with the results of the strategic planning process, 1994," outlining a six-month intervention. There were three agreed deliverables in this contract, which was to run through the end of July:

(1) one month after the start up, SMG was to give FS a memo with the guidelines and process of organizational evolution;
(2) then, within two months a diagnosis of coherence between strategy and present structural resources would be provided; and then finally
(3) a final report would be issued.

Necci expressed the need to involve more people in FS in his thinking, and so the format of small, intensive seminars and learning trips was abandoned. Breadth gave way to depth.

Necci again seemed under a lot of pressure from forces he did not communicate about. He told Normann that "we have to focus on the core business, and not on diversification and far out strategies." He said he believed FS was more and more situated in the "C scenario" of their book, the most political and "mafia-intensive" one. In early April, SMG suggested to Necci that FS should consider:

1. A clear internal reconfiguration, a new constitution.
2. Making business and quality elements in the core business visible.
3. Planning for a real, fundamental cultural change, and change of management practices.
4. An interactive process of external reconfiguration of the core businesses.

But this supposed that "the management group can agree on a strategic agenda which is close to these four points, and then operationalize it in a program and stick to it." Normann underlined that time for operationalizing the vision was running out, as stakeholders not interested in FS succeeding had been given ample time to gather their forces.

Failure in supporting the strategy process and function

The first workshop in the planned series of larger and more broadly attended sessions was held in Tivoli on the 5 and 6 of May 1995. Outside speakers had been invited. Necci made his own executives and the invited outsider wait. When the outside speaker started to speak, Necci asked Vaciago to follow him outside the meeting room on some urgent matter. Normann recalled (in 1999) that for him this was a key turning point, in which he saw that the process he and Ramirez and the internal strategists had tried to get going would fail: Necci's behavior did not appear to embody the interactivity that was required for success.

In his Tivoli speech, Normann forcefully reiterated the above four points. He felt (when interviewed for this book in 1999) that this was

probably the most personal and open speech I gave in the whole FS relationship, at least to a larger group. The red thread was that they had to build a business, or businesses. This I also saw as the rationale for changing the kind of discussions they had had with the unions. Unless you have a business rationale, an idea of the business you are trying to build, and how you do it, and why you are doing certain things, you can never have a discussion characterized by policy rather than politics with the unions. So these two go together.

Normann told participants: "Two and a half years ago in late 1992, I and my colleagues got the mission to do the core business analysis. You (managers) in FS have developed considerable knowledge around the business." There has been a lot of progress, Normann said. He suggested that "last autumn in the Foligno conferences the corporate vision became clear." The "theme around the team," and "integrated diversity" were underlined leitmotifs.

"The future is now," Normann said. "The moment of truth is to move the strategic plan into an operative plan. Consistency and persistence come from a joint perception of the situation. From taking joint responsibility. One has to start from oneself. No white knights will come. Concentrate on the factors that can be influenced. Increasing industrial efficiency, improving quality, information systems, distribution cost effectiveness. Better marketing segmentation, more communications with the market, improving the sales force. How to develop new offerings. How to invest in human resources." Normann said of investing in human resources "(I think this) is crucial for you, it goes right across the line. Investments in culture, middle management, sales organization."

External constituencies

Another issue to be addressed was how to handle external constraints. These involved negotiations with the State, with ENEL, with the European Commission, with the environmentalists.

The unions were a special concern. In Normann's view:

"You need to find new formulas, and of course this is critical to this kind of process.... Investing in new resources and negotiating with the unions has to go hand in hand. So there are a number of negotiations that have to go on, to loosen the constraints." And he quoted Necci: "When we negotiate with the environmentalists and Europe, this cannot be a substitute for being efficient internally, because this puts us in a weak position. We have to negotiate from a position of strong internal efficiency. There is no substitute for becoming the bench-mark in Europe."

In mid-May Normann sent a document to FS management:

"Our institutions are made as if all people wanted and needed to work eight hours a day to make a living..., but on the job demand side we have people who don't need as much of a job as before...and on the supply side scarce resources have changed. Entrepreneurship and flexibility are insufficient." He added, "I really don't see where is the place of labor unions and industry associations in the future as negotiators. I can see service organizations catering to the competence and flexibility development of member subscribers. Is this a naive view? ... We have to understand what kind of behavior our institutions create among the parties in the labor market."

Was Normann right? Are union-centered negotiations incompatible with flexible organization? Some German examples—like Volkswagen—and Swedish examples like Volvo and Swedbank seem to prove him wrong. But the role of trade unions in Italy is different from the one they have in Germany and Sweden. No trade union official was at that meeting. Looking back, a missed opportunity in the intervention was the possibility of debating such issues with the counterparts involved in such interactions. The issue is real, and no closure has been reached by the authors of this book in collectively studying it in three countries and two continents over half a dozen years. The only recommendation we can make is to engage unions and managers in determining the future of this interaction. Two of us—Ramirez and Tixier—have been engaged to do just this in an international, European-based, institution. Heckscher and Maccoby have done likewise in North America. But opposition to such efforts is real, and the results are—so far, at least—not encouraging.

Seeking alternative approaches

At the end of May SMG acknowledged that "it is important that the established organization can function in parallel, in a 'business as usual' mode." That is, a fairly fundamental change in strategy while simultaneously obtaining important gains in the efficiency and effectiveness of existing operations could not be forced upon the existing organization simultaneously.

But the failure to address this dual demand within a single organization made the value of the new strategy more questionable, as its enactment kept on being postponed. If management capability is a bottleneck, if managers cannot make operations and strategy interact (through plans, budgets, action priorities), then operations undermine strategy. So, a lesson is that an interaction between operational targets and strategic aspirations must be designed as depending on each other. Strategic change must be framed and fed by operational improvement, and this must be implemented as a single development for interactive intervention to succeed. With the benefit of hindsight, it is possible to conclude that SMG probably relied too little on institutionalizing ongoing interactivity, and too much on transitional events. Perhaps this reflected its being too thin on the ground locally, and having to concentrate interventions into several-day chunks for the economics of travel to pay off.

As the reality of the failure of the intervention strategy and the limitations of action its key customer could provide sank in, another possibility began to appear. This involved developing a business idea not "in" and "of" FS, as the consultants had been attempting to do, but "with" FS. The idea was to develop one of the strategic vectors they had identified—cities—as a joint venture between FS and SMG. FS had customers and local know-how, SMG had competence FS lacked and international networks. This alternative intervention gained support from Necci and others.

More planning and strategy workshops were held during the spring and summer. And then ... in September of 1996, Antonio Lorenzo Necci, the CEO of the Italian State Railways, was arrested on multiple charges, including corruption ... two days before the formal contract creating a joint company between SMG and FS was to be signed. To this day, the courts have not determined his guilt, and all convictions have either been overturned thereafter or are still being appealed.

Recent (2002) exchanges with FS strategists confirm that the strategy proposed by SMG is currently—over a decade later—being implemented. Some of the sources have stated that Necci's successor has a more engaging, co-productive, low-key style—and that the interactions he has managed to obtain with key stakeholders are beginning to manifest the promise the strategy held. The question is whether such results could have become visible earlier. This shows that luck, as well as patience, modesty, and perseverance, are all needed for the interactive approach of intervention.

5

Lucent: Toward Strategic Engagement

INTRODUCTION

The Lucent case pushes union–management dialogue to its limits. It began as a simple attempt to recreate Workplace of the Future (see Chapter 3) in an AT&T spinoff; but it soon confronted problems beyond those that WPoF had dealt with—problems of extreme turbulence in the industry, of fundamental shifts in management strategy, of major divestitures and layoffs. AT&T, faced with similar pressures, abandoned WPoF and fell into a declared labor–management war; but at Lucent the unions and the company continued to stagger along with some semblance of continued cooperation, although with a very high degree of tension. As we write it remains very uncertain whether the parties can work through the huge changes under way without also falling into major conflict.

The story passes through four main stages.

1. In the first, the problem was to rebuild relations, strained by a contentious bargaining round, as a foundation for new WPoF committees.
2. Very soon, however, the focus moved to a more fundamental strategic choice facing the company: whether it would or would not continue to do most of its manufacturing internally rather than subcontracting it. The problem in this phase was to build trust between the parties in the future of the company. After much discussion, at a level of depth and intensity greater than had ever been reached at AT&T, the company affirmed that manufacturing was core to the company's future; this gave a new foundation for dialogue.
3. Within a year internal and external pressures led to a reversal of that strategic decision, leading the company toward divestiture of virtually all its manufacturing operations. Now the problem was whether the parties could find a way to navigate this dramatic change without tearing each other apart; in some ways, it was like negotiating a divorce. They developed a level of union involvement in financial decisions almost unprecedented in the US and nearly completed that arduous course.

4. This process broke down abruptly near its close for a number of reasons, the most obvious of which was the intervention of the government in support of a union legal charge. Relations did not quite collapse into open warfare, but they did shift largely back to traditional adversarial bargaining with much posturing and bluffing. The question at the end is whether the process could or should be brought back from this state.

In many respects Lucent is the perfect model of a knowledge-service firm, focused on a high level of innovation (sparked by the Bell Labs) and development of end-to-end solutions for customers. It is also a model of the turbulence and uncertainty that has beset such firms for the last decade. It began with many advantages: the long history of QWL and WPoF described above had created a deep wellspring of understanding and relationships that could be drawn on in times of trouble, and both the company and the union held strongly to a basic commitment to work things out rather than fighting. The case therefore gives us almost a clear test of how far one can push union–management dialogue in dealing with new post-industrial environments.

THE STORY

Background

The business: strategic challenges
Soon after its divestiture from AT&T in 1995, Lucent started on a roller-coaster ride. It was initially viewed by investors as something of a dog—a hodge-podge of stodgy, old-economy, low-margin parts. But a sudden burst of investment in telecommunications infrastructure turned Lucent into a star of the dot-com economy. Then in 2000 it abruptly fell off a cliff, at first by itself, but soon followed by most of its competitors. The stock price dropped by over 80 percent within a few months, the CEO was fired, and the company had to deny rumors of bankruptcy. These rapid shifts and the high level of uncertainty about the industry's future have put enormous strains on the relatively positive labor–management relations that were carried over from AT&T.

Lucent's primary business was the development and manufacture of telecommunications equipment: switches for voice networks and data networks, fiber optic cable, integrated circuits, and software. It also had a substantial service operation focused on the installation and maintenance of equipment for small and large businesses.

The basic strategic challenge was clear: Lucent was the dominant force in an old technological arena approaching the end of its life, and it was aiming to move into a new area experiencing rapid growth. The old area was switches and networks for voice communication: a large share of Lucent's profits came from the 5E switch which drove voice networks in nearly all phone companies. But the

5E was inefficient for the rapidly growing needs for data communication and everyone expected that within a few years it would become obsolete. The data arena, meanwhile, was dominated by new player—Cisco Systems.

Cisco was nearly the antithesis of Lucent. Lucent was large, bureaucratic, East-coast-based, internally focused, heavily unionized, and with a long and proud history. Cisco was small, nimble, scarcely a decade old, with a California "dot-com" culture. In 1998, the two companies had nearly equivalent market capitalization (about $170 billion); but while Lucent had 160,000 employees, Cisco had about 14,000. The difference resulted from the fact that while Lucent produced most of its products in-house, Cisco outsourced almost everything.

The marketplace was extremely turbulent in all time frames. The telecom market was projected to grow at the dizzying pace of 15 percent + per year. The entire sector was seized by what, in retrospect, looks like a bubble mentality. Lucent's CEO aimed at 20 percent growth in revenues and 15 percent growth in productivity year over year, even though he recognized that no large company had ever been able to sustain such numbers. There was a frantic emphasis on speed—the ability to deliver cutting-edge products to market and to customers. The technology was evolving so rapidly that customers had no patience; products that used to take months to deliver were now demanded in weeks.

The organization: relational challenges
The market uncertainties created great strains on the organization. Lucent inherited at its formation two major components of AT&T: the manufacturing arm (Western Electric) and the research capability (Bell Labs). It also inherited a slow, highly bureaucratic, stovepiped culture in which Bell Labs was accustomed to working on important science and then telling the manufacturing people what to do.

Soon after Lucent was spun off its CEO, arguing the need for a sharply more entrepreneurial culture, decentralized the company into 11 businesses to gain greater focus and independence. There was much complaining about lack of coordination; the CEO acknowledged the problem but felt this is the only way to get the speed and focus needed in the new markets.

Lucent, like its competitors, also made heavy use of alliances and acquisitions to speed product introductions. These often led to considerable cultural clashes and increased the internal coordination problems. The Ascend purchase, in particular, led to systemic tensions between "new-age," "Silicon Valley" types, and the more traditional Lucent managers. There were continual vociferous debates within management at all levels over the basic strategic direction, with the old AT&T managers largely favoring a continuation of a manufacturing-based model and the newer employees pushing for a more knowledge and service-based business.

The unionized parts of Lucent, with about 45,000 of the 160,000 total employees, included over a dozen plants, making everything from metal cabinets, the flagship but aging 5E switch, to state-of-the-art microelectronic chips and fiber-optic cable; and a highly-skilled installation and maintenance workforce. Most of these units had never participated very enthusiastically in Workplace of the

Future. On the whole WPoF was seen as marginal, with some occasional successes and general usefulness in keeping tensions down, but not very important for the management of the company.

The two unions, CWA and IBEW, were roughly equal in strength at Lucent, each representing about 20,000 employees. The IBEW members were nearly all in manufacturing plants, while the largest bulk of the CWA members were installers and maintenance workers—highly skilled, very proud of their abilities, oriented to their local craft units, quite independent of the national union despite the latter's formal authority. The unions had historically negotiated separately, but for the previous decade had managed to maintain bargaining unity despite periodic skirmishes over jurisdiction.

The consultant's engagement in the Lucent partnership process
In the spring of 1998 Ralph Craviso, who had been hired a year before as the new labor relations VP, visited Heckscher to discuss the experience of Workplace of the Future at AT&T. Heckscher stressed that WPoF had become over time imprisoned in the Labor Relations ghetto, viewed as peripheral and expendable by operations management; his sense was that any successful continuation of the effort could not be driven by Labor Relations. Having so thoroughly put down Craviso's function, he was rather surprised to be asked a few weeks later to help with the reconstruction of WPoF at Lucent.

Craviso had worked for the most part in airlines, for TWA, American, and Continental. Deep-voiced and strong-willed, Craviso aroused strong reactions from most who met him. He became a very effective player on the management side. The top union players, including Morty Bahr (the President of the CWA), generally trusted him; but many further down the line on both sides found him abrasive, and some accused him of excessive bluff and bluster.

In his first conversation on a consulting basis Heckscher again stressed the need for line sponsorship. Craviso suggested that the best candidate for line sponsorship was Pat Russo, then one of the five top players in the company and in charge of many of the unionized sections. When Craviso and Heckscher met with Russo she focused on the strategic challenges facing the company, especially on the problem of *speed*; she believed that Lucent was standing on a "burning platform." The current success, she said, was built on legacy products; unless Lucent could leap to a new platform of data switching, very foreign to the traditions of the company, it would be left behind by nimble new competitors like Cisco Systems. She agreed to host a meeting with the two unions on the theme, "How do we create a high-performing unionized company?" and to persuade other top officers to come as well.

These encouraging signs from the management side were matched by the company's two unions, the Communications Workers of America (CWA) and the International Brotherhood of Electrical Workers (IBEW). Heckscher had had an especially long connection to the first of these: almost 20 years before, his first post-graduate job had been 4 years in their research department. Many of those whom he had become friends with at that time were now high-level officials in headquarters.

The CWA was also one of the most innovative and progressive unions in the country. In the early 1980s they had been one of the first to conduct a strategic planning process, engaging local officers throughout the union in thinking about the changes underway in their core telephone industry. They had consistently been among the leaders in pursuing worker participation, the promotion of women, and novel organizing strategies. Morty Bahr, the President (whom Heckscher had known when he worked in the union's research department), was now an elder statesman of the labor movement, and one of the few in my experience to understand that simply holding on to existing jobs would not enable the union to survive.

The person in charge of Lucent bargaining for the CWA was Jim Irvine, another old-timer and a power within the union who was often mentioned as a possible successor to Bahr. Irvine was an unusually articulate leader with a strong grasp of the business issues facing the company; he had also been one of the leaders of the WPoF effort at AT&T and had a long track record as a highly creative, as well as effective, leader, with high credibility both within the union and with the company. He could talk about business strategy better than most top managers, and then turn around and rouse a crowd of militant installers to battle.

The IBEW was a very different union—with a craft tradition, far more decentralized than the CWA. Heckscher had worked with some of their leaders over the years during his involvement with the Workplace of the Future effort, but his roots there were far shallower than in the CWA. The IBEW's headquarters representative, Mike Quinlan, was a true manufacturing man, believing to his core that value lay in making things well, scornful of managers who followed fads and juggled numbers on their way to the next job and the next company. During his long tenure he had built connections to many managers in Lucent with the same beliefs, so he often had a direct pipeline to secret decisions at the heart of Lucent. Time and again he pulled the covers back from company plans.

But while Irvine at CWA could exercise considerable control over his local officers, Quinlan had much less power at the IBEW. The holder of the contract was Steve Lynn, the leader of a council of local manufacturing presidents. Lynn was slow, methodical, often seen as stubborn; he made no apologies for focusing on the issues of his own constituents rather than on some larger vision or on integration with the CWA. He had been elected very recently and his political position was always insecure; he was constantly under pressure from the other presidents in his council.

On the whole this array of union leaders was supportive of efforts to improve relations and revive the Workplace of the Future principles. All of them had been leaders of WPoF and felt it had accomplished much good; they were already very sophisticated about the potentials and limits of joint efforts. It seemed that on both sides the foundation for a new structure was solid.

For the first six months of Heckscher's involvement the parties' focus was on the triennial collective bargaining process, concluded in the summer of 1998. He stayed largely out of that. The bargaining was quite acrimonious: it ended in a brief national strike which, although quickly resolved, left all parties blaming each other for miscues. The company felt that the unions, especially the IBEW, had failed to control their own locals: in the decentralized tradition of that union, a handshake at the main bargaining table was ignored by a number of local leaders. For their part, the union bargainers felt Craviso had been hard-line and overly aggressive; a CWA official told Heckscher, "We want him out."

In order to get his own sense of what was happening on the front lines, Heckscher arranged to visit three factories on his own and interview in each a cross-section of management, including supervisors; union officials; and union members. One thing he found in these discussions was that no one below the level of the plant managers had any real sense of the challenges facing the company. The "burning platform" about which Pat Russo spoke so fervently was never mentioned; on the contrary, everyone felt that the company was doing extremely well and could grow indefinitely on its current course. Issues that people were concerned about—both management and occupational—were almost entirely local and divorced from the strategic issues which dominated the discourse at headquarters.

During this period he came to two conclusions.

1. First, the company was not taking responsibility for its part of the problem in relations. The management attitude for the most part, in the plants as well as in headquarters, was that the union should realize the company had pressing problems and should just fall into line and help. Unions' concerns were consistently dismissed as petty and unrelated to business problems.

2. Second, nothing could be resolved until the company's strategy became clearer. In a meeting with the unions a year before, Rich McGinn, the CEO, had talked about Cisco as their major competitor. This worried the unions greatly, because Cisco outsourced almost all its manufacturing and maintained a far smaller employee base than Lucent. But all of this was tentative and incompletely explained.

The first active phase: exploration of the company's strategy

In the fall of 1998, once bargaining was truly concluded, Heckscher began a series of discussions with union and company people about the strategic choices facing the company and their effects on the unions. He met with three members of Lucent's strategic planning group, where it became clear that they embraced the "Cisco" logic: they said that in a turbulent environment it was too slow and expensive to maintain an internal manufacturing capacity and that subcontracting was a necessity. He then went to the unions and began a discussion about whether this direction was indeed inevitable, and how the unions could respond to and shape the strategy. But these efforts were not very successful. When a meeting was held between the strategy head and the union leadership, the union people did not engage in a discussion: they listened politely, and offline said it was "bullshit" and "nothing new." It seemed as if the parties were talking different languages. While the company was talking about revenue growth, the unions were hearing a presentation about job loss. There was little communication between those worlds.

The first outsourcing crisis
All this came to a crisis unexpectedly and suddenly. Mike Quinlan's management contacts told him that Lucent was developing a secret plan to outsource circuit packs, a mainstay of IBEW jobs. When he confronted Craviso and other managers about this, the company soon admitted that there was some discussion and contingency planning around such an initiative. The unions reacted swiftly, threatening major confrontation.

The most effective threat came from the CWA. They had developed over the prior decade the capacity for "mobilization," which meant direct local membership actions. The installers, a highly skilled segment of the union, were particularly effective in picketing Lucent customers when they felt aggrieved; such picketing was viewed with great alarm at the top of the company. When CWA threatened mobilization in November 1998, it got the attention of senior management.

Within a few days Craviso had set up a meeting for Heckscher with the CEO and the top team of the company. Heckscher's role was rather unclear: he was not really a representative of the unions, but the union leadership agreed that they would trust his report of the meeting, and Craviso apparently felt he could better present the issues to management during the crisis than the union leaders themselves could.

In that meeting McGinn made clear that he was very unhappy about past union picketing of customers. He also expressed a basic suspicion of unions, saying that his sense was that they valued growth of the unions as institutions above actually helping their members. As they talked about the strategic direction of the company, he put out a vision of a more high-tech, nimble company. He asked Heckscher three times in slightly different ways, "Why can't unions function effectively in Silicon Valley?"—suggesting that unless they could solve that problem they could not work effectively in the new parts of Lucent.

As the conversation moved to the more concrete level, McGinn vehemently insisted that the company had no intention of getting rid of manufacturing—that, he said, was a "stupid" inference by the unions. Heckscher said that such assurances were no longer enough: the unions needed a clear explanation of the company's logic, credible involvement in the process of strategic planning, and solid protections against sudden changes in direction. He pushed hard on the question: Is it really worth it to you to pursue a policy of engagement with the unions under those circumstances, or would it be better to push through unilaterally? McGinn paused, looked around at his team, and said, "Engagement is preferable by far."

On the basis of that conversation, CWA called off the mobilization scheduled for later that week. The company followed up with several meetings that were meant to elaborate the strategic direction and its implementation. Pat Russo met with the unions in Washington to add details to the claim that it was not in the interests of the company to severely cut back on manufacturing: their manufacturing capability, she argued, gave them a competitive advantage over their competition, because they could maintain higher quality and control proprietary information better. There would be some move to outsource products that were at the end of their life cycles, but no major shift in employment.

Reestablishing the cooperative relationship
In January 1999, McGinn met for a half day with the unions to try to start things off on a better footing; he said, "Let's stipulate: we haven't done a very good job of engagement so far." He further detailed the competitive challenges faced by the company and committed himself to actively leading a process of dialogue with the unions. At the end of the meeting he said to Heckscher, "Let's do a full day next time." In the following weeks he and Pat Russo spoke personally to many of the business leaders to make sure they were on board. McGinn and Russo developed a detailed explanation of the strategic logic for keeping manufacturing: they believed it would contribute to quality, speed, and intellectual capital. There appeared to be an opportunity for progress.

Here we need to jump ahead in the story: within less than a year the company did indeed announce plans to get rid of most of its manufacturing capacity, and within two years it had divested almost all its plants. How should we understand what happened? One possibility, of course, is that the leadership had those plans all along; another possibility is that the situation evolved so rapidly during the following year that they were forced to actions which they were not contemplating earlier; a third is that there were disagreements within Lucent—so that while at this moment those who favored manufacturing were winning, it took only relatively slight shifts to push the balance to those who opposed it. The third was probably an important factor. Heckscher's experience from many conversations was that managers within the company had sharply different views on the strategic future, and the process of setting a course was an ongoing "political" struggle that developed constantly. It is also true that the competitive and technological landscape was shifting constantly during this period.

Nevertheless—whatever the reasons—the fact remains that Lucent's commitments to the unions in December of 1998 did not hold even for a year. In the most fundamental way the union's expectations were violated: where they were told that union membership in Lucent would remain roughly flat, it was in fact rapidly decimated; the IBEW in particular retained almost no members in the company. It raises the question—explored further in other parts of this book—of whether our interventions and our roles can have any hope of succeeding in this kind of environment.

But that lay in the future; at that time it seemed there was a stake in the ground which would enable the company and the union to explore ways of working together. During the spring and summer of 1999 the parties tried to lay the foundation for an improved relationship. They began a series of monthly day-long meetings involving about ten union leaders dealing with Lucent; the company side was led by Craviso but also included operational managers appropriate for issues under discussion. Once again Craviso demonstrated his ability to get the involvement of line managers in all parts of the business: visitors included plant managers from two of the largest manufacturing facilities and the head of the wireless business to describe their business plans and think about how to work with the unions.

These meetings also began to develop a definition of what the parties were trying to do together—continuous with Workplace of the Future but taking on some new dimensions. The parties called it a "partnership" founded on "dialogue," aiming at openness of exchange and shared problem-solving. Two points in particular pushed the boundaries of WPoF. One was an emphasis on the need for change: draft language said, "The partnership will succeed only if it advances needed change," and "The partnership will succeed only if the employees see a positive future in change and share in the success of the business." For the unions, especially at the local level, "change" was often seen as a code word for layoffs and restructuring—as indeed it often was. The attempt at this point was to find a way, to the extent that layoffs or restructurings were inevitable, to do them in a way which opened, rather than closed, opportunities for the unions and their members.

The second issue was whether growth in union membership should be seen as a shared objective of both parties. Management's strong reaction was that while business growth was a shared responsibility, membership growth was the union's concern—that somehow business issues were universal but union issues were selfish and particular. They were resistant even to the idea that they should avoid opposition to organizing campaigns, to say nothing of the idea that increased union membership should be a goal of the partnership. But the unions saw little reason to trust management if it did not accept one of their fundamental interests. With Heckscher playing a role of developing language and testing it back and forth, the parties developed draft language saying, "The unions have a legitimate interest in growing membership in order to maintain bargaining strength." These principles were never formally adopted—they were intended to be the focus of a long process of discussion and education, a process which was soon cut short by crises in the business.

On a more practical note, development began on a training program for local union officials. It became clear during the discussions that the relatively positive atmosphere of the meetings was not shared by many local leaders. Heckscher believed that it was essential for the unions to have space and opportunity to develop a coherent understanding of the forces around them and of the strategic choices open to them. The best chance to develop a genuine dialogue which maximized the chances of a peaceful solution, he argued, would be for the unions to have a chance to work it through so that they could develop a point of view that they "owned," that reflected their own values and traditions, while incorporating the reality of the changes around them. To Heckscher's surprise, Craviso agreed readily with this point of view. Unlike almost every other labor relations manager the CWA had faced, he saw the value of a prepared partner in dialogue.

There remained one major source of resistance to the attempts at dialogue: Steve Lynn, the leader of the IBEW's manufacturing council, was highly skeptical of Craviso and had become increasingly sour on the joint process in general. He had filed an Unfair Labor Practice charge before the National Labor Relations Board in February, and in meetings through the summer he repeatedly said that the only legitimate outcome to the circuit pack outsourcing problem would be through collective bargaining, and that all the business information and dialogue they were receiving in the monthly meetings was merely a smoke screen intended to pacify the unions while the company moved ahead with its plans. Naturally this put him in conflict with Heckscher, who represented the dialogue process. The two spoke often and maintained outwardly cordial relations but were clearly pulling in different directions. Lynn was also often in conflict with the CWA, which had not joined in the Board charge, and with headquarters representatives from his own union who saw value in the discussions under way.

The position Heckscher took as a consultant was that his role was to support a process of dialogue, including an honest assessment of its problems as well as its potential, but it was up to the parties themselves to decide whether it was a process they wanted to engage in. His role was to give his best judgment of how to build the dialogue. During the previous winter, when Heckscher felt that the company was often acting arrogantly and failing to hear union concerns, he told both sides his point of view; now he was equally open in saying that the pursuit of a strong collective bargaining approach by the IBEW would undermine efforts to build a more open relationship.

The company shifts its strategy

But now, during the summer of 1999, a new and more basic challenge began to emerge. So far the process had remained essentially within the basic parameters of the old Workplace of the Future effort: trying to build an operational partnership to help the business function better. Now Craviso began signaling that a reassessment of the company's strategic direction was under way and that some of the things being considered could change commitments made in January. By September it became fairly clear that far more extensive outsourcing was being contemplated, which could lead to a great deal of job loss at Lucent. No longer was it possible to assume a stable overall picture; the question was whether the parties could work through, in a mutual way, challenges to the core values of the unions and indeed the very existence of many of their parts.

In September Heckscher met with the headquarters staff at CWA responsible for the Lucent contract. He was beaten up for $2\frac{1}{2}$ hours—not personally (since some of these were people he had known as friends for 20 years) but because he was the closest they could get to yelling at the company. They were absolutely furious at the increased outsourcing. The conversation moved directly into the realm of defending core values and identity; there was no way to think calmly and analytically. One exchange went:

U: "F— them. Let's go to war."
Heckscher: "What would you accomplish in a war?"
U: "I'll feel a whole hell of a lot better. Until they're ready to acknowledge who we are we can't talk to them."

At the September monthly meeting the IBEW headquarters representative, Mike Quinlan, challenged Craviso: the dialogue, he said, could not continue until the unions had a better sense of whether the company's strategy did or did not include the unions. Future meetings were put on hold.

Building a "new deal" for the new strategy
At this point it seemed clear that the company was going to go through major upheaval; the question Heckscher posed in his role was whether the parties could find a path through the change that would minimize damage. He proposed to management and the unions a notion of a "New Deal" in which

(1) the union would help the company achieve greater strategic flexibility and operational effectiveness;
(2) the company would put resources into providing security for members through training, placement, buyouts, support for union purchases of facilities, etc.; and
(3) the company would encourage (or at a minimum not resist) union organizing in unorganized facilities.

Steve Lynn at the IBEW was clearly not interested in this approach, but the leadership of the CWA was open to it. Morty Bahr had for some years been preaching the notion that the union should help with career mobility and development, rather than focusing on simple job security; he had pioneered contracts that set up training and professional education for union members. On the management side, Craviso saw it as a possible way forward and took it to the senior management team; he reported back that they were open to exploring it.

So for the next nine months the parties entered a new phase with two streams. Steve Lynn at the IBEW continued to pursue the collective bargaining route, especially by pushing the NLRB charge; while the CWA (and to some extent Lynn's colleague Mike Quinlan at the IBEW) explored the possibility of developing a partnership that would embrace change and make it beneficial to all parties. This would be a new level of ambition for the labor–management relation: where the previous effort at Lucent, and the entire WPoF project, had essentially tried to develop an operational partnership within a relatively stable strategic environment, the thrust now was to raise the level of discussion to a shared understanding of the strategy itself, so that fundamental changes could be discussed and worked out in an interactive way.

The first major step was a meeting with CEO Rich McGinn in December 1999. McGinn was nervous about meeting with the unions because he realized he would have to retract a lot of the assurances he had given less than a year before. Management was also worried that the unions were so hostile and angry that the meeting would degenerate into a confrontation. Craviso was clearly putting his neck on the block by advocating the meeting.

Heckscher worked before the meeting to prepare both sides for a proactive role. One of his goals was to get each side to show that they actually understood the other's issues and feelings. He also hoped that the unions would come with some developed statements of their perspective on the company's changes, rather than sitting back and listening. This is important because the parties have over many years fallen into a self-perpetuating cycle in which the company came in to give a presentation, and the union reacted negatively. This inevitably left the union feeling that the company had done bad things, and the company feeling that the union did nothing but criticize.

So Heckscher proposed a shift from the usual pattern of the meetings: he suggested that Irvine *start* the discussion. This notion of having the union lead off the meeting seemed unfamiliar and discomforting. Both sides were somewhat taken aback by and wary of the suggestion. Irvine asked Heckscher to write down the basic points for him; the IBEW decided they didn't want to speak at the beginning. McGinn, again at Craviso's urging, accepted the notion.

Craviso did most of the preparation on the company side, holding meetings with all the main players. Heckscher wrote a memo for the leadership team to help them see how their actions, such as outsourcing, affected the basic identity and sense of value of the union participants. He also pointed a number of ways in which he himself felt management had violated trusts and ignored the unions' legitimate concerns. This memo, according to several members of the top management team, made some of them think more seriously than before about the union participants as people with a sense of legitimate pride and responsibility, rather than as narrow-minded negativists.

The meeting, to everyone's surprise, went very well. The participants, crammed together in a too-small hotel room, were initially tense and uncertain; there was an uncomfortable silence in which it was not clear who was going to begin. Then Irvine launched into his opening speech. "We understand that the business is changing," he said—and he gave a detailed overview of the strategic challenges facing the company. He insisted that the union could deal with such changes if they got advance notice; but he said that trust was currently at a low ebb because of consistent lack of notice and involvement of the union. He closed with an impassioned plea: "There are ways to get through this change together if we are open and honest."

McGinn looked taken aback: he said it was "the best explanation of the union's perspective that I have ever heard." After that start, McGinn did not do the usual canned presentation with its inevitable implications that the speaker knows it all; he spoke more openly and interactively about the problems facing the company, including significant cash flow issues. Eventually, and reluctantly, he got to the main point: it was likely that there would be plant sales or closures. "We lost a year trying to do something different," he said, "not recognizing that there was this wave about to sweep over us."

Steve Lynn saw it as the end of an era: "This is like finding your wife in bed with another man. Our factory people are interwoven in the life of the company: most of the people feel it's their company, they're tremendously proud of it—as opposed to other companies where there's no loyalty." Now, he said, that seventy-year tradition of dedication and loyalty was ending.

But other unions' officials were less bleak. To soften the blow, McGinn offered "successorship"—a condition in any sale that the buyer would have to take on the union contract. This was a potentially significant concession, since a successorship clause could lower the sale price of any facility; Lucent's estimate was that it could cost them $1.5 billion in a series of sales. This was a result of extensive behind-the-scenes work by Craviso before the meeting, and a tribute to his influence.

McGinn also offered the CWA a particularly attractive opportunity. He stressed that installation and maintenance, the core of the CWA membership at Lucent, was essential to the new strategic direction because it was key to building customer relationships; but the nature of that work would soon be shifting from the old voice world to the new technology of data transmission via Internet Protocol. The company offered the union to help them migrate their members into the new "data space" by providing training, and was even willing to include in the bargaining unit some of those titles which were currently classed as managerial.

Thus the union contingent was on the whole positive, working to develop next steps: even Lynn said, "I'm not going to hug and kiss you, but we have to move forward." The top managers were, as one put it privately, "awestruck" that the meeting had gone so well; Craviso was called a "miracle worker." McGinn expressed surprise at how good an understanding of the business the unions demonstrated.

The rocky road to implementation of the new deal
This hardly meant that all mistrust had been resolved and all obstacles overcome. Meetings in the following weeks with local leaders went badly: they were far less willing than the national union representatives to accept the divestiture of manufacturing. On the IBEW side, Steve Lynn amended the National Labor Relations Board charge based in part on information given by McGinn at the meeting in December.

This highlighted an issue which everyone had been trying to finesse for months: it is dangerous to develop a dialogue when all parties don't buy in. The rules of negotiation and the rules of dialogue are different and essentially incompatible. In negotiation the parties give a minimum amount of information in

order to preserve their bargaining leverage, while in dialogue they give a maximum of information in order to build buyin and trust. In negotiation one uses
whatever leverage one can find; in dialogue one does not bring in unrelated
issues to create leverage. McGinn's statements actually went rather far toward the
dialogue model, revealing concerns that were not yet public among analysts;
when they were then taken into a context of legal challenge it really raised the
question of whether the IBEW could be part of the dialogue process, and whether
the company should continue to reveal more information than it had to.

Meanwhile, in early January, the company issued its first-ever earnings warn-
ing, and the stock dropped like a stone. This not only increased the urgency of
management, but it also created great turmoil among union members, many of
whom had the bulk of their retirement funds in Lucent stock. Irvine thought this
might create a greater sense of realism about the company's needs, but for the
most part it had the opposite effect: local presidents and members became more
angry at the company, feeling it had let them down and failed to protect them.

Now things began to move really rapidly. In part as a response to the stock
woes, management reached a decision to spin off the enterprise equipment unit.
They met with the CWA, which was most affected, over two weeks before the
Lucent board approved the move, and well before the public learned of it—a
highly unusual level of openness. For the next few months the company kept
holding meetings and laying out new divestitures under consideration. The
unions reeled under shock after shock, reacting often with fury, sometimes with
despair, but were unsure what kind of action to take. Heckscher's role in all this
was to keep making phone calls to talk through the overall picture and to work
with union leaders to think about possible ways of responding coherently and
effectively—from a concerted mobilization to a negotiated union buyout to successorship agreements, and various other possibilities.

Gradually the unions began to grasp the magnitude of what was going on and
to converge on a broad response. They decided that successorship was not what
they wanted, because any company that bought a piece of Lucent and was forced
to take the union contract would simply be able to kill the union the next time the
contract expired. For the same reason they wanted to avoid piecemeal divestiture
which, even if formally protecting union membership, would make the unions
much weaker in relation to new employers. They pressed instead for a "big bang"
divestiture of as much as possible in one chunk, to one buyer, possibly with the
union as a financial partner. This would have the concrete benefit of maintaining
the unions' strength as much as possible. Equally important, it maintained their
sense of pride and identity: they could see the move as a re-creation of the old
Western Electric, and a chance for unions to show the business world that they
really could be partners in a successful manufacturing enterprise.

The company, having gone through much internal struggle to get used to the
idea of successorship, now had to wrestle again with whether to restructure the
whole way they had planned the divestiture. Their initial reaction was that a big-
bang, single-buyer approach proposed by the union would not work: it would

put too many eggs in one basket, making Lucent too dependent on a single supplier.

As the parties moved through these debates they began to sketch out (with Heckscher facilitating and making suggestions) a process for involving the union in a systematic way in the decisions about divestiture. First, the company agreed to pay for two financial advisors, chosen by and responsible solely to the unions. Then Lucent agreed that the unions could have input into the bid specifications sent out to potential buyers. Finally, they laid out a series of steps by which the advisors would be able to look at the actual bids and report back to the unions; the unions could meet with potential buyers before the finalists were selected; and they could give their input on what buyers they preferred (though without formal decision rights). The final step would be a complex three-way simultaneous negotiation with the preferred bidder, in which the union would negotiate a labor contact with the buyer and severance issues with Lucent while the buyer negotiated sales terms with Lucent.

Through the late spring and summer of 2000 they worked painfully through this process. The unions in fact had a substantial impact on the structure of the offering: though it did not end up as one big package, it was put out in significantly larger chunks than the company had at first envisioned. The Mergers and Acquisitions unit at Lucent, who had never listened to unions before and saw no reason to now, was forced to meet with them and pay attention to their concerns. The three parties then withdrew to a set of hotel suites in New York to hammer out the tricornered agreement. From Lucent the unions got substantial improvements on the contractual severance package; from the buyer they got a strong contract with good protections of their future rights. Most union members would suffer little harm: they would be working for Lucent one day and the buyer the next, in the same job at the same rate of pay, but with a large lump-sum payment added to their bank accounts.

So in August 2000 most of those involved were ready to congratulate themselves on a real breakthrough. They had navigated a set of shoals that had broken companies like Eastern Airlines, and they had done it in a way that preserved both the strategic flexibility of the company and considerable security and pride for the unions and their members. Along the way they had created a level of co-management rarely seen in the US. They had gone a long way towards integrating union concerns into the strategic planning process of the company at all stages; and they had made progress in getting unions to think proactively rather than reactively about how to deal with change.

The NLRB intervenes: the triumph of bargaining over dialogue

And then came the fatal blow, from a completely unexpected direction. Everyone had discounted the National Labor Relations Board charge filed two years earlier—everyone, that is, except Steve Lynn. The company's lawyers and the CWA leadership were equally convinced that the charge would go nowhere. Yet days before the parties to the sale were to sign their agreements, the regional board announced that it was prepared to find that the company had violated the law in 1998 bargaining by not telling the unions about plans for subcontracting.

Abruptly everything shifted. The IBEW role in the discussions to that point had been filled by the national union representative, who had in effect shouldered Lynn aside; now Lynn had his own base of power. Celestica would not close the deal with the threat of a board charge hanging over it. Lucent found itself compelled to go back to the bargaining table with Lynn to renegotiate the terms for the sale of assets to a subcontractor. Bargaining trumped dialogue.

Lynn's lawyer now entered the scene and largely took over the process. One of the first things he did was to tell the two financial advisors that he did not need them around: as he told them, "The company doesn't need to know why I take positions; they just need to know that I do." There could be no clearer demarcation of the line between bargaining and dialogue. For the next month discussions followed the most traditional patterns of collective bargaining imaginable: coming in with extreme demands, bluffing, brinkmanship time after time. In the end it required the National Labor Relations Board to come in to help settle the matter.

The settlement in the end gave the IBEW somewhat more money than they had prior to the entrance of the NLRB; in that sense it was a victory for Steve Lynn and the bargaining approach. If there was any downside it was more hidden: tensions with the CWA increased exponentially; the IBEW was clearly labeled in the contract manufacturing industry as an adversarial and aggressive union. But these were no more than potential negatives to offset the real and visible gains. It should, however, be noted in assessing this outcome that if the union had taken a consistently aggressive stance *from the start* they would not have gotten as good a deal, because they would not have influenced the choice of buyer and the structuring of the offering. In the end they got the maximum benefit—though not through any plan—by being cooperative till the last moment and then hitting the company with a powerful weapon to extract some more. It was a kind of accidental "good cop/bad cop" approach.

The reason Heckscher felt that the bargaining approach was a mistake in this context, despite its immediate success, had to do with his vision of the future. His belief, which guided his approach throughout, was that companies in general would increasingly become information-based, fluid, with career paths that were more open and more individually constructed and with less bureaucratic stability and rule-boundedness. If this is true, then the bargaining victory at Lucent was a Pyrrhic one: it cemented the union into a classic approach of defending the past and extending it step by step, and allowed it to avoid confronting the task of rebuilding its strategy and capabilities for a different kind of economy.

What role for an intervener?

By this time relationships were in tatters on every side. The CWA was furious that the IBEW had ended up improving the deal (even though the company promised the CWA that they would get whatever final package was negotiated). There had always been serious tension between the two unions, and now the CWA felt that their rivals had in effect been rewarded for bad behavior. The conclusion they drew was that they should stop trying to be responsible. One of them said, "I've just decided that the IBEW has it right—f— them before they f— you. It worked for them, so it should work for us."

Heckscher figured it was time to end his involvement in the process. His motivation had always been to see whether one could achieve a new kind of union–management relationship that could deal openly and constructively with the turbulent "new economy." Now the answer, at least for this case, seemed to be "No." All the forces, since the NLRB charge, had shifted toward the conclusion that fighting was better than talking.

And yet—when faced with the choice neither party really wanted to put aside the hope for a better relationship. As Heckscher spoke with various parties they asked him to stay on; he had in a way become the symbol of a possibility, and if he really pulled out it would be a sign that the possibility was dead. He debated whether the right thing to do would be to force the parties to face that consequence.

In May 2001, Craviso began to look toward the day when all the restructuring would be complete. At that point almost the entire unionized force would be composed of installers and maintenance people, represented by the CWA. They could be the company's front-line representatives with the customer, and key to the successful implementation of a solutions approach. Clearly a continuation of the existing mistrust and hostility would be very damaging to the company.

Craviso circled back to some of the themes that he and Heckscher had discussed $2\frac{1}{2}$ years earlier: the need to place the labor relations strategy to a broader transformation of the company's management culture. He met with key line leaders, from the top of the house down through the areas most involved with occupational workers, and got support for broadening his role from "labor relations" to the champion of "workforce engagement," with the union as a partner in sponsoring this approach. He asked Heckscher whether he still thought this was a viable way to go and whether he was interested in trying once again to take the process forward.

REFLECTIONS: THE DYNAMICS OF STRATEGIC DIALOGUE

The core of this effort was an attempt to establish strategic dialogue: discussion between the union and management of fundamental issues of direction. The Workplace of the Future effort at AT&T had essentially stopped at the operational level; though there was a high-level "strategic Human Resources Board," its meetings were sporadic and largely informational. At Lucent these problems moved to the foreground because the high turbulence and growing crisis of the industry led the company to rethink long-held assumptions that deeply impacted the union work force.

Many of the stars were lined up for success. Not only did management make this decision, but many of those down the line in middle management—where engagement processes often are smothered in resistance—had had experience in Workplace of the Future at AT&T and understood the unions far better than their peers in other companies. The unions, based on this same experience, also understood the business and the functioning of management unusually well. Nevertheless, the effort at strategic dialogue largely failed in the period of this case study. It apparently moved a long way, but at the end turned into a quite traditional adversarial bargaining process around contract language. There were obstacles both within and beyond the two parties.

Management

In situations of strategic change the near-universal approach is for the top strategic layers of management to make their decisions and to toss the resulting organizational and labor problems "over the wall" to HR and Labor Relations to solve. The structure of most US companies makes it virtually impossible for the issues of concern to the unions to be included as part of the strategic planning process. The planners, both staff and top management leaders, are too distant from the unions' concerns. They are unwilling to engage the union on territory that is unfamiliar to them: they do not understand the subtleties and complexities of the unions' issues with employment security, and they do not want to be dragged into such discussions.

Over time this distinction has become enshrined in a whole set of structures and procedures. The labor relations and HR functions have become highly specialized and bureaucratic, with a clear "place" down the chain in the decision-making process. The idea of "managerial prerogative" has been elevated to the status of doctrine, especially in the US: it is taken for granted (after several major battles were fought over the issue in the 1940s) that management must keep an unfettered hand in deciding strategy. The day-to-day lives of middle managers rarely intersect with union leaders or members, and they develop very little understanding of those concerns. As long as they are able to operate successfully in that way, they have no incentive to change—no matter how much pressure this may put on the labor relations director who is then caught in the line of fire.

Lucent's management had the same instincts, and acted in many of these ways. There was continuing resistance to giving information to the union. The strategic planners focused on market positioning; union reactions were simply not part of their calculus until Craviso forced them in. On a day-to-day level, as well, many managers also continued to tread on the toes of the union and its members through actions, often small in themselves, that indicated to the unions that their concerns were not being treated seriously.

But for a number of reasons Lucent's management reconsidered this approach and took a somewhat modified path. One reason was that it recognized that the unions were capable of disrupting the change process. A second was that Craviso was unusually effective in persuading his leadership that dialogue with the unions might provide the best way through the transformation. Thus management, starting with the CEO, made a conscious decision that engagement was better than confrontation.

This decision did not end the matter. The long history of bureaucratic relationships, the lack of understanding and skills in middle management, the political turf issues between Labor Relations and other functions, and many other organizational habits continued to be obstacles to a consistent policy of dialogue. A particular problem was the role of the Mergers and Acquisitions (M&A) department. This group had never dealt with unions before, and felt very uncomfortable in dealing with them now. They typically resisted disclosing information to the unions, and a number of times they agreed to aspects of deals that exacerbated union–management tensions, without checking with Labor Relations. This was in part a matter of pride—they tended to see themselves operating "above" the level of union rules and relations—and partly a matter of lack of understanding.

Craviso was a consistent and very effective warrior within the management ranks for the policy of openness, but he did not win all his battles.

Unions

The obstacles on the union side were probably higher. They had an opportunity to be involved in and influence fundamental decisions well before they were made; why did they show such ambivalence about seizing the opportunity? The answer involves many layers of what we call in Chapter 7 their "identity."

1. The common uniting symbols of both unions—the parade-ground marks of pride—almost all had to do with battles fought against management. Stories of "standing up to" oppressive or stupid bosses are the common currency of the convention cocktail hours as well as of speeches. These stories won respect, and they also built a sense of security in the union. Few people spoke with pride of cooperative relationships or problems solved peacefully, and those that did were a bit marginal.

2. There was the matter of resources and skills, which should not be underestimated. These unions had neither the time, the resources, nor the information necessary to develop alternative to the company's business scenarios. The IBEW had only one national staff member working on Lucent, CWA had the equivalent of perhaps 2–3. The rest of the union people relating to Lucent consist of local officers, most of whom also represent other employers, and who are naturally focused on the local level. When the unions and the company CEO meet, the former spend certainly less than 1/10 as much time in preparation as the latter. It was therefore virtually impossible for them to

prepare themselves effectively for these complex strategic discussions. They felt, with justification, that if they got drawn into that discussion they would be playing a game in which the company had all the cards. So they were safer simply insisting on their own interests as aggressively as possible and forcing the company to figure out how to adapt to them.

3. For both these reasons the union leaders tended to win their elections through visibly tough action rather than through problem-solving. The most "statesmanlike" leaders, like Jim Irvine, were constantly under attack from those who felt they were not being militant enough.

4. Most unions are poorly structured for strategic action. They are built around local jurisdictions and local politics. Strategic change almost by definition requires shifting resources from some existing areas to other, often new, ones; this is extremely difficult when local officers have their own budgets and political constituencies, with weak accountability to the national union. Though the CWA was far more centralized than the IBEW, and had two strong visionary leaders, it was still not able to develop a strategic commitment that would be reliably implemented by the locals.

5. Simple organizational habits also played a role. The pattern of action to which most union officials have become accustomed is reactive: they expect management to make the first move, and they react. It is very difficult to get unions to prepare for meetings on strategy: they prefer to walk in unprepared and wait to see what management will say. They very seldom meet among themselves ahead of time: management would spend many days of staff and leadership time preparing for a meeting such as those between McGinn and the unions, while ordinarily the union participants did not get together at all ahead of time and frequently asked for no staff work.

For all these reasons the unions found it difficult to play a role of real interlocutor seeking to solve problems at the strategic level. They were highly motivated to pick on management lapses—of which there are inevitably many—rather than developing positive proposals. As one CWA officer said, "I'll be honest: it's much easier for me to yell and scream and call management [expletive]s. I'd much rather do that."

Strategic dialogue, in sum, requires moving out of well-worn grooves of habit for both sides. Collective bargaining involves a whole set of established routines: unions typically establish bargaining committees, gather demands from locals, establish communication channels, draw up lists of demands, prepare strike votes, and so on; on the management side Labor Relations has an equally elaborate set of routines for polling its constituencies and preparing its positions and fallbacks. None of these habits is appropriate for strategic dialogues.

And we have not yet touched on an equally powerful force that had a major impact in this case: the government, in the shape of the National Labor Relations Board, which reinforced the traditionalists in the union and undercut the dialogue process. One can imagine a role in which government could help the parties to work through strategic issues—in the EDF case, for example, the government's adoption of the 35-hour work week as national policy gave great impetus to those who were advocating this as a win–win solution within the company. But in the Lucent case at least, the government put the companies back into the most traditional of conflictual, win–lose bargaining processes; it took power out of the hands of those union leaders who advocated dialogue and gave it to those who had been trying to undermine it.

Thus the "pull" back to the traditional relationship on both sides was very powerful. The experience is Sisyphean: one can roll the rock uphill but it takes a very long time and hard work to get it over the top. At Lucent, in fact, it has not gotten over the top: it takes all of the unceasing strength of supporters in both management and unions to keep it from rolling back and crushing them.

EPILOGUE

We have ended the story somewhat arbitrarily at one of its many twists and turns. It is worth at least mentioning, however, that that moment of crisis was followed by a year of doldrums—meetings with low energy, leading nowhere; Heckscher's involvement became less and less. Then suddenly, unexpectedly, the configuration of forces shifted dramatically: company and union leaders were once again interested in serious discussions about the strategic future of the business. A joint team was put together with direct support from the CEO and the active involvement of the head of the Services business, with Heckscher as facilitator and (as he described it to the participants) "strategic mediator." As of this writing its work is unfinished, and the only thing predictable is that there will be more unforeseen turns.

6

Electricité de France: Moving Toward the National Policy Level

THE FRENCH CONTEXT

The European electricity market was opened to competition in June 1996 by a decision of the European Community. This directive established a timetable for change in the member countries, with a target of 25 percent of the market open to competition by 1999, and 33 percent by 2003.

Until this decision, Electricité de France (EDF) had been in a kind of "Waiting for Godot" condition: everyone had long expected an opening to competition, but it never seemed to come. The French context in general has been characterized by a collective fear of globalization (especially manifest in the presidential elections of 2002), which has led widely to conservatism and resistance to competition. In 1996, EDF, with 118,000 salaried employees, still held a monopoly within France. To the great annoyance of the surrounding nations, however, it had also used this base to develop a larger reach—becoming the foremost electricity producer in the world, with 57 nuclear stations with a production overcapacity enabling it to sell electricity in adjacent countries.

Only after the EU directive did the frozen system begin to crack. Since 2000, 30 percent of the electricity market, including major industrial customers on French soil, has been opened to competition. Since 1998, EDF has pursued a strong policy of buying subsidiaries and aims to earn 50 percent of its revenues abroad by 2005. It is well on the way to realizing this target, with 35 percent foreign revenue in March of 2002.

The EDF situation originated in a national strategy developed after the Second World War. Faced with the collapse of private firms, France chose to create nation-wide public enterprises in key strategic sectors, including power, the post office and telecommunications, Air France, Renault, and rail transport. Each of these was granted a monopoly and a specific legal status corresponding to the mission of collective interest the nation had granted it. EDF was created in 1946 as part of this move in order to (re) construct an electricity grid that had until then been divided among a multitude of private operators with concession contracts.

This approach involved a double compromise. Gaullists and Communists reached a political agreement that oriented development around large national-ized and nationally owned industries; and unions reached a compromise with engineers, by which the latter took charge of technology, while the unions took charge of social affairs. This set of institutional arrangements constituted what was called "the French model," with a highly centralized decision-making system composed of a set of state-controlled industries and geared to a tacit pact that linked modernization to the quest for technical excellence.

Although the French trade unions gained a very strong position in key sectors at that time, they have been generally weak in the economy as a whole: member-ship at a national level is at 9 percent of the work force. The system has been highly affected by divisions resulting from a plurality of unions with ideological roots. By law several unions can be present in the same company, competing for members. This makes it difficult to reach needed social compromises, and in turn often results in widespread protest movements outside the "regular" system.

In this whole arrangement, EDF occupied a peculiar position. In 1946, the Minister of Industry, the Communist Marcel Paul, wanted to make it a model of collaboration between productive forces in order to foster national development by creating a principle of co-responsibility in performing public service. Therefore two major unions (the CGT, dominantly Communist in the post-war period, and the CFTC, largely Catholic) became co-founders of the electricity corporation's public sector status. This political will was translated into the establishment of four sectors that orchestrated discussions between unions and management: production, personnel management, social security, and health. This whole institutional system encouraged a constant debate over the direction and objectives of a nationalized industry that has been called a *"cité entreprise"* (corporate community; literally "town-enterprise").

Starting in 1947, the idea of explicit co-management was abandoned as the Cold War developed. There was a return to the traditional French model of social relations within the public sector: a form of consultation ("paritarisme") in which management had to explain its policies to the unions but without the need to reach explicit agreements. This way of functioning satisfied the tradition of the French elites of making expert decisions over the heads of local actors; it also suited the Communist CGT union, which avoided contractual agreements for ideological reasons. Any contract, in their view, would imply compromise between classes and a slide into reformism.

This system of ideological choice and institutional architecture led to an unusual way of functioning in other public sector industries at the time: a *de facto* co-management or codetermination in which the union was able to influence management choices as well as to administer the internal labor market without formal agreements. (We will translate this concept of *paritarisme* henceforth as "consultation" or "consultative system.") In some local affiliates, management went so far as to delegate to the unions both recruitment and the management of employee careers. This allowed the unions to have high-quality information about a corporation's strategies, but without necessarily having an explicit share in strategy-making. It worked efficiently for many years. In the 1970s, this form of formal consultation permitted the development of nuclear power—despite resistance from the ecology movement. Its technicist and industrial vision was in harmony with the industrialist values of the CGT.

The other main player on the union side, and the chief rival to the CGT, was the CFDT, which had emerged from one of the company's founding unions, the CFTC. This union, centered among the technicians and the lower management, never succeeded in broadening its base or attaining a majority of the work force, garnering around 23 percent of the employee votes. It was known for a more cooperative, humanist view of unionism, in contrast to the fierce anti-capitalist militancy of the CGT.

"TO MAKE THIS A COMPANY LIKE ANY OTHER"

In the middle of the 1980s, EDF's policy changed profoundly as a result of two factors. On the one hand, there was a drop in the growth of demand for electricity, from about 7–8 percent a year to around 3 percent. On the other hand, there was the need to modernize the corporation and to improve its performance. At this time, EDF controlled about 95 percent of French electricity production and held a monopoly on its transportation and almost all distribution. Faced with these two pressures, management sought to augment labor productivity and especially employment productivity. Between 1985 and 1992, therefore, the corporation decreased its workforce by 1000–1500 persons a year (by way of natural retirement and severance). It began to decentralize itself and set up a policy of human resource management oriented to personnel job evaluation and re-training.

This strategy provoked a rupture in the implicit compromise that had structured relations with the CGT. EDF directors now perceived consultation ("paritarisme") more as a formal obligation, a "shadow play" that had been polluted by the atmosphere of conflict. They considered that this system no longer produced effective social regulation[1] and so they tried to disqualify the consultation structures and the CGT. This strategy of bypassing the CGT, however, was manifestly ineffective. The union continued to play a role in career management, it hung on to social services, and more generally, made the consultation system work. In employee elections, it got (and today still regularly gets) the majority of votes: 90 percent of EDF's wage employees vote in regular elections to choose union representation, and more than 53 percent of those voting since the corporation's creation vote in favor of the CGT.[2]

The start of intervention

In 1989, Gerard Anjorlas, the Director of Human Resources, asked Tixier to participate in writing a social forecasting report for EDF. This initial contact was made on the advice of two of Tixier's former students then working in the department, Lorraine Fauconnier and Alain Poupon. The first study led to consulting work with the industry as a whole.

In 1991, when Tixier took over the directorship of GIP Mutations Industrielles (a research body financed by both the state and major industries), Philippe Saimpert, an HR director, asked him and his team to study the EDF labor relations system.[3] Their hope was that new understanding would help them find a way to reduce the role of the CGT. They chose Tixier because he was then known for his doctoral study of the internal functioning of the CGT's rival, the CFDT, a modern union that had become the leading one in France and upon which the directors wanted to rely in undertaking their strategy for change.

The results of this research project, presented to management in 1993, were not what management had hoped for. The study showed that the CGT had gained a sort of functional legitimacy among employees that enabled the current system of labor relations to work. Management well understood that the results of this study undercut their strategy of trying to go around the union. But after difficult but in-depth discussions, the new head of Human Resources, Jean Louis Mathias, accepted the study's conclusions. In this sense the dialogue was productive of a new diagnosis, this one co-produced by management and researchers.

Management then attempted a modified strategy: rather than ignoring the CGT, they tried a "soft" form of avoidance. They announced their willingness to "re-equilibrate" the system of co-management, which was widely seen as obsolete and overly formal. Management felt, furthermore, that it fostered union irresponsibility because discussions were not required to lead to formal commitments. They proposed an alternative process of collective negotiations, an approach that was highly unfamiliar in the public sector but that had been encouraged by the Auroux Laws of 1982. They thought this experimental strategy would allow them to modify the relative influence of the social partners,[4] since they knew that the CFDT was ready to enter into collective negotiations to modernize the corporation.

The 1993 agreement and its consequences

After ten months, an agreement "For the Development of Employment and a New Social Dynamic" was signed on November 19 1993 at the national level by the general management of the EDF and by four union organizations, including the CFDT.[5] The agreement stipulated that if a union did not sign at the national level it could not sign at the local level—a clause that had been demanded by the CFDT. The CGT, however, feared that signing the agreement would weaken the status of the consultation system, which it dominated. It therefore refused to sign, immediately cutting itself off from the negotiations within local branches.

When Tixier's team was consulted during the negotiation process, they reminded management of the results of their prior study: in their opinion, the attempted strategy could not succeed since it bypassed the CGT. Their advice was ignored. The managers saw the consultants as "mere" academics who, though capable of analyzing the labor relations system, could not understand the constraints upon action that the business world needed to observe in order to succeed.

The follow-up committee created by the 1993 accord, which consisted of all of management and the signatory unions, called for an evaluation of its effects 18 months after the signing. The management of the CFDT, the principal union signatory, turned to Tixier and the GIP team because of the confidence gained in the course of the first study; they knew that the team would be accepted by the other unions, including the CGT, which had been able to gauge their autonomy from EDF management at the time of the first study.

This second inquiry showed that—as Tixier had predicted—the results of the agreement fell short of the signatories' hopes with respect to both its principal objectives: adjusting the level of employment and changing the system of labor relations. Unevenness in management practices (with some departments forecasting job losses and others not) and the indeterminacy of job accounting were constant sources of disturbing rumors and uncertainty for employees. The logic of "job sharing" was far from winning acceptance. A key issue was whether to hire from outside before reabsorbing "supernumerary" EDF personnel (those without posts). Most of the actors involved agreed that the first priority was to preserve the boundaries of internal employment. Many wondered whether contingent jobs—temporary and part-time work—would undermine the statutory jobs.

Nor were the results any better in terms of "social dynamics." The agreement was translated into a sometimes-difficult *cohabitation* between incompatible systems: consultative bodies and collective negotiations. The formal consultative system and the culture of involvement were still a shared point of reference, including for the signatory unions.[6] Most of the latter were, however, unwilling to move to a wider kind of power-sharing, especially without the support of the CGT, because they feared that they would be manipulated by management without having the power to confront it when necessary.

The agreement also had the effect of distancing the union officials who did take part in negotiations from their base in the membership, a phenomenon already widely observed in France in agreements on managing future employment. The agreement had a sort of "club effect": there were interesting debates among participating union leaders and management—but cut off from the rank and file. Union leaders were less and less present on the ground to inform workers and to debate with them, since they were spending much of their time in expert committees, studying dossiers, and meeting with management. Moreover, competition between the signatory and non-signatory unions played itself out in debates between the paths of conflict and of collective negotiations, with each camp trying to prove that its strategy was the most effective in job creation. Management, of course, found itself ultimately in the position of referee, having to "drop" jobs to solve a conflict or "grant" jobs to support the signatories. In many cases, the created jobs appeared as much (if not more) linked to tactical considerations than to needs that were clearly identified in economic terms.

The 1993 agreement nevertheless launched a process of cultural learning by fostering exchanges between unions and management, without the dramatics of the formal consultative system in which the game was always either to prove that management wanted to pressure the workers, or on the contrary that the unions were refusing to adapt to the company's situation. The agreement helped both sides to become aware that employment in public enterprises could not be reduced to "defense of the public service," a sort of intangible patrimony supposedly shared by the French in which the interests of the personnel and the interests of the consumers somehow were amalgamated. At the level of the company's strategic head—the heads of the union federations, the operational departments, and Human Resources—the agreement undoubtedly stimulated the most significant learning experiences. It created a locus of communication and negotiation that was translated into new capabilities, manifest in risk-taking in negotiating more ambitious agreements.

The search for a new compromise

Nevertheless, the company was still far from prepared for open market competition. During this first period, while the Maastricht Treaty (signed by the European Union in 1991) was theoretically calling for the free circulation of goods and people starting in 1993, the question of the market was absent from debates inside the EDF, and the energy monopoly was not challenged as part of a debate on the quality of services—even if users where now being referred to as "clients."

In November 1995, Edmond Alphandery was named EDF president—just when nationwide strikes roiled the country in what the press came to call "the events of '95." A former Minister of the Economy, Alphandery had a mandate after the crisis to calm the social situation and to prepare the industry for competition.

EDF management's diagnosis put the spotlight on the company's social fragility, illustrated by the invasion of several nuclear plant control rooms by young employees, and by the more general uneasiness of personnel about the employment issue. Major social tensions were manifest everywhere at the local level. The promised reforms were difficult to put across. Management was advancing only "less" (a reduction in personnel, a reduction in overtime, uncertainty over retirement, etc.); its reforms promised only pain and suffering for employees, without a positive vision. And the industry management was ill pre-pared: What type of social regulation should it construct now that the European directive was allowing competitors to enter the market starting in 1999? How could the company prepare itself for such competition?

In this context, the Human Resources Department asked Tixier and a colleague, Henri Vacquin, to intervene as advisors to its head and members of top management. Management made a calculation: first, they knew that the two consultants had been accepted by all the unions and they knew of Tixier's long-standing relation with the CFDT. Second, they wanted consultants with profound knowledge of the industry. The company wanted to use them as a sounding board, considering their familiarity with how the EDF and the unions functioned, but it also wanted them to involve the unions in the process of change and try to find a framework around which an agreement could be reached.

The 1997 agreement

In February, 1996, negotiations opened around the task of preparing the com-pany to enter the market. Management aimed to improve flexibility by using the negotiations to gain reductions in work hours and recruitment. They promised "15,000 hirings" to win support from the work force.

The negotiations went through several phases. The first was a period of explora-tion of the positions of the various parties concerned, which were initially quite far apart. The signatory unions of the 1993 agreement thought a new accord should reinforce their legitimacy, which presumed that new negotiations would produce clearly identifiable gains in terms of employment. The CGT asserted that any eventual accord should above all preserve the special protected status of the industry and of the consultation system. During the first meetings in February 1996, everybody still bore the scars of the previous autumn's conflict. Setting aside their quarrels, the five union federations presented a united front to demand a 24-month moratorium on workforce reductions and structural reform. Management made an initial commitment on April 17, 1997 to recruit 2,500 people, including 400 apprentices. Moreover, it promised to stabilize the workforce during the negotiation period.

From Tixier's standpoint, renouncing reforms for the time being contradicted the corporation's aim to adapt to the market context and amounted to a denial of reality. But the industry management delayed reforms for six months. These tokens of goodwill were nevertheless not sufficient for the unions. Dialogue was difficult, punctuated by several one-day strikes, some of them unit-wide.

In this first phase, Tixier's role was largely to educate managers who consulted him: explaining to the new president the characteristics of the company's social regulations and, on a more detailed level, helping managers to understand the rationales of the union and personnel negotiators. He sought also to build bridges between the world visions of managers—who were forecasting a future of competition—and of employees, who were attached to the ways things worked in the past, and for whom the market remained a disturbing abstraction.

Meanwhile, the French business context was extremely negative; a sort of collective anguish was seizing France over its future; unemployment reached an unprecedented 13 percent of the active population, and there was a general sense of panic.

In this period, the operational departments wanted to play at negotiation as they had in 1993, without really making a commitment. They refused to give credible figures of prospects for the future of the business. Along with the Director of Personnel, Tixier explained to them that maintaining this position made an agreement impossible. Without credible information on the economic situation and the forecasting of industry jobs, the unions were refusing to budge and they held several days of sporadic strikes in the spring.

In July 1996, after six months of negotiations, the steering group met in a particularly somber mood: the faces of management negotiators were particularly tense and drawn. They had the feeling that the situation was going to get worse. Tixier, pushing strongly, persuaded them to make a major concession—giving the unions "real" job forecasts. These were calculated on the basis of different development hypotheses in relation to the market, culminating in a memo of November 13, 1996 about "prospects for change in employment at EDF and GDF." Presented by the directors of the two major operational departments, it contained a series of scenarios and testified to a coordination between departments that had been lacking in 1993.

In November the operational departments publicly supported the negotiations approach, including the "15,000 hirings" pledge. This initiative opened the way to a third phase of intense negotiations that unfolded "outside" the CGT, which refused (as in 1993) to take part in collective negotiations, and without the Force Ouvrière.[7]

The agreement was finally signed at the national level by three unions—CFDT, CGC, and CFTC—representing 33 percent of the personnel. It was titled "The Development of the Public Service, Working Hours, Employment of Young People, 15,000 Hirings: A Project for Us All." This mouthful of a title indicates the complexity of the agendas at work. On the one hand, management wanted to advance the economic dimension with the chapter "Development." On the other hand, the unions were partly in agreement and partly split over the objectives. They were split over measures regarding the working week but agreed on the employment of young people and on the public service.

In the period that followed, Jean-Louis Mathias, the operational directors, and Tixier participated in numerous road shows for unit directors in order to explain to a resistant management why such an agreement had been signed and what benefits the corporation might expect from it in terms of work flexibility.

The effects of the 1997 agreement

In September 1998, Jean Louis Mathias asked Tixier for a new analysis of the company's social system, with the idea that the company would be making major changes with the forthcoming entry into the market and that therefore social affairs had to change profoundly. This study was carried out by researchers from GIP as well as some from Tixier's former research group (LSCI). LSCI acted as a control on the analysis, since Tixier had been deeply involved in work on the 1997 agreement.

In contrast to the aftermath of the 1993 agreement, internal observers pointed to the importance of the social debate unleashed by the new one. It introduced the goal of asking each person at EDF about his relation to time and to work, and even about the balance in his lifestyle. The tradition of the *cité entreprise* and the consultative system had always encouraged a culture of vigorous internal debate; these new discussions were therefore in this sense a continuation of the past.

The agreement proved, however, to be difficult to implement. To enable the promised recruitment of the minimum of 11,000 people,[8] the agreement presupposed that a large number of current employees would voluntarily embrace reduced working hours. This was a serious gamble, since it ran strongly counter to company culture: when the accord was signed, only 2.5 percent of salaried employees of EDF–GDF worked part time, as opposed to 16 percent of the national workforce. And it did not pay off at first. Despite opinion polls showing that 20 percent of the personnel were in favor of a reduction in working time, the requests for reduced time remained modest during the first five months. This was a vivid demonstration of the stability of traditional social behavior: the continued prevalence of full time work, the relative marginality of part time, employees' fears over career prospects. Most of the workers who opted for the new arrangements under the 1997 agreement were young women with children.

Prime Minister Lionel Jospin gave the company's scheme a boost of legitimacy in July of 1997 by announcing the drafting of a law to reduce the legal working week to 35 hours, using the EDF agreement in part as a model. Eighteen months after the national agreement was signed, an assessment of the "control group" showed positive results: 179 local agreements had been signed, and a total of 16,855 workers were using the measures for work time reduction in various forms.

These results were criticized by the signatory unions, however, because the number of hirings was less than the commitments made by management (3,567 hirings instead of the 6,000 promised). In June 1998, they threatened once more to renounce the agreement. Management then agreed to strengthen the national agreement with measures favorable to salaried workers in order to make the option of a shorter working week more attractive. Among the indirect effects of the agreement was to strengthen local managerial oversight of labor relations, which until then had been governed at the top of the organization, and to create means of decentralizing dialogue.

During this period Tixier worked simultaneously with the CFDT union as well as the company management. The Secretary General of the CFDT for Chemistry and its Secretary General for Energy established a steering group with the aim of constructing a powerful union federation capable of confronting the effects of globalization, which was the center of frequent debates on changes within EDF and within CFDT's strategy.

But the work with the unions soon came to an end when Tixier voiced his criticism of the way in which the union leadership conceived their relation to members. The CFDT leadership, as Tixier saw it, emphasized work with company leaders at the expense of their relationship with their rank and file. In his opinion, the strategy of participation chosen by the CFDT risked making it appear as a "management union"; at France Télécom, similar CFDT positions led to the downfall of the union in employee elections and to the rise of a left-wing alternative. The CGT, meanwhile, presumed inter-union competition and focused strongly on constructing a very solid base.

Another point on which Tixier insisted was that the new federation should have only one Secretary General, which would mean the outgoing one should leave quickly so that the new one had time to fully occupy the post. This did not occur and there was a bitter organizational fight that weakened the federation. The great difficulty of intervention during this period was the fact of working partly in common and partly in parallel with each of the actors and then trying to unify their viewpoints on the transformation of the corporation faced with a free market.

CONSTRUCTING A "POLITICAL EXCHANGE" TO CREATE A GLOBAL GROUP

In September 1998, there was a moment of high drama: just as the results of the study of the agreement's impact were presented to the unions and to management, the agreement was nullified by the Court of Appeals in Paris upon a complaint by the CGT that it did not respect the corporation's special status.

When the new EDF president, François Roussely, arrived at the corporation in October 1998, he made it clear to management that he did not intend to construct an enterprise "against" 53 percent of the personnel, meaning the employees who voted for the CGT in the representative elections! The annulment of the 1997 agreement by the courts allowed him to quickly apply his own conception of social relations. The attempt to find an agreement that would be signed by all the unions, which had failed in 1996, was therefore successful in January 1999.

During this period, Tixier experienced the frequent fate of advisors when there is a change at the top—an interruption in his involvement. For management, the main objective was to increase the CGT's capacity for dialogue and mediation. It was a question of increasing the union's resources (to develop its ability to control) in exchange for its participation. Management in this period began to involve the union in major decisions affecting the corporation, while reinforcing its legitimacy among employees by allowing it to derive significant concessions for personnel from among its demands. The political exchange was thus in the reordering of forces with a view to increasing the effectiveness and legitimacy of company policy.

Various factors may explain this success. At EDF the CGT was on the defensive: it had seen its legitimacy crumble during the elections that followed the annulment of the 1997 agreement. The 1993 and 1997 agreements had destabilized it; by its continued refusal to participate in negotiations it ran the risk of isolating itself from the expectations of workers. It had therefore begun to engage in discussions with the Department of Human Resources and to take part in collective negotiations. The CGT was also forced to evolve due to changes at the head of its Confederation, with the arrival of a new Secretary General, Bernard Thibault, who proclaimed a strategic shift toward negotiation that brought it nearer to the CFDT approach. The Jospin government wanted public enterprises to set an example in the implementation of the 35-hour law. All these factors contributed to creating a favorable situation for a collective agreement to be signed at EDF–GDF[9]—but what agreement?

What was expected from the agreement

The 1999 round of negotiations was introduced as echoing the 1997 one by strengthening work flexibility. It had the same institutional characteristics: a national accord followed by local ones. It called for follow-up arrangements at both national and local levels. The preamble was in the same spirit as the previous one: competitiveness, the need to modernize "the public service," development, and the availability of services. However, one could note significant differences. In the preamble, the social objectives preceded the economic dimensions, and respect for the special statutory nature of the company was pointedly restated. The wording was carefully drafted to be less provocative and less centered on management concerns. The form adopted was certainly more acceptable to the organization's culture. It was more ambitious than the preceding one regarding employment (foreseeing between 18,000 and 20,000 hirings, which meant a net creation of 3,000 jobs). Finally, the involvement of the CGT and the FO profoundly affected the significance of the agreement, since the unions now had a larger capacity to influence the corporation's policies.[10]

From the perspective of company competitiveness one can interpret the 1999 agreement in two contradictory ways. One interpretation sees in this agreement a formidable opportunity for the corporation to undertake the necessary modernizations in a more peaceful internal climate, and thus obtain the necessary mobilization of the workforce regarding the corporation's objectives, which would foster the creation of a world player. It would permit a beneficial interplay between improving working conditions and new flexibility in work schedules. On the other hand, the agreement can be interpreted as a sort of new administrative detour by which the rights of actors were increased without there being any clear advantages for the corporation. Under the latter hypothesis, the agreement would appear a "fool's bargain" in which modernizing efforts would be unilaterally supported by management, while the unions were merely playing the role of demanding benefits regardless of the corporation's need to adapt.

Transforming the dialogue between the major players

Two months after the agreement was signed in January 1999, the new Director of Human Resources, Claude Hue, asked Tixier to help set up a new agreement at the local level. In fact, the role quickly changed to coaching and advising when Hue took Tixier to meet with the new president, François Roussely, to discuss the evolution of the corporation. This first meeting dealt with the characteristics of the corporation and ways of making it evolve to adapt to the market. The context in which the president arrived—an organization traumatized by the previous conflict—made discussions with managers very difficult. Tixier had not been involved in this fight, but knew the corporation very well and so could help Roussely understand the rationales at work and offer him interpretations that no one else had offered. The president then asked Tixier to play the role of sounding board and to participate in formulating new strategy, in forecasting its internal consequences, and considering ways to conduct change. The strategy had several parts.

Sustainable development
The development of an international group meant buying up companies, particularly in Europe. EDF had bought London Electricity, EMW in Germany, and Montedison in Italy in conjunction with Fiat. Its objective was to participate in the development of companies in which the group had a share by giving contracts to national and local companies that respected the economic and natural environments. The North American model of free-market competition had been shot down in Europe due to the energy problems encountered by California and because of the attitude of George Bush and US big business to environmental projects—an attitude that appeared illegitimate to Europeans. The EDF strategy of decentralized globalism would be more easily carried out in countries with a concession system where the chosen corporation had a monopoly for a given length of time. It would be less easy to implement when there was full competition within open markets.

The success or failure of this policy depends on the behavior of social actors, their collective capacities to build the compromises to permit adaptation of the corporation to the market. Therefore we should analyze the stakes of both union and management actors. Any political exchange presupposes playing with the majority organization—or else on the union side, radical factions would appear and grow stronger, or at the very least the discourse about change would have low credibility among employees. On the other hand, this strategy risks destabilizing management.

Profound dialogue with the unions
This strategy has been in effect since 1999. The gamble is that by implicating the unions in defining policy, management removes their capacity to mobilize personnel against the corporation's objectives. The passage from public enterprise

to a competitive international group therefore occurred with the agreement of the CGT—unlike the positions the union had taken in the twenty preceding years. The idea is to co-construct strategy, which means negotiating incentives for personnel who must adapt to the transformation of its market environment. New fields of negotiations are opening today, with the transformation of Human Resources and performance incentives, but also with the creation of a European Group Committee. Let us examine the positions of the two main unions.

CGT: historic legitimacy being questioned. At the start of the 1990s, the CGT still referred to the class struggle. It relied on an institutional system of consultation and on the legitimacy it had acquired through the special status of an industry considered an accomplishment of the working class. Above all, it tried to maintain the boundaries of the monopoly by relying on the resources it possessed, forcing debate to occur in political bodies. It also tried to mobilize the workforce against the 1993 and 1997 agreements. Its goal was to deconstruct the legitimacy of these agreements, at both national and local levels.

But this strategy unfolded in a context of strife within the union. Union officials did not always follow the positions taken by the rank and file. Debates turned principally around two aspects. (1) Was it wise to exercise a "right of opposition"[11] that would result in blocking the opportunity to take advantage of the individual benefits that were being offered in local agreements? (2) Did a primarily defensive strategy risk isolating the union from the employees at a time when many militants subscribed to the necessity of the corporation becoming a European public service? The CGT knew that the stability of its electoral successes did not necessarily imply that its choices were shared by workers.

The strategic shift the CGT made by signing the 1999 accord allowed it to escape the trap of appearing to resist change at a time when the corporation was entering into competition.[12] Today the CGT is ready to accept a partial privatization of the corporation. But this strategy carries a weakness: some resistance from local militants who do not share the preference of the federation.[13] Will this strategy survive the test of market realities or will it result in the development of an anti-globalization wing, close to the radical union SUD that has arisen within the corporation?

The CFDT: a gamble on modernizing the "Cité entreprise"? With the 1997 agreement, the CFDT completed the about-turn made in 1993 by offering to renew the *"cité entreprise"* model, by participating, in alliance with management, in redefining the corporation of the future. Replacing the previous coupling of CGT and management, a new coupling of CFDT and management was in effect during the 1990s, one approved and followed by other, minority unions. As we have seen, the tradition of debating the role of the corporation through consultative institutions was now oriented to new issues: the reduction of work time, and flexibility in order to respond to the market, both through collective negotiations.

The CFDT engaged in an explicitly participatory strategy. Its representatives had participated closely in meetings with workers, sometimes in tandem with management, in the course of the 1997 agreement. The goal of these meetings was to explain the different measures and to convince workers to take advantage of them. In the beginning, the CFDT positions often met resistance among employees—including its own supporters. After a period of uncertainty, the rank and file followed the federal leaders. The CFDT was the only important union to support the agreement. Its engagement alongside management sometimes led it to be perceived as a "management union." So this has been a risky choice, particularly in a pluralist system. And so the CFDT had to bear the negative effects of political engagement without having the necessary resources in order to build employee opinion and so to influence management policy. Creating a new policy meant modifications in routines and a series of difficulties.

To understand the CFDT's choices, one might compare the alliance between CGT and management in 1946, and the CFDT's alliance with management in 1997. It is apparent that, to the CFDT's detriment, the stakes are not the same. In the former case, the aim was to foster the construction of France. In the contemporary situation, in order to build an economic and social Europe, it is a matter of adapting the industry to competition by limiting the abolition of jobs—a less rousing issue because these choices are not clearly made by French politicians, whose speeches present Europe more as a constraint than an opportunity.

The oppositional strategy played out by the CGT over the previous decade offered the CFDT a strategic opportunity. The 1999 agreement seemed to the CFDT to continue the one of 1997,[14] but this continuity did not protect it from a new alliance between CGT and management. Some of its local leaders fought strongly against the CGT, feeling that it was now preempting their own viewpoint, but this did not protect them. The CFDT found itself faced with a CGT with superior resources and more able to convince employees. The CFDT participated closely in the transformation of the corporation—but it gained little institutionally from this involvement.

An interactive dialogue with the workforce
The dialogue with the unions was also nourished by desires expressed by employees. A process of wide-scale participation concluded in June 2001 with a huge meeting in the stadium at Bercy to which 7,000 employees were invited. The process began with regional forums (one per unit of 200) with all employees who wanted to participate. In each unit, personnel were invited to discuss with management the corporation's challenges and how to meet them. After these forums, employees could make proposals on targeted themes (6,000 were offered) and a small number were retained, becoming "commitments to change" from management, who set up mechanisms to evaluate them. This process aimed to foster a common awareness of the challenges to the corporation on issues where employees and management clashed, and implicitly to bring pressure on management to modify its behavior, still often bureaucratic in approach. Through the collection of proposals, this process also allowed an analysis of the main internal dysfunctions. Numerous proposals were made concerning human resources—for example, problems linked to remuneration and to professional

evaluation meetings. The existing blockage between personnel expectations and union politicking had nourished a need for negotiation through this direct expression from personnel.

Management reform
While relations between management and unions were characterized by recurrent conflict, as at EDF before 1999, the move from an oppositional game to a strategy of political exchange at the top poses a challenge to local management; they are losing their credibility and are being questioned by unions. This challenge is compounded by new demands being made on management. Previously oriented to technology and the application of rules, management now has to develop the capacity to react and adapt to the industrial market. The leadership has to circumvent the resistance of those local managers while relying on the continuing efficient functioning of bureaucratic mechanisms—but then those bureaucracies feel abandoned by management.

It has been necessary to develop management strategies through a series of meetings on group policy and development. These exchanges have given rise to lively debates with the top echelons, which have been carried over into regional meetings featuring discussion between the president, board members, and management personnel at a regional level.

REFLECTIONS: THE WORK OF INTERVENTION

Tixier has occupied various positions since 1989—researcher, facilitator, advisor, and sounding board—that linked his experience as sociologist and psychoanalyst. Today his role is mostly to assist in the steering of a multinational corporation with historic roots and a French identity. The question is how to make a bridge from an industry founded upon monopoly to the new modernity of the global market.

What are the available tools?

In a country like France, characterized by systems of professional relations that are deeply conflictual and split, where relations are built upon distrust and unpredictable social movements, research is often one of the few possible ways of intervening at the strategic summit of a company, since research is based upon the hypothesis of the neutrality of the one who intervenes. When research uses large surveys, it offers the advantage of a deepened knowledge of the company. It allows the researcher to meet all categories of actors, to bring out the sources of their identities, to understand the social regulations that underlie relations between social groups, and to cultivate among actors a more complex vision than the one each possesses as a function of his position in the organization. This is done by "restitution," meaning furnishing partial elements of interpretation and formats for interviews, a technique used at EDF especially in the committees that followed up on the agreements. It is a matter of joint interpretation on the part of unions, management, and consultants, whether at the base or at the top of the organization, which allows the social representations of the actors to be transformed; an analytical to-and-fro shifts the benchmarks and the company's views of itself.

This work of elucidation is followed by a second type of work, consisting of putting management objectives into tension with the characteristics of the company's social system. It is also necessary to spend time at board level analyzing the effects of the decisions it makes and helping it to produce new strategies (after gaps between goals and observed functioning have been identified)—which sometimes means modifying the goals. This type of work over the long term allows a "cultural learning" that brings about a much better understanding of problems. The research set-up thus creates a space of mediation between the different logics of the actors, allowing a cognitive framing through diagnosis and thus a new kind of dialogue.

This methodology of diagnosis derived from the sociology of organizations ended at the moment when Tixier's contacts asked him to get involved in company strategy and to help them to resolve the dilemmas that he had studied. Moving beyond the work of research and facilitation in the first phase, Tixier now had to deal with the anxieties of his clients about the strategies they were implementing; and so he began to lean on his psychoanalytic experience.

In effect, while the methods of sociological diagnosis and their variants (especially Crozier, Friedberg, and Sainsaulieu) had helped Tixier to understand organizations' rules and the behaviors of organizational actors, these methods leave untouched what accompanies change and the subjective aspects that arise at the moment of choices. This is particularly clear when one works regularly with company directors. Psychoanalysis works on the transferential and counter-transferential dimensions and includes them in the work of intervention. For example, at the start of Tixier's intervention he was considered (as a researcher) to have "an objective eye" in analyzing the corporation's social system, but at the same time he was supposed to share the views of certain managers regarding the CGT. His proximity to the CFDT implied that he shared an anti-CGT sentiment. In explaining to management to what extent the CGT held legitimacy for the employees, Tixier became "the bad object."

Transference in the work of intervention has a dual aspect, a positive one in which the client lends the intervener certain qualities—even to the point of considering him a sort of magician. The intervener can let himself be seduced by the positive grandiose image his correspondents reflect back to him. But transference can also be negative when the intervener does not respond as the correspondent wishes—in this case, to validate management's strategy. This moment of negative transference is always strategic, because it requires overcoming the wound inflicted and presumes analyzing what is at stake.

Relational configuration, legitimacy, and transference

Large organizations use "scouts" when they purchase advice, people who know about the various types of intervention available for each task. EDF, in particular, is always buying the services of numerous researchers and consultants and it has a profound knowledge of the intervention market. A request, once formulated, implies a goal on the part of the initiators in the company. Moreover, one can hypothesize that the transference to the intervener is in a certain way prerequisite to intervention, due to the effects of reputation. Tixier's correspondents at EDF had clearly formulated their demands to understand the changes at the corporation a year before he became a professor at the Institute of Political Sciences in Paris. His new position, in a French social context strongly attached to academic traditions and conferring prestige on intellectuals, strengthened the positive dimension of the transference. For his clients, it conferred on him the aura of comprehensive expertise in the mechanisms of internal change—and also of an understanding of the political dimensions of change. In effect, the transformation of public enterprises presupposes analyzing their complex corporate identities. In this sense, the changes EDF was going through cannot be summarized as a simple opening to the market but rather dramatize the cultural dimensions and institutional arrangements that govern the place of this industry in French society.

The ability to intervene in such a complex system requires various alliances. Without retracing all of them (because they are unstable and fluctuating), Tixier's interventions were made possible from the start by acceptance from both the Human Resources Department and the CFDT federation for energy—and by the neutral attitude of the other unions. When the corporation asked Tixier to be an advisor in negotiations, this ability to cooperate with multiple actors allowed him to occupy a mediating position, either explicitly or implicitly, according to the situation. This mediating work took place within a framework that was at no time either stable or clearly enunciated. It was not a matter of resolving conflict between clearly defined actors, as when a court appoints a mediator or arbitrator, but rather of pushing the issues to and fro among the actors and helping them to construct a common vision of their present, to diagnose their situation, and to construct a shared vision of their future.

The question of Utopia in intervention

The enterprise that requests intervention expects that it will clarify its problems, help to solve them, but also that it will dramatize a partial dream on the part of directors, employees, or unions about the future of their organization. They ask the intervener to put into effect a sort of social utopia, especially when it comes to professional relations. They make him a sort of "medicine man" capable of inventing a reconciled social world. The intervener must be able to offer the remedies of a miracle doctor: interests will no longer be divergent (if not contradictory) and identities will no longer be defensive, regressive, or schismatic.

Tixier had been known for his work on the CFDT but also for having worked on the problems of organizational democracy. He was therefore invested with a transference of values expressed in his writings about a potentially more just and more democratic world. What was Tixier's counter-transference? He was caught between two pitfalls: satisfying the fantastic expectations of the organization and becoming its foil, its guru—at the expense of helping it to understand the root problems. In this respect, two moments gave rise to negative transferences, one with respect to management when he announced that their strategy of circumventing the CGT was ineffective, and the other with respect to the CFDT when, faced with his insistence on its working on relations between union officials and its base, they put an end to his intervention.

Intervention implies agreeing to be both the object of transference, accepting the utopian portion of the demand (and its echo in the person of the intervener) as well as being able to respond in timely fashion to this demand.

What new social contract?

In the case of EDF, the work of intervention consisted largely of participating in the construction of bridges between historical identities built around the public service and a new identity corresponding to a global group. Tixier's role in these changes was to help put this strategy into words and to strengthen awareness by negotiators of the choices they were making, to help them to unite over a common vision of the corporation of the future. This work involved the construction of "scenarios of alignment" that produced coherent equations in which one element of a rationale implies another element, which implies a third: "Market = need to react $\rightarrow$ decentralization + adaptiveness $\rightarrow$ management through goals $\rightarrow$ negotiation of the social implications of economic choices $\rightarrow$ a new HR policy $\rightarrow$ collective negotiation + commitment via contract $\rightarrow$ constructive unionism." At the same time, it was a matter of constructing the social acceptance of change by proposing new possibilities of interlinking private life, corporate life, and society.

This policy involved the construction of a multi-actor dialogue in which interactions among union, management, and personnel could be managed. The bargaining process became a means of general consciousness-raising about the economic stakes. The logic of the market is explicitly the reference point and horizon that establishes a new accounting of personnel needs. The agreements of the 1990s rested on an analysis of the French situation that posed the critical situation of employment at the national level, and so successive governments asked businesses to share employment while adapting to the market.

When EDF–GDF mobilized on the issue of employment, it reinforced its legitimacy in French society and at the same time applied the internal tradition of discussion within the *cité entreprise*. The corporation's actions unleashed intense debate, with job creation constituting a sort of civic trigger relating each person to membership in the company, to participation in its mutations. The agreements functioned on a sort of metaphor of "war effort," which echoed the collective unconscious of the corporation at the time of its foundation. Finally, the agreements proposed an alignment between economic efficiency, relation to the market, civic effort, and employee well being. Not only did the corporation have to perform better, but at the same time it had to recruit and offer the possibility of well being to individuals, thus creating a sort of new totality articulating the social and the economic, and starting to sketch a new kind of company.

The CGT's workerist myth had persisted since the creation of the industry— with typical factory working hours, an internal labor market allowing social mobility through worker education and entry into the consumer society, debates organized by the consultative system around the "class against class" mode (management on one side, workers on the other). By contrast, the agreements proposed the vision of a postmodern society in which each person constructed his or her own destiny, with new equilibria between life at work and life outside work. The possibility of individual trajectories replaces the previous model's notion of class destiny. The logic of collective negotiations seals the new social pact heralding the society of the future.

The previous model of the corporation made the *cité entreprise* function on the basis of an internal socio-political order—co-management (*paritarisme*)—that allowed a constant debate on the purposes of the industry and working life, but without commitments. Collective negotiations link this tradition of debate with a new prospect in which the corporation positions itself on social issues while involving the union actors in decision-making. Symbolically it projects another definition of social relations. Today EDF is abandoning the public service image (now that the goods it produces and distributes are subject to competition) but it is creating, through a strategy of sustained development, new public goods, desiring to outline a new legitimacy for the industry, both internal and external.

III

THE INTERVENTION APPROACH

7

A "Full Engagement" Approach to Intervention

Our interventions have centered around increasing the competitive capability of monopoly/bureaucratic cultures. We have not usually started with that aim. Sometimes we have begun with narrower organizational goals like enhancing labor–management cooperation or worker participation; at other times we have started with the strategic problems posed by growing competition. Yet, in each instance, the transformation of relations has become increasingly central to success. As these organizations have struggled with change and competitiveness, they have found that they could not adapt without reconstructing relations at all levels—not only between unions and managements, but also within each organization and with other stakeholders, partners, and allies. One lesson of the Italian case (Chapter 4) is that the relational dimension cannot be ignored even in strategy-focused interventions; a lesson from the other three cases is that changes in relations are complicated, long, and painful.

Relational interventions in these complex situations have three basic requirements:

1. They must be *interactive*: that is, consultants cannot effectively change relational systems through predefined programs or expert solutions. They must work with the clients in helping them define their own problems and develop their capacities for dialogue and problem-solving.
2. They must confront *sociodynamic* aspects of organizations—the group identities and memories that produce resistances and "irrational" behaviors. It is not sufficient to facilitate problem-solving dialogues; consultants often need to dive into the dark waters of the past to overcome obstacles to change. A corollary of this point is that it is often necessary to work separately with different stakeholders and units, rather than building a single dialogue for all, because each needs to go through its own distinct process of examining and changing identity.
3. They must be *systemic*, crossing all the major divides among stakeholders. It is not sufficient to work at the plant/production level, or at the middle

management level of operational planning, or at the top strategic levels; nor is it sufficient to work with just management or unions. The problem involves holistic reconfigurations of all these levels and the relations among them. It requires aligning measurements and incentives and developing new skills. Indeed, in the end (as we will discuss in Chapter 10), our interventions have not been systemic enough: they have been limited by our inability to reach levels beyond the firm that are also crucial to the transition we are describing.

This combination and complexity of elements that we are describing is not needed for every social change; but it is needed, we have found, wherever organizations are going through shifts that profoundly touch their core beliefs and ways of functioning. The move from monopolistic to competitive positioning in our four cases has turned out to involve such a "step" change. Partial and narrowly focused approaches are insufficient in those instances—they require "full engagement" across a range of actors, levels, and dimensions of action.

THE INTERACTIVE APPROACH TO INTERVENTION

There have historically been two broad approaches to intervention, though they have no widely accepted names.[1] We follow in a long tradition which we will call *interactive*, in contrast to the more widespread *expert* approach.

Expert consultants—to draw a somewhat simplified "ideal-type" picture—come with methods and specialized expertise; they do analyses of the clients' needs using the tools and knowledge; and they present reports on what needs to be done. They remain "outside" the dynamics of the organizations with which they work: their reports are presented rather than developed in conjunction with the clients, nor do they become part of a critical dialogue. Their interventions tend to be relatively brief and intensive. If these consultants get involved in implementation of their recommendations, it is usually in a highly structured way, "rolling out" a "program."

The expert approach to management consulting may have been initiated, and was certainly exemplified, by Frederick Taylor around 1900. He studied work processes, determined the "scientifically" best way to perform them, and imposed them on generally unwilling workers and supervisors. In the modern world Taylorism lives in the work of reengineering consultants like Michael Hammer, and it has also spread to many new domains. The same philosophy is now applied to many other areas: it predominates broadly in firms like McKinsey and the Boston Consulting Group, focusing on strategy; or Accenture, focusing on information systems; or the many firms preaching total quality and process management.

It is hard to resist the expert mode, even for those who want to. Large consulting companies are almost forced into it: they need reproducible methodologies that can be taught to young associates, and that can be broken down so that labor can be efficiently divided. Human nature also pushes in this direction: after one has conducted a few interventions one almost inevitably seeks out rules and starts to refine them, as a way of simplifying and making things more reliable. The economic logic of efficiency is also compelling. Thus many approaches that start out as interactive tend to drift towards an expert orientation. A recent example with which we are familiar is the "balanced scorecard" approach to accountability: as originally formulated by Kaplan and Norton,[2] it stressed involvement of all members of the organization in understanding strategy and relating their work to it. But, as it has become popular and widely used as a consultant tool, it has become increasingly "refined" into a method with predefined categories and processes that often fit badly with the client organization. Recently the listening, interactive dimension has dropped out entirely: Kaplan and Norton now sell the method as a software package.

Interactive consultants, then, follow a difficult path: they do not come with solutions, nor do they present reports. They treat client organizations as living systems with their own dynamics, and seek to establish a relationship with people and groups so that solutions are created with the active involvement of the clients.[3] The approach dates back at least to the famous "Hawthorne studies" conducted at Western Electric in the 1930s, which produced some of the first challenges to the Taylorist world view—demonstrating that by involving workers in planning their own work they could achieve greater productivity increases than the scientific experts. The theme was picked up notably by Kurt Lewin in the 1940s, and memorably formulated in Douglas McGregor's contrast of "Theory X"—expert—and "Theory Y"—interactive—views of human nature.[4]

The authors' approach to consulting owes a great deal to descendants of these pioneers, especially the work on participation, group process, and sociotechnical systems carried out at the Tavistock Institute of Human Relations in the 1940s and 1950s. The Tavistock core group of psychiatrists, clinical and social psychologists and anthropologists had their prewar roots in the Freudian Tavistock Clinic but had worked together in the British army in the Second World War.[5] These social scientists saw their application of theory, through "action research," as a way of both improving productivity and the quality of working life.[6] They stimulated projects to improve work in Scandinavia, the US, Australia, Canada, and India.

A notably successful project carried out by the Norwegian Work Research Institute in Oslo was directed by Einar Thorsrud, a social psychologist who worked with Tavistock researchers. Thorsrud brought together representatives of management, unions and government to sponsor experiments in worker participation in redesigning factory and office work as well as the design of ships. The rationale was that young Norwegians refused to work in the Tayloristic work structure of factories and authoritarian hierarchy of ships. They demanded greater participation and active engagement in their work.

When Maccoby was asked in 1973 to direct the Bolivar Project—which was the first US joint union-management attempt to improve work through employee participation in its design—he traveled to Oslo to seek guidance from Thorsrud, who became a close adviser to that project. Thorsrud also became an adviser to the Program on Technology, Public Policy and Human Development at the Kennedy School of Government at Harvard, which Maccoby directed. Heckscher was one of the first fellows in this program and also learned from Thorsrud's approach. Ramirez studied and then worked with Eric Trist, one of the principal founders at the Tavistock Institute.

Russell Ackoff, who worked with both Maccoby and Ramirez, developed theories of system design and interactive planning.[7] His work is in the tradition of American pragmatism as developed by William James, John Dewey, and later, C. West Churchman. Our work shares this philosophical basis of testing democratic values through experiments in the workplace, and the idea that practice is the best test for theory.

The authors have also been influenced by other descendants of the Lewinian tradition. All four have worked in different contexts with Michel Crozier, who also brought social science methods into the workplace. Other major proponents of this tradition with whom we have worked include Chris Argyris, known for the concept of double loop learning; Donald Schön, who has analyzed how expert thinking blocks change and has further developed the approach; Richard Walton and Robert McKersie, whose work on negotiation laid the foundation for the more recent field of "mutual-gains" bargaining.[8]

Widely dispersed as these approaches are, they share core characteristics. The interactive tradition as a whole centers on *involvement*—involvement of the clients in the consultation process, and also involvement of employees in management decision-making. These consultants focus heavily on creating dialogue among stakeholders—on building fora where groups can openly discuss issues that have previously remained hidden, where information can be shared, where consensus can be created. They tend to place their main emphasis on establishing discursive *processes*, elaborating the rules of openness and fairness. Lewin originally relied heavily on the concept of democracy; later versions have tended to use less philosophically loaded words, such as "participation". But in either case they have tried to reduce power differences by establishing "rules of the game" that bind leaders as well as lower-level employees, and by using consensus as a measure of success.

At times the interactive approach moves towards *pure* process. Some consultants define themselves simply as facilitators, bringing no substantive knowledge of the particular situation and making no recommendations at all; their "expertise" lies entirely in bringing people to agreement. Similarly, mutual-gains or "win–win" bargaining consultants usually help the parties to understand each other but avoid explicitly injecting their own views.

For most of these authors and practitioners the goal, at least conceptually, is an effort to replace power plays with dialogue among stakeholders whenever possible. Most of these writers believe that conflict, when bounded by the principles of rules and collective bargaining, can be constructive; but they also believe that power can be moved, as it were, into the background, allowing greater space for problem-solving and the creation of new solutions.

Recently the interactive tradition has stressed the importance of building shared visions of the future. This was perhaps a less crucial issue in the early days, when it was more often possible to conceive of change as a transformation of the operational routines without fundamental change in the business model or culture. Now, however, the theme of rapid change has become widely accepted and has been incorporated into interactive methodologies. Consultants in the interactive tradition are generally critical of "top-down" visioning exercises, in which the core leadership go off and develop a vision and then come back to preach it to the masses; they favor instead, as one would expect, widely involving processes of study and information-gathering, building towards shared understanding, and eventually to a vision that everyone can actively "buy into" and contribute to.[9]

This kind of dialogue-building has been an important aspect of our work. We have often suggested new forums in which unions and management talk directly to each other outside the collective bargaining context. In this dimension of our work, we often act as coordinators and facilitators, framing the topics of discussion and establishing ground rules that give the parties equal access to the discussions. We have urged the parties to envision and study "ideal futures" together.

Limitations of the interactive approach

Yet the interactive role of creating open dialogue, while important, turns out to be inadequate on its own. It is by no means always true that good process will lead to consensus and commitment. Often solutions offering clear gains to all parties will spark anger and mistrust rather than cooperation. Frequently, too, initiatives that are developed and endorsed through highly participative methods nevertheless languish and drop quickly from sight. When one examines problems closely one often begins to see layers of emotion and collective memory that have been largely ignored by the interactive tradition.

Even the best forms of interactive process have a bias towards focusing on the present and future—the links between people and their goals—and to downplay the past. One of the most developed approaches, for example, is that of *facilitated problem-solving*. These interveners try to get the group to run through a structured analytic process, getting groups to define problems, analyze them, and develop solutions.[10] They use methods like brainstorming, "root cause" analysis, and structured prioritization; they pay particular attention to documenting decisions, allocating responsibilities, and making sure that there is followup. All these are very important in getting groups to work effectively together, and we sometimes use them as aids in the creation of dialogue. These approaches do move beyond the assumption that the analyst's rationality will overwhelm all defenses; they get down into the "nitty-gritty" of daily interactions and relationships and try to build commitment through involvement.

But this problem-solving approach also downplays or oversimplifies the issue of relations among groups. The assumption—not always explicit—is that one can overcome emotional tensions by focusing on accomplishing a shared task. Though there are certainly cases where groups need to be turned towards an external problem rather than continuing to obsess about their internal relations, this only works where the focal problem is really shared. In our cases, the changes are great enough that they create basic splits around what should be done, even within management, to say nothing of between management and other stakeholders. In these circumstances the facilitative approach rapidly breaks down and is seen as "artificial" or "manipulative"; it obscures the root problems, and therefore makes everyone suspicious that it is merely a cover for what is "really" going on, merely a justification for the imposition of a vision that they do not share.

There are other variants of the cognitive approach to facilitation. The "win–win" method, for example, differs from facilitated problem-solving in that it recognizes that there are real differences in interests and visions, but it still tries to resolve them through rational analysis and development of options that meet all interests. The conflicts in the cases we have described are not entirely driven by rational interests: they cannot be reduced to profit for companies or membership for unions or wages for employees. There are cases, as mentioned above, where employees will literally embrace the destruction of their livelihoods as a way of expressing their refusal to accept humiliation and disrespect. Win–win methods are at a loss to incorporate these motivations.

Another cognitive approach is the highly developed approach of Chris Argyris, which seeks to break defensive patterns in organizations by surfacing relational issues, using a structured "ladder of inference" to move people away from emotional reactions and towards verifiable statements based on directly observable data. Argyris' approach, unlike the pure facilitative problem-solving approach, clearly focuses on relationships among people, but it is also extremely cognitive: his assumption is that one can overcome relational tensions by doing in effect a scientific analysis of the "truth" in various points of view. The method, despite its powerful expression in Argyris' work, has not spread widely because, in our experience, people tend to get angry when they are told that their deep beliefs have to be subjected to objective testing and justified by observable data.

The broad transformations we have engaged, in short, have brought up layers rooted deeply in "irrational" group emotions based on past experiences and relations. The sources of these obstacles to change are ones that cannot be talked about or resolved in even the most well-run discussion, often because the participants are themselves unaware of their resistances. This is the world of "culture" and "identity"—poorly mapped in the current literature, but crucial to the successful navigation of change. The sunlit world of discourse and consensus stressed by interactive consultants largely ignores this more mysterious and only partly conscious side.[11]

BEYOND INTERACTIVE METHODS: THE SOCIODYNAMIC
DIMENSION OF INTERVENTION

The dimension that cannot be accessed by classic interactive methods can be called "sociodynamic": it consists of *the persistence of past patterns of group behavior and emotion into the present.*[12] These sociodynamic patterns are most clearly seen in the identities that groups build up and cherish, rooted in events and traditions from long ago, but generating strong feelings of pride in the present. In the interrelation of groups with distinct identities, this pride can quickly turn into equally powerful variants such as humiliation and envy. At AT&T, for example, the concept of universal service was the core of a tradition which was such a source of deep pride; it was very painful for employees to give it up even when the policy and competitive environments no longer supported it, and many resisted the change overtly and covertly. Similarly, the deeply held image of the Ferrovie dello Stato (FS) as one of the creating forces of modern Italy became a source of resistance to the growing pressures for transnational competitiveness.

Why "sociodynamic"? We are deliberately drawing an analogy to "psycho-dynamic" forces that can drive individuals to self-destructive behavior as well as to accomplishments beyond the reach of mere self-interest. But whereas psycho-dynamics concern individuals' sense of self, sociodynamic patterns involve *group* identities. They remain "dynamic," however, in the sense that they generate power-fully motivated behaviors that are not reducible to rational self-interest, and may at times conflict with it—ignoring the "objective" needs of the present.

Continuity with the past is a necessary and vital aspect of the healthy function-ing of organizations as well as individuals: it is the foundation of motivation and meaning. Managers faced with pressure for change often forget this—they talk as if all that counts is the future and the external environment. Yet without an inner sense of direction corporations and individuals lose their way and their focus.

When ignored, the past also tends to reappear in distorted forms. Groups within corporations develop subcultures and ways of seeing the world that are initially appropriate to their function and place and fit well together into a whole. As the environment changes, however, their understandings of what is going on (and what *should* go on) diverge because they see it differently. When they interact with each other, these differences are likely to create misunder-standing and, increasingly, suspicion. Unless there are successful processes for re-alignment, the variations originating in the past can easily produce patterns in the present that become more and more disconnected from what is actually going on outside, and more and more centered on the internal rifts—which become known as the realm of "politics."[13]

Typically these sociodynamic aspects remain largely hidden from the outside. Occasionally, however, they trigger dramatic and visible conflicts. In a case close to our own field, the unions and management at Eastern Airlines—once proudly united in a strong corporate family—simply destroyed each other, killing the company and the locals and putting most of the employees out of work. Management was driven by the military instincts of its CEO, Frank Borman, who felt that to give the unions a significant say in strategy would undermine his control. The union felt such disrespect from Borman that they entered into a final battle knowing full well that the outcome would almost surely be mutual destruction; but their pride, as they said explicitly, was worth more than their jobs. Nor was Borman driven entirely by rationality, despite his insistences: he would surely not have driven off the cliff if he had not seen the conflict as involving his sense of self-respect as well.

We see such counterproductive conflicts on a frequent basis in our work. One was cited in the Lucent case above (Chapter 5)—the sentiment: "F— them, let's go to war. It doesn't matter what it would accomplish, I'll feel a whole hell of a lot better." The key words "pride" and "respect" are a useful signal when these issues drive the parties. The negotiations over the unfair labor practice at Lucent were nearly intractable, in large part, because a key union leader felt, "I've never been so disrespected in my life."

Such patterns do not yield easily to facilitated discussion and dialogue. Frequently, in fact, the most well-managed process only increases everyone's anger, because it does not deal with the real problems: group feelings of anxiety, resentment, and humiliation built from long experience. This is the source of many failures of interactive intervention. Mutual-gains bargaining, for example, frequently fails to achieve the benefits that are evident when rational interests and options are laid out, because the meeting of visible needs may conceal threats to group identity and solidarity. The CGT union in the EDF case (Chapter 6) at first rejected many deals which other unions accepted, and which it itself later accepted, because it was struggling to deal with its anti-capitalist and anti-cooperative traditions.[14]

The roots of sociodynamic patterns

Identity has many dimensions, which is what makes it so hard to change. It is first of all a set of shared symbols and meanings that defines a group and is a source of pride for its members. The national flag, the union label, the company logo may be such focal symbols; for unions there are often key struggles in the past that give "meaning" to being a union member; companies have their myths of the founder and of critical moments in their history. These are sources of pride and unity: people "rally round" the symbols when threatened, and "parade" them to show their uniqueness. The symbols and myths of identity express a deep human need to be part of a valued group, and they play a powerful role in defining who can be trusted.

These symbols are not, however, powerful in themselves: they are powerful because they represent entire "ways of life"—that is to say, *multiple* concrete and interconnected aspects of organization. Patterns developed over time become increasingly embedded in every aspect of organizational functioning. We can distinguish some key ones:

1. Social identities are embedded in organizational systems—formal structures, routines, and systems. In many companies, for example, it becomes extremely difficult to change the role of functions that have been historically important, such as the engineers in technology companies at IBM or DEC; when CEOs in these situations attempt to raise the profile of marketing, they consistently run into a buzzsaw of opposition based on the feeling that "we're not that kind of company."

2. They are embedded "below" organizational systems in the normal routines and habits of daily life. An important obstacle to building union–management trust, for example, was simply that most managers were not in the habit of including union representatives in their planning memos. Thus, even when the will was good, mistrust was frequently reinforced by unions finding out something a little too late. More generally, shifts in values and formal structures may not be enough: these small daily patterns often continue to have powerful effects.

3. Social groups come in time to define themselves in part by their relation to other groups. Sometimes, in union–management relations and others, this can be like a bad marriage: each side stores up grievances and images about the other. Letting go of those grievances is difficult because it would also mean changing one's perception of oneself, and giving up justifications and reasons for the way one behaves. Unions generally define themselves by their opposition to management; efforts to redefine this cause great anxiety because it is no longer clear what the union is if it is not in opposition. Managers, meanwhile, frequently use unions as convenient excuses or scapegoats for their own inability to pursue change.

4. Social identities become embedded also—sometimes most powerfully of all—in individual personalities and values: what Fromm and Maccoby have called "social character." Some companies have traditionally rewarded "jungle fighters," who build personal empires and fight for position; others have encouraged "craftsman" personalities, focused on care and quality performance. As the competitive environment heats up new types come to the fore, especially "marketing personalities" oriented to interpersonal persuasion and networking. These patterns lie deep in personality, connected to family structures and life experiences, and so are not easily shifted when the organizational needs change without wholesale replacement of employees. Thus, craftsmen, for example, build ideologies of what the organization should be—high-quality, service-oriented—which fit their own orientations and lead them to resist strategies based on marketing or innovation.[15]

In healthy and stable organizations, these rooted sociodynamic forces are hard to see because they are aligned with the more rational and visible dimensions of self-interest and organizational purposes—the past does not conflict with the present. But during crises and transformations, the sociodynamic aspects rooted in pride and memory of the past may become detached from organizational and individual interests.

From this perspective the story in all our cases has been remarkably similar. During the heyday of AT&T, EDF, and FS, the core value of high-quality universal service met multiple needs simultaneously: it brought power and rewards to managers and employees; it made the companies successful; it was a source of pride to employees, something recognized in the community at large as having great value, and contributing to national strength; it drew on the dominant social character of craftsmen, focused on service, employment security and quality of performance; it anchored employee expectations of stability. During the 1980s and 1990s, however, several of these previously aligned factors shifted dramatically: markets became more differentiated, so that universal quality became a less successful business strategy; the companies lost their standing as exemplars of national identity; social values of innovation and customer respons-iveness rose at the expense of universal service. Yet the sense of identity and pride of the employees in all these companies remained rooted in the older values. Thus for many years—even down to the present—the "old" way of extreme focus on quality and rejection of short-term consumer pressures has continued to shape many behaviors at the heart of the companies, among both managers and union members, acting as a continual source of conflict with those who would make the company more "modern."

When identity and tradition become split off in this way from current realities, social pathologies may result. The images of the past become highly "sacralized": behaviors which began as pragmatic solutions to problems now become undis-cussible values, symbols separating the good from the bad, quite apart from whether they "work." Denial and defenses fill in the gap between what is believed and what is observed. Vicious circles of blame are locked into place: dif-ferent groups accuse each other of not "getting it," and they look for every evid-ence they can find of the other's errors while turning a blind eye to their own.

Some key sociodynamic patterns

Sociodynamic patterns are not universal but have to be observed and inter-preted for each particular situation. Some, however, reoccur regularly in the kind of situation we have described—the move from semi-monopoly to competitive business in unionized situations. Two stand out especially.

Relations of inequality
The parties have not historically approached each other as equals. Management has been the dominant party—better-educated, richer (individually and organi-zationally), more mainstream; unions have had to fight for recognition and

influence often with great self-sacrifice. Managers do not see themselves as needing unions—indeed, unions are an affront to managers' self-image, because the unions suggest that they have succeeded in winning the loyalty of managers' subordinates. They do not see unions as potentially constructive partners. They see them as external to "their" firm, "third parties," a reproach to the management of people. Unions, meanwhile, cannot exist without management, but they have to shout to make themselves heard.

Over time this relation has affected all the dimensions of identity, becoming much harder to change. Union leaders (for the most part) take *pride* in their ability to disrupt. Those who make it through elections are often those who have been able to (to use common phrases) "stand up to management," "show them that they can't walk all over us"; they find that they unleash tremendous energy in their constituents by taking management down a peg: the battle for self-respect in effect becomes a win–lose struggle, in which defeat for the enemy is automatically a victory for self. There is no pride to be had in being constructive about business matters, because that puts the union and its members entirely on management's ground, needing to be tutored and "educated" in order to participate, and highly vulnerable to manipulation. Instead there is clear joy in thwarting the adversary: this joy is enshrined in the collective celebrations of great strikes, in songs about defeating the bosses, in the ritual chants and slogans of the movement. In Europe even with legal co-determination that puts union leaders on supervisory boards, the unequal relation has often developed also into a systematic anti-capitalist ideology, with a vision of the future in which the capitalist will be permanently brought low and workers will be on top.[16]

The union defines itself in a kind of David–Goliath relation, with management seen as untrustworthy but also highly incompetent, leading the company into disaster. There is always *some* truth to these charges, but it is also clear that union leaders pick out those pieces of the truth that support this picture of management and of the relationship. In this way they steadily strengthen a picture that becomes more and more difficult to change.

The patterns become in time more and more self-reinforcing: the leaders are selected for their aggressiveness; if they are persuaded (perhaps by our intervention skills) to enter into dialogue with management, they risk becoming isolated from and losing the understanding for their base; they have little history or shared symbolism to appeal to in trying to bring along those members. Their leadership is challenged by people who claim cooperation means getting in bed with management, enjoying good dinners and losing sight of traditional union goals.

Management, being far more in control, prides itself on avoiding such petty vindictiveness and generally sees itself as both rational, responsible, and caring. But this self-image consistently blinds it to the political realities of unions. Almost all managements treat the "human relations" side of the business as a secondary nuisance: the job of top management is to make strategic decisions related to capital accumulation, and they delegate to their HR and Labor Relations staffs the job of working through the consequences in the most humane or least disruptive way possible. "Real" managers, in effect, are ones who can be "serious" about business strategy that involves "serious" amounts of money, while those who talk about human needs and wants are seen as immature, like a boy who cries when he stubs his toe. Real managers always look to the future, turn lemons into lemonade, seize opportunities, do not dwell on the past, focus on getting the job done rather than on the human dimension; those who are most revered are often the most ruthless.

This obviously does not produce a highly respectful attitude towards dialogue with union leaders. Many managers who dealt with union leaders in AT&T Workplace of the Future (WPoF) meetings complained that it was not worth their (by implication: important) time to listen to the unions "bitching about some worker who didn't get his upgrade." They are also extremely impatient with unions' tendency to bring up long-ago events to justify their suspicions or values. When unions do try to talk about strategy managers are tolerant, perhaps a little amused—isn't it nice that these union leaders are trying to grow up and be real businessmen? But they certainly don't treat the unions as worthy partners in the serious business of strategy formulation. This does not give a highly rewarding feeling to those union leaders who risk their political futures and put into question their own histories and identities by trying to change their relation to management. It is no wonder that these dialogues tend to boil over: even for those union officials who see a real need for better relations, it feels a lot better just to be oneself, bring these know-it-alls down a peg, show them they can't mess with us, than to try to engage them in this painful way.

Thus, the circular tension between "higher" and "lower," between those who control and those who seek to assert themselves in the face of control, is one identity dynamic that continually undercuts attempts at dialogue.[17]

The "old" corporate family vs the "new" entrepreneurialism
The second recurring sociodynamic pattern in these cases is the difficult problem of identification with the company. In the "before" state of all the companies we worked with—in the period of bureaucratic/monopolistic culture—both the company and the employees expected that careers with the company were for life, that turnover should be rare, that people should sacrifice when needed and the company, in turn, should care for those who through no fault of their own were unable to perform fully.

Unions have often bought into this loyalist ethic. It is a seemingly paradoxical but nevertheless real position: they define their relation to management as highly adversarial, taking pride in their ability to block management, yet at the same time they see themselves as deeply intertwined with and dependent on the company. Even Marxist unions like the French CGT, with its strong anti-capitalist ideologies, have oriented strongly to the notion of an "entreprise-cité"—enterprise-community—with a sense of permanence. This seeming paradox is captured in a familiar term which applies perfectly to many union leaders: "loyal opposition."

The unions we have dealt with are first of all *structurally* committed to their companies: they set up their political structures around plants and geographical units. Thus, any major change in the company's structure disrupts the union's internal politics and threatens careers. Industrial unions in both France and the US are also fundamentally organized around a job-preservation strategy. In our cases many of their members have nowhere else to market their skills: locomotive engineers or telephone operators have no job markets outside FS and AT&T. These rational ties to the company are generally supplemented by deep emotional connections: faced with layoffs or corporate restructurings, union leaders often speak with feeling about the commitment that their members have, all they have invested in the company's success, how much they care. We quoted above a Lucent union leader's response to a new strategy of divesting manufacturing plants: "This is like finding your wife in bed with another man. Our factory people are interwoven in the life of the company: most of the people feel it's their company, they're tremendously proud of it—as opposed to other companies where there's no loyalty."

In the last two decades companies have begun to reject this loyalist ethic, but they have not yet found a clear substitute. At AT&T, leaders have emphasized competitive cost comparisons with MCI and Sprint and embraced a "tougher" performance ethic: they have begun to see it as legitimate to move people in and out to maintain high standards—to get rid of poor performers, even if they were doing their best, and to bring in new people. Throughout our four companies, managers have begun to talk more about growth than security, innovation than quality of production.

Yet the managers themselves have not given up the older values: they still want their employees to be loyal, they still want to be seen as caring. Managers still widely use images of a "family" to describe the corporation's relation to employees. At Lucent, CEO Rich McGinn spoke of wanting to build a "culture of ownership": this has implications of long-term commitment and mutual obligation which are at odds with many other signals—bringing in high-priced free-agents to management, making dramatic strategic moves that eliminate thousands of jobs promising "employability." As the unions noted, it is hard to feel like an owner when your ownership can be revoked at any moment.

In relation to the union, moreover, managers as a group are deeply enraged by the fact that unions disrupt the unity of the corporate family—their reaction frequently goes beyond rational concerns about strikes and bargaining. We have frequently seen high-level managers turn livid at the thought that unions were violating the unified commitment of the organization. They do not accept a vision of unions as entities with independent interests.

In effect there has been a kind of struggle under way within these managements between the "old" identity of company loyalty and the "new" one of entrepreneurial individualism.[18] Each has its own set of bases. The old one, on the organizations we have dealt with, is supported by formal and informal reward systems, by internal rituals, by organization traditions; financed by cross-subsidies; and reinforced by a quasi-tribalistic sense of mutual support and membership in a tradition. The new one is based more heavily in the teachings of business schools and in the popular press and is adaptive to the pressures of stock markets, pension funds, and investors. It sometimes caused AT&T managers to put on an identity that did not fit their personality, to act like corporate cowboys.

Paradoxically, management's self-image as a rational actor often prevents it from understanding the dynamics of identities within its own ranks, as well as with other stakeholders. AT&T, after its divestiture, consistently rejected managers brought in from outside to transform because they did not fit with and understand the culture and they challenged the identities of managers who saw themselves as providing universal service. This pattern continued fifteen years later at Lucent, where an external CFO favored by Wall Street was blocked by internal resistances, and where the "Silicon Valley" vs "Western Electric" identity struggle was manifested throughout the organization in tensions between managers grounded in the different traditions. In strategic discussions among top management, one can spot very quickly those who see themselves as "new economy," financially savvy, shareholder-oriented types, and those who see themselves as more traditional manufacturers or service people; these differences are extremely important in shaping strategic choices. Most dramatically, the near-merger of Lucent with Alcatel was scuttled at the last moment in part over questions of pride: who would have the bragging rights, what nation would be seen as the victor, and whether the Lucent CEO would be seen as abandoning a cherished history and exporting the iconic Bell Labs.[19]

Thus, fundamentally, neither unions nor managements know how to move beyond paternalism and long-term security: the move from quasi-monopoly to competitiveness has set them adrift. Management verbally embraces the new world, but without having a very coherent picture of it. The image is further blurred in all our cases by public institutions—government regulatory agencies as well as other "watchdog" groups—that call for rapid innovation and a new level of profitability, but retain strong oversight in the public interest. FS is no longer a government ministry, but it is still owned by the state, and the transport, labor, and treasury ministries use it as a battlefield. EDF is still controlled by the French government. AT&T constantly claims that the regulations and public obligations put into place at divestiture make it unable to compete freely with cutthroat competitors. They can all quite naturally ask, "Who are we? And what will we become?"

Consequences for intervention

The sociodynamic patterns that arise from the interplay of identities create enormous, usually unanalyzed, challenges for any organizational intervention that requires fundamental change. They ordinarily exert a deeply conservative force. In the relatively sparse literature on deliberate culture change, in fact, much debate has focused on the question of whether group identities can be deliberately modified at all. Many writers emphasize the depth and interconnectedness of values and emotions as an almost insuperable barrier to change; a few see them as more easily subject to linguistic manipulations and redefinitions.[20]

In our experience the task is indeed very difficult, going far beyond verbal exhortations and symbolic ceremonies, because identities are grounded in so many dimensions of action. Woven through the fabric of groups' internal structures and relations, identities define the expectations that people have of each other; individuals who violate these expectations lose influence and become marginalized. Transforming these patterns therefore requires in effect that everyone change at once. Leaders can help catalyze this simultaneous redefinition, but they too have only a relatively small margin for innovation without themselves being rejected and losing the commitment of their followers. Union leaders, being elected, are especially vulnerable, and we have often found that ones who try to lead redefinitions of the union away from simple adversarialism are open to attack from those wielding symbols of the militant battles of the past.

Four consequences follow for interveners. First, it is vital to spend time in understanding, in an anthropological sense, the backgrounds and histories of the various players in the drama. The consultant's credibility and ability to influence depend fundamentally on being able to respond and use the symbols that are crucial to each party. Consultants who do not understand the roots of union politics, for example, or the sources of the emotions around seniority, will not only be marginalized: given the strong *emotional* nature of the sociodynamic patterns, they will become lightning rods for those emotions. Again, this is true on the management side as well: we have had to understand and appreciate— though not always agree with—the feelings of resentment held by most managers about the unions' refusal to accept their assurances of good will and to fit comfortably within the corporate "family."

A second and related consequence is that interveners must often work with the parties separately. The development of a new mode of behavior for the complex pattern of union–management–worker (and other stakeholder) relationships is not just a single shift for the whole system; it also involves *different* dynamic transformations for each of the players. Unions need to wrestle with challenges to the ethic of seniority; managers need to wrestle with the transition from paternalist to performance cultures; operational managers must learn to incorporate strategic perspectives; strategic managers must learn the importance of relational capabilities; and so on. Failure on any of these deep shifts can easily cause the whole transition to explode. Consultants, if they are to help smooth the changes, must establish independent relations of trust in each of these realms.

Our intervention roles have often involved such reinterpretation of the parties' past to themselves. If one looks over the history of EDF one can stress its role as a pillar of national stability and collective French economic growth; these images tend to generate resistance to globalizing and competitive moves. But equally in the history one can find and stress traditions of service and innovation which are more easily linked to current strategies. Union traditions often focus on the wars with management; but Tixier has sometimes brought out through internal discussions other traditions as well, ones of mutual self-help and local self-management, that are more friendly to the entrepreneurial and team-based direction of current company policies. As consultants we have sought opportunities to encourage such self-reinterpretations within each of the stakeholder groups.

On another front the CWA has, with Maccoby's help, reexamined over many years the meaning of job security. This is a highly "sacralized" concept, symbolizing the power of the union won through many battles of the past; but it has become increasingly untenable, leading to defeat after defeat. Behind the concept of job security, however, is a deeper notion of security of employment, which can be won not through holding onto particular sites but by helping with retraining, mentoring, and so on. By helping both management and unions to focus on this core need in developing new solutions to a more dynamic environment, the consultants can contribute to a more constructive discussion.

Third, the parties must be given opportunities to communicate with each other not just about goals and tasks, but about their interpretations and perceptions of the changes they confront. Facing deep change, groups diverge on what they make of it—some see it as an opportunity, others as a threat; some see it as a denial of their value, others are thankful that their value is finally being recognized. When all communication is about surface behaviors, these differences almost inevitably produce increasing mistrust, observable as groups start saying of each other, in effect, "There they go again." More open discussions—about the ideal future, about obstacles to trust, about the values of the corporation—give people a chance to realign around fundamental aspects of meaning.

Finally, since identities are so multidimensional—grounded in structures, routines, relationships, and personalities—successful change processes (in these complex situations) must be slow and iterative. Crises, as has often been observed, may help catalyze transformation;[21] there is no question that in our experience crisis is an important element in forcing people out of the deep grooves of values and habits dug over time. But it is not sufficient: without patient attention to all of the elements of social identity, from routines to skills and personalities to values and meanings, transformations will remain incomplete. Even so catastrophic an event as the French Revolution gave way to a reaction in which many of the prior forces reasserted themselves; and in our own experience, the nearly twenty-year period since the divestiture of AT&T has not been enough to erase many core dynamics based on the old monopolistic culture.

In the union–management relation, one may begin by working on the level of conscious values and symbols, encouraging the parties to visibly demonstrate equality and partnership through joint releases and other means. But, astonishingly, often minor routines built up over years keep coming back to undermine the best intentions: union leaders are not in the normal communication loops; they do not like the same restaurants as managers; etc. Other symbols may also interfere: union leaders may insist that meetings not be held in the usual hotels because they are unorganized. And, still deeper, managers have usually gotten where they are by being authoritative, and union leaders have gotten there by being aggressive; both may lack the attitudes and skills needed for collaborative problem-solving. All of these issues need to be addressed through different means in interventions.

These interventions carry no magic. The transformations we have described, from traditional paternalistic relations with images of the family and built-in inequality, to more open relations of dialogue, involve social "identity crises" for all stakeholders. The changes move in the pattern of identity crises: long, uneven, punctuated by explosions and depressions. It is very common for stories of grievances long buried to reemerge suddenly as the parties struggle to move to a new level of understanding, seemingly forgetting intervening years of progress. The only lesson at that point for an intervener is patience, keeping focused on the problem and the vision, working over and over again to link values grounded in the past to the challenges of the present and the future.

SYSTEMIC OPPORTUNISM

The third aspect of these complex interventions—in addition to the interactive and sociodynamic dimensions—is that they are *systemic*. The transformations described in this book touch on every aspect of organizational functioning, from the shopfloor to the executive suite, from accounting to information systems to line management. For the intervener, it means constantly scanning the entire system for "openings" for action.

The organization development literature of the 1970s was full of discussions about the best place to focus a change effort: whether change could spread from the "top down," or would move better from the "bottom up"—or, according to some, from the "middle out." We have worked from all of these positions, but have found we could not count on a "spread" from any one of them: different parts of the organization have their own dynamics and identities that impede the logical flow of change.[22] The strategic visions flowing from the top of FS ran into severe obstacles in the middle of the organization; the shopfloor transformations of the AT&T Quality of Worklife program were equally boxed in and smothered.

Instead, we have found we needed to work on the entire system—not all at once, but piece by piece: on the internal identities of the key stakeholders, the relations between them, the different levels and divisions of the company. It cannot be assumed that change that "makes sense" in one of these domains will spread by osmosis to others. The large processes we have discussed are composed of *many independent* processes within unions, within divisions, within top and middle management, on the shopfloor, in joint bodies; processes of visioning, of dialogue, of study, of reexamination of the past. Only over a long period of time do these begin to meld together into a larger coherence.

Since one cannot work everywhere at once, the consultant has to be an opportunist, spotting and seizing openings as they emerge in different parts of the system. Frequently, changes in leadership will shut down promising initiatives, but, equally frequently, such changes open up new possibilities elsewhere. We have at various points found ourselves working primarily within particular divisions, or within a given union, or on the top management team, or on a joint committee; there are also moments—sometimes long ones—where the change process is becalmed, where everyone seems to be "hunkering down" to focus on dealing with what has already occurred. Thus, we are ourselves frequently taken by surprise by new initiatives that call on us just when we think that all is dead.

Our experience, then, leads us to doubt the possibility of intervention by diffusion, focusing on one spot and expecting it to spread. It bears mentioning that it leads us equally to be skeptical of "big bang" approaches, trying to hit everything at once through some massive coordinated initiative or corporate campaign. The process of building a new system of related identities, unified around shared visions, is too complex to be planned. One cannot lay a roadmap from monopolistic to competitive organization any more than one can plan and force a child's transition to adulthood: both require a great deal of experimentation and learning by doing. Change moves in rhythm of experimentation rather than according to prescheduled timetables.

Strategic, operational, and relational dimensions

Although we are opportunistic in finding parts of the system that are open to change at a given moment—and finding ways to deal with blockages—it is also worth having a broad road map of the key elements that need to be recombined in a competitive system. Two dimensions, in particular, have stood out. One has already been central to the discussion: the interrelation of *stakeholder* groups, particularly management and unions. Our interventions have been unusual in thinking about this relation as a central element of success rather than as a subsidiary annoyance within a management-focused change. We are arguing, in other words, that a successful intervention of this type must pay special attention to building understanding and relationships among stakeholders, including work with each of the stakeholders as units in themselves.

A second aspect of the system bears emphasis here. We have spoken before of the convergence of strategic and relational logics. These need to come together because companies involve both strategy—what they do—and relations—how people cooperate to get it done. But they are too often kept *apart* because the managers who think about these aspects are widely separated in terms of their views of the world and of each other; there are gaps of mistrust and misunderstanding that may be as wide as those between managers and outside stakeholders. The business strategy function typically produces analyses with little understanding of the cultural, psychological, and social underpinnings that they require for implementation.

We ourselves have come from the two ends of the spectrum: Rafael Ramirez focused primarily on strategy, the others on stakeholder relationships. Our interventions and our understanding have gradually converged on the interrelation of the two.

When interventions touch lower and middle management levels, an *operational* orientation also becomes crucial. Operational managers are often equally scornful of strategic superiors and relational functionaries. Their focus on improving production is quite different in tone and logic from the focus on developing strategic visions or of developing effective relationships.

These differences run deep. The strategic orientation reflects what William James called a "tough-minded" view; the relational is in James' terms "tender-minded."[23] James noted that these two types often have contempt for each other; so it is in the business world. Strategic thinkers often feel that attention to human relations weakens their ability to make the "tough choices," and they expect the HR functions to do whatever cleaning up is necessary. The operational types, meanwhile, typically view the strategic level as having their heads in the clouds, missing the "nitty-gritty" of actually making things happen. (A popular joke among middle managers at GM in the 1980s referred to the headquarters building as the place "where the rubber meets the air.")

Successful system change requires integrating these dimensions. We noted earlier that we as consultants needed to learn to combine strategic and relational skills, which are often divided. Even more important is to get operational leaders to understand these different views of the world. But these three categories are still not the whole story. There are, of course, many more such divisions within management: for instance, as mentioned earlier, marketers often hate engineers (and vice versa); at times, in each of our cases, that disjunction has been a crucial blockage and has required another bridging process. Our work has for various reasons focused on still another deep divide, stretching across the gap between the corporation and one of its key stakeholders, labor unions.

A systemic orientation, then, needs to build understanding across all the key divides within an organization. We are not claiming that every intervention must be systemic in this sense; but we are claiming that *this* kind of intervention, transforming from quasi-monopoly to highly competitive, does involve all of these elements. In order to succeed in working together in a changing environment, the parties need to build rational images of a future in which their interests can be reconciled. They also need to take a deep look at their pasts, and go through the task of revising their own sense of self in order to survive transformative pressures. They need to gain empathy for each other's values as well as cognitive understanding of each other's interests. They need to deal with their own defensiveness about these challenges to their identity, and to confront unrealistic fantasies about what they hope for from the future. Through all this, the intervener himself becomes a lightning rod, on which much of the anxiety and defensiveness is projected. He has to engage the parties in a rich network of relationships without himself becoming absorbed into any one relationship, though each party will try to co-opt him and may become angry if he fails to yield.

OVERVIEW: LINKING PAST, PRESENT, AND FUTURE

Pulling together the elements we have outlined, we can schematize the overall interplay of intervention processes in the following way: All relationships involve an interplay of past, present, and future. The past is the root of hidden dynamics that define identity and resistance; the future defines aspirations, fears, and direction; they come together in the present decision-making which, for our purposes, involves the "political" interplay of different groups.[24] Thus to transform an organization one needs to *create understanding and dialogue among the stakeholders which integrates their view of themselves and their past and leads towards a common future.*

One can thus distinguish three *major* intervention "moves": creating dialogue, building visions, and interpreting identities—though such a distinction is useful only if it is firmly remembered that the three pieces interplay constantly with each other. Of these, dialogue and building visions have been the core of interactive methods; the integration of the past adds another layer of complexity.

In other words, we view the culture both "diachronically," in terms of its history, and "synchronically" in terms of its adaptation to its environment. In this way we see how certain practices that were adapted to past environments persist when they are no longer adaptive.

In the next chapter we will sketch in more detail some of the particular methods we have used in each of these areas (Figure 7.1).

CONCLUSION: RATIONAL AND NON-RATIONAL DIMENSIONS OF INTERVENTION

The task of changing relational systems is fundamentally one of reconnecting dimensions and organizational components that are normally treated separately.

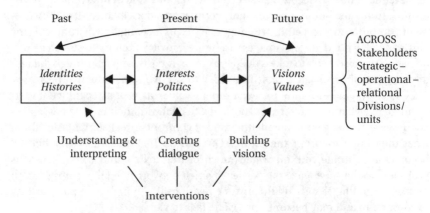

Fig. 7.1. Elements of intervention.

In a stable system various functions become specialized and develop their own points of view—strategic, operational, relational, or focused on particular sets of interests. But when, as in these cases, a system's purpose and environment are fundamentally redefined, the distinctness of points of view becomes an obstacle, encouraging "political" defensiveness rather than constructive rethinking of what each part can contribute to the system on which they all depend.

The task therefore involves redefining roles, but it cannot assume a blank slate: the parties involved have their own interests, histories, and sense of pride that can often turn into resistance to change, overt or covert. The change process involves another kind of recombination—of rational and non-rational elements. The parties have to both understand cognitively the emerging structures, and also to *feel* that they have a valid place in it. This can be summarized, therefore, as a matter of convening parties in direct conversations that transcend their normal roles, in which they build shared images of the future, in part by reinterpreting their own pasts and their historical relationships.

The rational and cognitive side is the easiest one to get hold of—either analyzing, or helping the parties themselves to analyze, the nature of a problem and its solutions. Many intervention methods focus on this aspect. But the problems we are dealing with have strong emotional components rooted in the past; they touch not only the surface interests of the parties, but their sense of who they are and what they stand for. Purely cognitive approaches ignore this crucial obstacle to agreement.

In terms of the framework suggested earlier, these cognitive approaches are oriented to the present and future—the analytic particularly aims to build future visions (solutions to problems), while the facilitative approaches try to build those future visions through dialogue among stakeholder groups in the present. These are vital aspects and should be the eventual goal of interventions. But our experience is that one cannot get there without going back through the past, redefining connections based on solutions to old problems that have acquired independent emotional charges. Thus, even when we use analytic methods such as win–win negotiation, we do it with an emphasis on leaving a great deal of space for the parties to "work through" their own core values and their relations to each other; we do not push immediately to focus the discussions on cognitive analysis, but encourage exploration of historical causes of mistrust and the sources of pride among each of the parties. The goal is always to build a shared ability to work together in the present; but developing visions of the future and interpretations of the past are essential to freeing people up to do that work.

Full engagement combines all these dimensions: past, present, and future, rational and non-rational, across stakeholder groups and organizational levels. In dealing with transformations involving whole systems, nothing less will do.

8

Techniques and Methods

The last chapter framed the work of intervention in general terms; there is also a more concrete world of tools and techniques. Diving deeper, we can detail the main methods we have used in terms of the three major tasks we have set out: creating dialogue, envisioning the future, and interpreting the past.

CREATING DIALOGUE

A thread in these interventions which we share with many other "process-oriented" interveners is the attempt to develop the area of dialogue and policy and to reduce the domain of power. In all our interventions a constant part of the job was bringing people together who did not normally talk to each other. The problems are not by any means always between unions and management; there are major gaps within each organization, and with outside groups, that need to be bridged. At times we have set up meetings between middle managers or first-level supervisors and their superiors, so that the latter can understand the stresses created by the change process; at others, we have brought together customers with top managers or union leaders; sometimes we have linked local unions with national leaders.

Building forums, starting conversations

Interactive interventions therefore involve building forums[1] that widen dialogue among parties that affect the functioning of the firm. Some of these are relatively informal—connecting people who are interdependent but who do not normally talk to each other. Others are more formal: creating new bodies that cross normal organizational lines.

The most obvious forums are those bringing together union and management: the attempt to overcome historical conflict and build a unified approach to new business challenges has often been the starting-point for our interventions. At EDF, for example, the followup groups created to evaluate the various labor agreements included both union leaders and managers. They enabled the two parties to teach each other their visions of the world and the key problems they faced. This learning process developed the habit of dialoguing and promoted the development of a shared cognitive frame, which gradually legitimized the company's shift towards a global competitive role.

Such forums are also valuable in dealing with other types of divisions: on the management side, Ramirez' intervention in reframing the identity of the Italian railroad is perhaps the most extended of our efforts. After the "conceptualizing" phase, the top managers recognized the need to bridge the gap with the middle "operational" layers, who tended to see these new strategic ideas as threatening and impractical. Thus, they created forums, co-designed between the consultants and the strategy staff unit, that brought together line managers with senior management to discuss the strategic future(s) of the company. In a first phase many individual and small group consultative meetings between the strategy unit and different Ferrovie dello Stato (FS) divisions helped to prepare the ground; then a larger group was brought together to attempt to align around a strategic vision.

The purpose here is not, of course, to create a huge bureaucratic infrastructure of new committees with unbearable numbers of meetings. As it has gradually become clear how important and powerful the creation of stakeholder dialogues is, it has also become more evident that they need to be structured in a flexible and efficient way. We have evolved towards a mix of permanent committees, like the WPoF business unit councils, and temporary or one-time groupings on an "as-needed" basis.

Union–management connections are only one part of the work. We have become increasingly aware of internal barriers within management, as well as within unions, that present obstacles to change. The ability to understand and problem-solve across those lines is crucial to breaking down the bureaucratic rigidity which holds back the move to competitive strategy.

Tools and techniques for creating dialogue

We have used three primary tools in building dialogue within these forums:

Research and feedback
At key moments in the development of the union–management relation, we have used our status as independent researchers to develop credible analyses of the effects of different strategies. Tixier began his work from this perspective: he was asked by management to investigate the union–management relation, and he built an institute of researchers capable of conducting interviews and

analyses in large companies. At EDF a key moment was Tixier's presentation to EDF senior management of the conclusion that their strategy of isolating the CGT union was counter-productive. The ability to do credible research with high legitimacy across all parties has remained the most solid foundation of his interventions.

Such research efforts have an effect of changing the tone of discussion, even in traditional bargaining settings and even when we do not ourselves facilitate meetings. The habit of basing arguments on data, rather than on the volume of threats, or on hierarchical position is a powerful one in avoiding senseless confrontations.

Though initial research was often done by the consultants themselves, it was still more potent when the parties themselves did it. At various times we have encouraged teams of managers and union officials to conduct interviews throughout the organization. This is a radical shift from the usual relations within organizations, where subordinates listen to superiors or (at best) try to influence them; here, we put the superiors in the position of trying to understand the subordinates' point of view, and to reproduce it in a report that could be circulated and widely seen as valid.[2]

Self-generated research can be very powerful in breaking through the tendency of organizations to gloss over unpleasant realities and to avoid confrontations; as Argyris has shown, this is a major obstacle to organizational learning.[3] In a recent intervention by two of the authors, for instance, they noticed that the managers were aware of a high level of cynicism, but avoided dealing with the problem. The consultants suggested they measure trust through a survey. When managers found that fewer than 20 percent of those they managed trusted them, they could no longer avoid the issue: they took these figures out in the open and made them discussible. Eventually, this led this division to recognize that resistance to the trade union was only making things worse.

Techniques of "mutual-gains" ("win–win") problem-solving
This approach, which traces its formal lineage to the enormously influential book *Getting to Yes*,[4] uses two techniques that have been central to our conversations with the parties, whether separately or together. The first is analyzing and understanding the interests of the other party (or parties)—their power bases, their long-term goals, their internal politics, etc. The second is thinking about as many options as possible to meet those interests.

Mutual-gains techniques were spread widely at AT&T as part of the Workplace of the Future (WPoF) training materials. For the most part, however, we used the method implicitly rather than formally, pushing the parties to think about how to meet the other side's essential interests. This has certainly helped at crucial junctures in resolving major disputes such as those over employment levels at EDF or over organizing at AT&T.

We have also always acted to bring into the open credible information. One critical moment in Tixier's intervention at EDF was persuading management to give the unions realistic projections about future employment levels, which they had previously withheld for fear of tipping their hands too much—a traditional bargaining frame. In the other cases, as well, we continuously tried to bring out hidden information as much as possible to build a basis for dialogue.

But in our experience, dialogue between the unions and management tends to be fragile. We analyze the basis for the frequent breakdowns in other contexts (see Chapter 10). Here, it is sufficient to say that acting as a facilitator and laying the groundwork for open discussion is simply not enough by itself to overcome the play of institutional and personal interests and values. The parties have long-established patterns of relationships which they do not give up so easily. They mistrust each other deeply; they are used to lying to each other—collective bargaining is nothing but an organized system of bluffing and lying, in which truth is never assumed; they have fundamentally different views of the world. It requires work at several other levels to transform these patterns, so that the parties can raise the level of cooperation and improve both productivity and the quality of working life.

Techniques of facilitation and process management

We sometimes play the role of classic "facilitators," with all the tools of that trade: building agendas, recording the discussion on easels, testing for agreement, making sure that all voices are heard. This is more often the case in the early phases of interventions as we try to bring out ideal futures or shared diagnoses of the situation. As interventions move along, we act less as facilitators than as commentators. Often we do not stand at the front of the room but sit with the participants.

We do try to make sure, by one means or another, that basic building blocks of process are put in place. In all four cases we pressed the parties to agree on basic ground rules to frame their discussions. At AT&T initial statements of principle defined the basic areas of discussion and set out norms of reciprocity and trust. At Lucent a similar effort to define "dialogue" has not been completed at the time of this writing, when the company is facing a financial crisis and has laid off thousands of employees. At EDF Pierre-Eric Tixier facilitated sessions after the 1993 and 1997 contracts in which the parties together reviewed the results of the negotiations. Otherwise, most of his work has been done with the parties separately.

The problem with the role of facilitator is that it is both well-defined and too limited to encompass all the dimensions of building interactivity. If we allow ourselves to be "slotted" into the position of standing at the front of the room and organizing the discussion, we lose the ability to make substantive comments and to stimulate new points of view. Such a role, furthermore, allows internal leaders to get away with not managing meetings well themselves. The interactive approach is guided by the intention of developing the capacities of the actors, not by taking over an ongoing specialized role in the system.

CREATING VISIONS OF THE FUTURE

A second focus of our role has been helping the parties to develop visions of where they were going. At AT&T, although our values pushed us towards involvement and dialogue, our initial aims were relatively modest: to get workers more engaged in decision-making on the job. But we found that this apparently simple goal was quite subversive to the bureaucratic culture; the parties began to see more and more that this was not just a new structure but a fundamentally new way of relating, and they felt it necessary to clarify the vision of what this change meant. As we articulated a picture of higher trust and teamwork, we found that people were excited and became motivated to carry out often-difficult changes. Later, as we moved into WPoF and beyond, the strategic challenges became so severe that no agreements were possible until we had some shared sense of what the future might look like.

Picturing the future has involved a convergence of the major viewpoints discussed above into a single image: a *social/relational* vision of participative involvement and equity; an *operational* vision of working more flexibly, in teams and with fewer bureaucratic props; and a *strategic* vision, specific to each business, but generally involving a move from quasi-monopoly to competitive adaptiveness and co-production.

1. In the QWL stage at AT&T the participants were thinking almost purely in social/relational terms. The key concepts were "participation" and "trust"; the vision was of a system in which managers exerted less overt power, in which workers could develop their capacities more fully, etc. The actors believed that such changes would benefit the business by improving productivity, quality, and commitment, but the weight of the intervention was clearly on the social side.

2. At the other end of the spectrum was Rafael Ramirez' involvement in the FS. The starting-point here was a fundamental strategic rethinking of the nature of the company, from thinking about itself as a State railroad to a competitive transportation company to, ultimately, a provider of services to cities. The focus on the "visioning" aspect of the intervention was so intense that the lead consultant actually co-wrote a book—*Reinventing Italy*[5]—with the chief client.

3. In the WPoF, EDF, and Lucent interventions, which lasted much longer than the FS effort, there was a concerted effort to bring the strategic, operational, and relational dimensions together. These were all cases in which the strategic environment of the firm was changing rapidly, and unions were inescapably part of the change. Managers often tried to ignore the union role, but found they could not: in all three cases there were major top level confrontations in which the interveners challenged management to consider explicitly whether they could make the needed change without the unions, and in all three cases they realized that the answer was "No." The

question then was whether they could find a strategic path that would incorporate the interests of the unions. The FS case did not get this far and this needed confrontation was never done.

We have found that in developing such visions it is valuable for the intervener to move out of the pure facilitative mode. By themselves, the parties tend to be either timid or vague and rhetorical in thinking about the future. In fact, imagining a future is a much more difficult project than is usually recognized: it takes considerable knowledge of a wide range of environmental factors and long exploration to put them into a workable pattern. Thus, we have provided strong input to these visioning processes—not as "final reports" that stand outside the interactive processes, but as contributions to the dialogues. All of us have written extensively about the fundamental forces that are reshaping businesses and stakeholder relations; we have developed views about what it will take to create healthy relationships in the future. Ramirez, for example, stresses the importance of "coproduction" as a key element of modern strategy; Maccoby has studied the social character dynamics that help systems move from bureaucratic to more open cultures; Tixier and Heckscher have written about emerging organizational forms and the responses required of unions to adapt to this world. These studies and views become inputs to discussions and sometimes, at least, have a significant influence on them.

In all the cases except Lucent, the emergent vision followed similar lines: they tried to retain the notion of the corporation as a community, with strong commitments to employees, but in effect shifted from a stable, internally oriented community to a "war" mentality in which everyone was to pull together to meet the external pressures. The unions and their members were asked to support crucial strategic shifts that involved some loss of jobs and considerable changes in skills and outlooks, but the company retained strong obligations to them rooted in the paternalism of the past. In this vision strategic decisions remain firmly in the domain of top management, and other parties are expected to support them; but in exchange the top management has to show respect for the others' needs.

This vision based on a "battlefield community," however, has proved insufficient to hold people together. It is at best a fragile and temporary form of unity. At EDF the unions have grudgingly accepted the inevitability of the entry of capitalism into their business, but the competitive challenges have not been severe enough to force them into cooperation with management; thus the CEO is in the process now of trying to build a more robust positive shared vision of "sustainable development." At AT&T the fear of competition was very important in overcoming differences in the early phases of WPoF, but it broke down when management was changed, chose a much more risky and transformative strategic path, felt itself unable to take care of its employees in the way that this approach demands, and no longer considered it necessary to partner with unions. At Lucent it was clear from early on (after splitting from AT&T in 1997) that management neither could nor wanted to take on the paternalist role; they embraced a different ethic, more open and individualistic and adaptive. This was the meaning of the CEO's question to Heckscher during their first meeting, "Why can't unions organize in Silicon Valley?" Heckscher's response was to propose a vision of a "new deal" in which the company would provide resources for helping employees with transitions—through training, placement—and would support the union as an institution, in exchange for new degrees of strategic flexibility and the right to involvement at the strategic level. Though leaders on both sides have found this attractive, it presented huge challenges to many traditions and expectations.

Tools and techniques for developing visions

We have tried various intervention approaches to developing these visions.

Scenario planning
Scenario planning—a technique that has been widely used since the 1970s—was used in the FS project at two levels: (a) to verify the viability of the strategies that the company was intending to develop under different possible futures; and (b) to help the company shape its environment to better enhance its viability.[6] The approach consisted of:

(1) identifying the stakeholders in the system with which the focal actor (the Italian railways in this case) interacts. These actors constitute the focal actor's "transactional" environment;

(2) identifying the factors in the wider "contextual" environment that create the action options for the actors in the immediate "transactional" environment;

(3) identifying discontinuities in the relation between the two environments;

(4) organizing these into plausible outcomes (draft scenarios);

(5) identifying implications by back-casting from the scenarios to the present/planned options;

(6) identifying actions to approach desired outcomes, or evaluating existing strategies in relation to the outcomes;

(7) further developing the draft scenarios qualitatively and quantitatively, and re-testing their plausibility;

(8) repeating steps 6 or 7.

Idealized design
At AT&T Maccoby led an explicit visioning process at a number of business units during the WPoF phase. At every level he urged groups into an "ideal future" discussion, in which the parties *together* would try to imagine what a good picture would look like.[7] To begin the process of change, he facilitated idealized design of a business unit and its functioning.

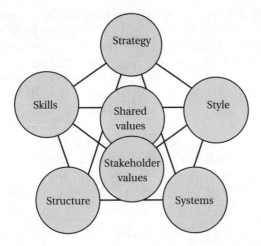

Fig. 8.1. The "7-S" framework.

The first step was typically a joint union–management discussion about their conceptions of a good firm. Typical elements, among the hundreds (perhaps thousands) that were written, included: business focus; a workplace spirit of trust; open planning and information; wide, fact-based involvement; employment security; and personal behaviors of honesty, trust, and respect.

The immediate response to these discussions was almost always surprise at how much overlap there was. Though these concepts may seem like clichés on the page, the parties typically failed to appreciate how much the other actually adhered to the same values. To the unions it was a surprise that management saw value in commitment or security; management did not expect union leaders to be so positive about productivity and business focus.

The discussion was sometimes pushed and focused through the use of a "7-S" framework, adapted from the widely known work of Peters and Waterman. The "Ss" are the elements of the business as a *system*:[8] see Figure 8.1.

They are extremely useful in helping people to think through the entire web of interlinked parts, rather than getting stuck on one or a few pet elements. In particular, they often start a valuable discussion about the relation between the "hard Ss"—strategy, structure, systems, the typical focus of management leaders—and the "soft Ss" such as style and shared values. The framework helped the parties develop more detail for the generalized principles from the initial discussions.

Maccoby then developed and administered "gap surveys" to measure the difference between these ideal elements and current practice, as perceived by the organization more widely.[9] The survey results generated a new round of discussion about priorities and actions required to close the gaps; actions were agreed on and assigned with time frames. These exercises proved to be quite powerful for many participants, giving them a glimpse for the first time of the possibility of a *shared* future in which the values of the parties could be brought together.

Tixier has another approach: he often asks the parties to conduct a self-diagnosis of the situation, bringing them to enlarge their perspective and to integrate dimensions other than those they are used to. This has been particularly effective in working with local union leaders, often helping them to develop their own strategies with a better understanding of the business.

Table 8.1 helps frame such discussions.

A discussion around these issues displaces the parties from their usual "ruts" and encourages the creation of a common framework which becomes the basis for a multidimensional dialogue. This is particularly important for unions whose members do not integrate characteristics of the business into their reasoning.

Table 8.1.

Diagnosis of the situation	Goals	Gap with current situation	Change strategy
Business			
Management			
Socio-technical system			
Human resources			
Cultural system			
Industrial relations			

Value-added analyses

An important aspect of our interventions has been the articulation of the stakeholder framework and the notion that a healthy business works best through the integration of values and stakeholder concerns. This viewpoint can be developed by working the parties through analysis of *what value each contributes* to the system on which they all depend. This analysis helps to pull together divergent orientations and to show their convergence in a shared future.

At FS the consultants used an analytic approach based on the results of the scenario planning process (above). They mapped stakeholders in terms of what they each could offer to the company, and built a strategy with an eye to maximizing the business benefits in relation to each customer, contractor, or stakeholder group. Two key state ministries—Treasury and the Ministry of Transport—were drawn into the process through their role in budgeting: budgets were drawn for each scenario, positing different relations among stakeholders (Figure 8.2).

At AT&T Maccoby proposed a conceptualization of three dimensions of value for a healthy business: *economic* value-added (EVA); *customer* value-added (CVA); and *people* value-added (PVA). He suggested a dynamic among the three kinds of value: that in the ideal world people value-added would lead to more satisfied customers, which would lead to improved economic results, which in turn would provide the resources for rewards, education, and improved

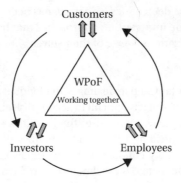

Fig. 8.2. Workplace of the Future framework.

working conditions. This helped in creating a sense of shared interest among the parties. The training materials then turned this into a more explicit stakeholder picture of the goal.

This picture provided a distinct function for the union, as a representative of employees; rather than becoming merely an ally of management, it could be seen as a partner with a distinct role in contributing to a healthy business. The picture proved a powerful tool in helping the parties to imagine a changed relationship in the future. Practically, it was used to evaluate proposed changes, requiring that they be positive for customers, employees and investors.

REINTERPRETING SOCIODYNAMIC PATTERNS

The third basic intervention move is the reinterpretation of sociodynamic patterns. This arena has less technique and planning than the other two—in part because it is harder to grasp, in part because by its very nature it must follow the unpredictable energy of the group.

Although identity is often defined from the "top" in the formative phases of a group, it is not so easily *changed* from the top. There is a substantial consulting industry based on leader-driven "culture change" which has not worked very well. A classic and well-documented case is Xerox, in which the CEO and a consultant during the 1980s led an intensive process to redefine the corporate identity—first around quality, later around the concept of a "document company." These elegant strategic concepts were "driven" through the organization by cascading educational processes. Yet as has become clear in recent years, they only partially redefined the identity of middle managers: relationships were not centred on quality or documents, managers did not internalize or take pride in representing those concepts. Although top-down approaches occasionally succeed, the record has persuaded us that the process is complicated.[10]

Our approach to these deep issues of identity has been essentially exploratory. We have developed some intervention approaches that have had partial success in reframing the organizations' sense of themselves.

Active understanding
The first and most important step in dealing with identities is *understanding* them. This seems a simple point, but it is difficult to accomplish and frequently neglected. "Expert" interveners may pay attention to the identities and aspirations of their immediate clients, but grasping the overall dynamics of organizations requires more than this. We generally conduct early on some form of "anthropological" investigation to try to understand these dimensions of identity. Thus, the first thing that Maccoby did in his work with the CWA was to interview a cross-section of leaders in an open-ended way about their views of the challenges facing them and possible futures; later he did something similar with supervisors at Long Lines. This has been repeated with more or less formality in every intervention. Tixier, for his part, wrote a major book, based on many years' observation, on the internal work-ings of the CFDT union federation, and then conducted observational research with managers as the first phase of his intervention. Heckscher worked for the CWA for four years, and he conducted a long interview-based research project with AT&T middle managers.[11] These served to steep us deeply in the cultures of the organiza-tions we worked with, so that we could interpret the many meanings of change.

These studies have always been based on open-ended clinical interviews or on in-depth observation. Understanding identity is particularly unsuited to any kind of standardized questionnaire, because identity is by definition the pattern of meanings that makes an organization unique. It needs to be grasped through empathy, being able to "put oneself in the shoes" of those in the group. This requires an essentially anthropological method of living with and dialoguing with its members until one can reliably interpret what things will mean to them and how they will respond.

Interpreting groups to each other
As consultants, we find ourselves very often explaining the parties to each other. Managers, to take a single example, have a very hard time understanding the unions' intense insistence on seniority; we need to explain its meaning in terms of the long historical struggles against management arbitrariness, as well as its current functions in stabilizing career expectations and shaping the unions' political systems. Conversely, unions have a very hard time grasping managers' stress on individual performance and rewards; from the unions' perspective this is a cover for arbitrary power. We often act as interpreters of such issues through conversations, memos, and speeches.

This is not a permanent role, however: it is transitional and at best dangerous. When a consultant tries to explain party x's view to y, it is difficult for y to trust that the consultant really understands *him*. Getting in the middle of such mis-understandings can create suspicions of the consultant on all sides. Therefore, we act as direct interpreters only in early phases or as a way of getting by some particular obstacle, but move as quickly as possible to getting the parties to talk directly to each other in a way that increases their understanding. At AT&T, the union showed managers films about union history and spoke about their meaning. Some managers had parents or relatives who were part of that history.

Re-experiencing relationships

Thus, a crucial part of the intervention process, particularly at AT&T, has involved getting the parties to talk openly to each other about their values and sense of self, and about what made them feel respected or the reverse. In most cases we organized retreats at which the parties could "get to know" each other over dinner, usually for multiple days, with much time for unstructured conversation that moved beyond the usual problem-focused agendas.

In the WPoF the experience-sharing process was structured as part of the training. The two parties—management and union—met separately for an hour and were asked to develop descriptions of their own strengths and weaknesses, and those of the other party, and what each contributed to issues of trust in the relationship. They then came back together and shared their views. The interchanges always started with great nervousness: both parties were convinced that the gaps were unbridgeable and that the anger stored up from the past would make any communication impossible. The lists—especially on the union side—did indeed focus heavily on perceptions of past wrongs, sometimes long in the past. Yet, both parties were surprised to find that there were human beings on the other side of the divide, with viewpoints that could be discussed and understood. When Heckscher went back to teams a year later to assess the effects of the training, it was consistently this discussion that people remembered, and it, more than anything else, seemed to have set a tone for openness and equality within many teams.

This "obstacles to trust" exercise, as it was called, shows clearly the importance of the third-party role. Managers and union leaders would never do this on their own: they resist it strongly, raising all kinds of objections. They need to be pushed into it. When they are meeting separately they joke nervously about what the other party is doing, and cannot wait to race back to see what the others are saying about them. But by the end this exercise always produces a strong sense of release and improved understanding within the group, and it is regularly seen as the most valuable element in the training experience.

Yet this little exercise just scratches the surface of the problem, and it cannot simply be generalized to a larger scale. It "works" because it puts an entire group at once into a new relationship, changing the patterns of expectations at one fell swoop; it would not work beyond the face-to-face level of shared experience. Nor does it begin to tackle many of the elements that hold identity together: institutional structures and rituals, skills, and so on. It creates a base for greater understanding within a team, but no more.

At EDF, management and the unions now have joint working seminars to explore the future of the enterprise. These discussions are made possible by the learnings and experiences emerging from previous debates, especially around the committees that evaluated the previous agreements. It must be stressed that this kind of relational learning requires a long process: the trust necessary for such exchanges depends on many previous demonstrations of mutual trust.

Reinterpreting the past

A key intervention approach in these efforts is a reinterpretation of the past: that is, thinking about the past in a way which connects with possible futures. We need to enable the organization's members to see it first of all as still fulfilling the same basic values, and, second, as still worthy of pride as an effective instrument of those values.

At the CWA Maccoby and Heckscher have been involved with this union for 20 years; Maccoby has led internal planning processes at the board level, Heckscher worked as an employee of the organization in the early 1980s and built relationships which continued to be important. Maccoby catalyzed a series of internal studies of membership needs and wants, and of the external strategic environment, which became the core for ongoing debates at many levels of the organization. He led members of the executive board in a study trip to interview managers and union leaders at a number of telecom companies which had participation programs. This resulted in a document approved by the full executive board which presented the rationale for participation (the need to represent members' interests in a rapidly changing industry) and the criteria for participation.

Over time, parts of the CWA have begun to see the union as an organization that can have a proactive strategy towards managing job growth and skill development in the industry. Morty Bahr, the union's President, tells a story of how in the mid 1990s he addressed a group of AT&T operators. "I took a deep breath," he says, "and told them something I'd never told an audience before: I said that most of them would not finish their careers as AT&T operators. I wasn't sure what response I would get. And they said, 'Finally! Someone is telling us something that makes sense!' "[12]

In his autobiography, Bahr reports that he initially opposed union participation in management, but was persuaded when Maccoby took him to visit offices in different parts of the country where he witnessed the enthusiasm of his members whose jobs had become more challenging and rewarding.[13]

This reframing is helped by reference to one dimension of labor union history: craft unions have long helped members move from job to job, from site to site, and have provided training and placement. Though this is new to industrial unions like the CWA, it helps to feel that they are not completely abandoning their reference group. It has also been advanced by some contract provisions: AT&T and the union established an employee retraining program in 1986 that has helped many people develop portable skills, and Bahr negotiated a pioneering program with Nynex in 1994 that provided master's-level education to employees during slack times. These programs have become, over time, very popular with members.

Tixier has at times formalized this "reinterpretation" process by giving semi-structured material to the parties, consisting of interview material with a partial interpretation by the consultant. This stimulates the parties to develop their own opinions. Repeated over time, this work helps the actors reshape their understandings and to accustom them to in-depth diagnostic processes. If one tries instead the simpler approach of presenting fully developed analyses, they are often rejected: this puts too much strain on the parties' visions of the world, creates too strong a sense of anxiety, and can produce a collective denial of reality.

Yet, with all this time and experience, and a series of planning discussions and processes from the top to the bottom of the union, the change is far from permeating the institution: most local officers and members still orient to fighting for existing jobs rather than developing members' abilities to get new ones. The other unions we have dealt with—the IBEW, CFDT, and CGT—are similar. Tixier has struggled for years with a deep dilemma of the CFDT and other unions: the more the leaders take a wide, creative view, proposing new forms of management and new approaches to maintaining employment, the more they alienate themselves from their local bases.[14] The obstacles to change within unions, to which we will return in Chapters 10 and 11, are among the most fundamental blocks to the long-term success of our interventions, and a principal reason why we believe something more is needed.

Tixier has found it necessary to work over time with the CEO of EDF to help him to understand the resistances he encounters from stakeholders, not only unions but from workers and his own management. Because the CEO must be a decision-maker, his focus often narrows according to the political situation to one or a few dimensions. It is too simplistic to think that middle management is always close behind the leadership; at times it is more estranged than the unions. The consultant's task, then, is to explore through dialogue the CEO's vision of the situation.

Redesigning systems

Identities are supported not only by ideas but by a myriad internal systems—rules, habits, procedures—that have momentum of their own. Very frequently change processes attack these systems first. An implication of the interactive change analysis is that they should rather be dealt with *after*, or at least in the context of, the broader issues of identity.

Most systems' aspects of companies—and of unions as well—reflect in this way basic patterns of relationships that initially grew out of the value choices of the organization. Changing even the most innocent-seeming procedures can, therefore, if leaders do not pay attention, set off fears about what this "means" in terms of the direction of the organization, its basic mission, and the futures of the employees. These tensions are of course much higher in periods of deep change such as the ones we have experienced. In those situations the identity issues come more quickly to the surface and spark great distress. It is necessary to make some progress on redefining identities not after but *before* tackling the systems. If mistrust between units is high, for example, efforts to build trust need to precede installation of an information system that links them. Conversely, interveners need to pay attention to the systems involved in redefinitions of orientations and visions, and make sure that those systems are reconstructed to support the new orientations.

CONCLUSION

The techniques described in this chapter clearly do not add up to a "method." Some consultants focus on one or another method—scenario planning, win–win bargaining, and so on; in our work, they are tools in the toolbox, to be used at the right moment. The determination of the "right moment" has to do with the larger approach sketched in Chapter 7. Any of these techniques can be effective or, if mistimed, disastrous: it might be seen as a threat to the identity of certain players, or (by the powerless) as a cynical move in a predetermined power game, or (by the leaders) as a way to win support without too much real change. Such dynamics would require drawing on other tools.

In an engaged approach the techniques depend on the clients, and are often constructed with them. The listing of techniques for exploring the future, building dialogue, or interpreting the past is no more than a way of bringing to mind some possibilities as one faces a complex situation.

9

The Consultant Role: Transference and Counter-transference

The last chapters describe the various dimensions of "What must be done?" to transform systems of interactions; but there remains more to say in the active voice: "What can *we* do?" For interveners, as we have emphasized, are not technicians above the fray; we function as actors in the drama, attracting feelings—respect, suspicion, admiration, dependence, anger. Success in the role depends in large part on how we handle these connections, and how we leverage them into learning on the part of the clients.

Expert consultants, though they tend to *see* themselves as outside the battle, in fact have a very clear position in it. They are hired by and serve a particular leader or function—they are in effect "subcontractors" to some part of the organization, extending its capabilities. Some firms are best known for helping CEOs with strategic planning; others for helping Information Systems departments; still others for supporting finance or HR or legal. Some expert interveners provide "off-the-shelf" offerings, such as courses on how to transform the culture. This expert role is clear; one understands what the consultant is supposed to do and be accountable for. We have generally been brought in initially with that set of expectations—hired for our expertise on participation or labor relations or strategy.

But expert consultants are by their nature blocked from the crucial task of redefining relationships because they are tied directly to one node of the existing system of relationships within an organization. They are a *part* of the existing "political" system; they serve power and are therefore bound by the limits of the existing power relations. They may be involved in changing the structure of a bureaucratic organization, but they reinforce the overall logic of bureaucracy. Thus expert consultants typically become part of internal "games": they serve as scapegoats for managers who need someone to blame for failures; they give a cover of legitimacy to actions that managers want to take for their own reasons; they enable managers to look like something is being done without actually having to do anything. These are among the reasons why consultant reports so often line the shelves of managers' offices, looking important but clearly unopened and unused.

The most important characteristic of the full engagement approach, by contrast, is the fact that we are *not* located or tied to any person or organizational function and stand outside the play of organization "politics." It is a difficult and uncertain position, one that we have explored through trial and error, raising considerable anxiety in ourselves as well as our clients. We have pursued it, in retrospect, because it has critical advantages. Because we stand outside the organizational/bureaucratic dynamics of empire-building and career positioning that typically are major barriers to change, we can better perform some major tasks:

1. We can often build new connections and conversations by moving across functions, levels, and individuals, as well as across stakeholder organizations; we can "float" more lightly than organizational actors, who always cause waves when they cross more than one level or trespass into other areas of responsibility.

2. When we propose visions and changes, we do not generate automatic responses from different groups assuming they know what we are really aiming at. The difficulty of pinning down "who we really are" can paradoxically provide openings for new ideas.

3. We can act as safe "speaking partners" for leaders (and other actors) who cannot speak openly inside the organizational web of relations. We constantly find that people at all levels are hungry to talk to someone—anyone—in our position who gives them a space to reflect without worrying that their uncertainties might be seized on as weaknesses to be exploited by their organizational peers.[1]

4. By diminishing the psychological pressure felt by organizational leaders, giving them a safe place to voice their anxieties, we help "open up" the imagination of new possibilities.

5. We can break the circles of collusion that block learning in many organizations, by preventing discussion of key problems. Very often learning is blocked by a kind of mutual hostage-taking: if you do not raise uncomfortable issues for me, I won't raise ones for you. Our status as outsiders gives us an opportunity to pose uncomfortable questions and surface difficult facts.[2]

Yet this is, on reflection, a very strange and contradictory position. Someone has to bring us in to an organization, yet our effectiveness depends on not being seen as an agent of that person. Someone has to pay us, yet we cannot be seen as "in the pay of" any party. We must develop very close and trusting relations with leaders without becoming an organizational ally of any of them.[3] We have to persuade members of conflicting organizations that we are fundamentally on their side, pursuing the same values as they, without behaving in the ways that they expect.

These contradictions cannot be resolved once and for all by establishing a fixed role or position; rather, the consultant is involved constantly in an unstable process of construction and resolution of tensions. In this role, we have to speak multiple languages and be trusted by multiple parties; we cannot simply put our knowledge in the service of someone with the power to make it happen. The role calls on us to combine the hard macho logic of strategy with the soft emotionally sensitive, consensual role of social relationships. It requires that the stakeholders invest considerable trust in our integrity as well as competence. and we must honor this trust while at the same time challenging our clients' logic and sense of identity. Our goal is to be tolerated by all actors and trusted by the key actors. We must over time establish trust through our scientific integrity and competence. This includes political understanding but also convincing participants that we not only understand their thinking, but also respect them and their creative aspirations.

All this results in high ambiguity and stress. We constantly have to "push in" to places we are not wanted in order to build the necessary connections for organizational change. We have to tolerate, without defensiveness, projections by all parties that we are somehow playing a secret game, trying to further some hidden interest. We also must accept that we can rarely see direct results of our actions: we do not give much advice to anyone which is merely taken as the expert gospel; indeed, when this does happen, it puts us in a dangerous position because it usually means someone is setting us up to take blame away from themselves in the game of organizational politics. Our only real success is when the parties internalize changes to a degree that we become invisible and forgotten. If the parties take our advice, at least after the early phases, we are failures; if they generate their own transformations we are successes—but we do not have the satisfaction of knowing exactly what we have accomplished. We take on this uncertainty because it is the only way to create sufficient tension in our clients, so that with us, they question their fundamental views of the world and their own identities.

We have almost always acted as lone wolves, or in packs of no more than two or three. There are several reasons for this. The establishment of trust is a highly personal matter, driven by concrete relationships, and cannot be delegated to others. Experts can flood an organization, conducting research or enforcing orders or implementing technical changes; but the core of our work, the crossing of relational barriers, has to be done through the patient work of one person at a time. In addition, consultants in large numbers tend to create dependencies. Full engagement requires that the actors themselves internalize new relations and understandings; adding teams of outsiders simply gets in the way of the work that needs to be done internally. We act as catalysts, in almost exactly the chemical sense: by creating new connections in organizations we encourage the parties themselves to generate new and stable configurations. If the connections do not work the chances of success cannot be improved through brute force of numbers.[4]

ESTABLISHING INITIAL CREDIBILITY: CREDENTIALS AND LOYALTY TESTS

The first task of any consultant is to establish credibility; this is much harder for an interactive consultant than for an expert, because we make no claim to providing answers to problems. In the bureaucratic world, the consultant's credentials are extremely important; in the interactive world, credibility is more complicated. First, we have to be seen as "on the side of" multiple parties—they have to believe we share their basic values. Second, we have to be viewed as competent and knowledgeable—but we have to establish that not by showing specific expertise on a particular problem, but by winning trust in our general ability to tackle as-yet-unknown issues.

Organizations and leaders apply certain types of "loyalty tests" to see whether the consultant understands and sympathizes with their concerns. One key question is about their associations and memberships. It is not sufficient that they be affiliated with prestigious organizations; they have to be the right kind of organization. Thus, EDF executives told Maccoby and Heckscher that they considered Tixier's connection with Sciences Po to confer greater objectivity than would be the case if he were at HEC ("too management oriented") or the Sorbonne ("too leftist"). Similarly, Heckscher was brought in to Lucent after the unions had rejected a Harvard Business School professor, who was assumed to be too management oriented. His affiliation with the Rutgers Labor Studies program was a plus; at the same time, his past position at the Harvard Business School gave managers a sense that he understood their side of the issues.

Tixier also was trusted by CFDT, the union that had the best relationship to EDF management during the 1990s. He had studied the union, written his doctoral thesis about them and had been a consultant to them. Similarly, Maccoby had worked as a consultant to both AT&T management and CWA, and his connection with the JF Kennedy School of Government at Harvard gave him legitimacy as a certified academic expert. While AT&T management would have preferred a business school professor as consultant, CWA leaders considered such a person too pro-management. Although the Kennedy School's ties to business were not so strong, Maccoby had been a consultant to the top management of AT&T Long Lines before working with CWA and had friends among the executives there. He had also worked with the UAW and AFSCME in quality of work life projects, all of which strengthened his union credentials. The participants knew about his writings in which he made explicit his goal of improving work according to both economic and social values.

Establishing our competence, as well as our value-orientation, is complicated by our rejection of the expert role. Academic prestige can be a factor in legitimizing us as knowledge experts, but experience becomes the overriding qualification, and consultants are chosen on the basis of their reputation as interveners. We are invited as consultants in part because of our established track records. In Maccoby's case, the participants knew about his work in the US and Sweden (with Volvo and the metal workers union), and with Harman International and the UAW. Ramirez was part of a joint Italian/foreign consultant team in FS led by Richard Normann whose research, writings and consulting experience earned him a role as the major European strategic thinker about service strategy. Tixier began with a more expert role as researcher, but gradually established his reputation within EDF and beyond as an effective intervener.

The issue of payment is particularly fraught with dangers. It is natural for everyone to assume that the person who pays us also controls us—that we are in some sense his "agent." If we were unable to break out of this trap we would lose all credibility with the other actors whose trust we must win in order to develop new relations. The question of pay becomes a lightning-rod, attracting all the suspicions and political dynamics that divide the parties.

We partly escape these dynamics because we are usually anchored in more than one stakeholder group: managers who hire us to help with union–management relations must understand that our value has to do with our credibility with the union, and so they cannot expect us simply to be management agents. The fact that we have often drawn our main salary from academic positions, so that we are not dependent on the consulting work for our livelihood, is also helpful. We have occasionally gone further by having our pay split between the union and the company. These factors help mute, though not eliminate, the suspicions about whose side we are really on.

TRANSFERENCE AND COUNTER-TRANSFERENCE

Since the interactive intervener stands outside any of the political positions in an organization or web or stakeholder relations, the parties tend to try to make sense of him by projecting familiar roles. In these expectations, there is an organizational analogue of what Freud termed "transference." In psychoanalysis, the patient transfers onto the analyst the qualities of adult authority a child has experienced in childhood. At first these tend to be very positive as the patient expects the analyst to solve his problem. Later, when the process becomes more difficult, the transference can become negative and the patient transfers all his frustration and disappointment on to the analyst who has not accomplished a magical cure. To resolve the transference, the patient must work through memories of the past and accept responsibility for his own future.

In our cases, the transference is institutional as well as individual. The organizations we work with have established patterns of interactions—expectations of who will do what to whom. When we come in from outside the system, there is a generalized need to make sense of us by fitting us into one of these patterns or inventing a new one. The fact that no one knows exactly what to expect from us creates a threat that we might disrupt established patterns, which is in fact exactly what we are trying to do. Thus the organization as a whole tends to develop defenses against this outside agent to protect itself—by assimilating us to some existing role as an agent of one or another actor, or by pushing us "out" with images of academic ineffectiveness or conversely of magical powers; all of these, even the most seemingly favorable, work to keep us from really *connecting* with people to help them work through the challenges facing them.

The danger for us as consultants has been to slip into a "counter-transference" by playing into the projections of the parties and acting out roles in the existing political system—of manager, or union leader, policy maker, leader, or cheerleader.[5] This happens when we become fed up by the actors' inaction and resistance and we think we can push the actors toward our own ideals of a more democratic, more effective enterprise. As in psychoanalysis where a danger for the analyst is to over-idealize the patient as a promising child and to want the patient to be healthier than he or she can stand, the patient may for a while act healthier to please the analyst. But when there is the inevitable regression to more sustainable behavior, the analyst is rightfully blamed. Some of the so-called negative transference in psychoanalysis is anger at bad interpretations. But there may also be a realistic resentment for supporting or even demanding that the patient realize the unrealizable. The result can be not only disappointment, but also a corrosive cynicism. This may account for some of the negative accounts of consulting.[6]

Once we move away from the relatively safe role of detached researchers to the more clinical role of interactive consultants, mediators, and facilitators, even designers, we face not only increased complexity, but also increased dangers of transference and counter-transference. As with psychoanalysis, where the analyst becomes a partner with the patient in a research project aimed at both understanding the causes of problems and trying out new approaches, the relationship can both facilitate and itself become a resistance to progress. We, like psychoanalysts, have had to become aware of the fantasies or irrational beliefs and emotional attitudes directed at us by both union leaders, members of staff units, line managers, and corporate leaders. We also have had to recognize how our own fantasies and attitudes could deform our role and weaken our effectiveness. Because of this, we have had to use the emotions stimulated in us by organizational work as data that could help us to understand how others were experiencing uncertainty and change. For example the feelings of being put down, not included in key discussions were experienced by many of the actors we worked with. We would not be able to understand this if we were not able to distance ourselves from some of our feelings when we were put down and left out.

We have come to realize that it is essential to analyze and understand our own motives for doing this work. What did we expect to achieve? Perhaps the most legitimate motives, in the sense of being generally accepted as rational, are those that further our careers as researchers and consultants. However, this is not our only motivation for choosing the kind of work we do. Inasmuch as we develop useful knowledge and improve the effectiveness and efficiency of the organization and the quality of working life, we remain on solid ground, particularly when our ideals are shared by our clients. It is when our motives become too visionary, with ideals that are not fully understood or supported by the actors, that our grounding crumbles and we are in danger of "acting out"—playing out our own ambitions and anxieties rather than helping the situation.

Our approach relies on an "identification with" stakeholders which results in a blurring of identities between the intervener and his clients, leading us into a permanent identity debate which touches us emotionally. A rational view would see such emotions as obstacles to understanding and would seek to deny them. For us, however, they are at the heart of our work, because the only way to understand others is by starting from the emotions that they provoke in oneself. We cannot understand from the "outside," by objective observation; nor can we persuade clients that we understand them by showing them correlations and scientific propositions about their actions. It is by observing the effects of the client's identity on ourselves, acknowledging this effect, and connecting it back to the client's own anxieties, that we disarm his projections and suspicions; we enter into a relationship of mutuality that gives him confidence to proceed with us into unknown territory. This interchange is especially intense when we work one on one with leaders.

This intervention work, in which self-transformation and understanding goes hand in hand with understanding of the stakeholders and the system, crosses the boundaries of academic disciplines. We must link the analysis of emotions— of our interlocking fears, understanding subjects in their psychological complexity—with understanding of the organizations and of their management processes. This work on the tension between the dynamics of the system and of the actor in the system is contained within no existing body of theory.

Varieties of transference

Though we avoid making claims about what we can accomplish—we provide no glossy brochures, set no stretch targets, reject the role of expert—our clients form their own ideas about our role which reflect, in one way or another, the limits and blockages of the existing organization—either slotting us into familiar political roles, or treating us as magicians come to dissolve all barriers and create an ideal future.

The magic helper
The first kind of transference is, almost of necessity, positive in form—otherwise we would not be hired—but no more realistic for that. We have often been seen as magic helpers who could give each side what they most wanted: a utopian workplace free of conflict for AT&T and EDF, or in the case of FS, a transformed and entrepreneurial company. AT&T and EDF management expected that the union would become more helpful and flexible. Union leadership expected that management would make it easier to satisfy worker demands; thereby they would become more respected and electable. At FS, all parts of the company were supposed to become more customer-oriented, more results-oriented, less political, better aligned with their bottom line targets, more entrepreneurial, more cost-conscious, less subsidized, more transparent and accountable, more effective (punctual, safe), and ... even profitable! Perhaps, all the leaders thought we would make their work easier rather than, as was the case, considerably harder.

While we were helping the client move toward dialogue and reduced conflict, we knew that in the real world some conflict is inevitable. We wanted to do away with unnecessary conflict and create better processes to deal with necessary conflict. Yet we did not want to throw cold water on the client's utopian dreams, and our collusion with this fantasy helped to establish a positive transference. To some extent, therefore, we accepted the role of gurus who would lead the actors to utopia. At the same time we needed to use the energy of the positive transference to move the actors to the best possible relationship, recognizing that conflict is not only inevitable, but if structured can even be constructive. The same logic applied to the FS case, in which management was at the time considered by the Italian press and community as the spearhead in the modernization of Italy's cumbersome public sector. Working on this initiative was inherently worthwhile, and publicly praised.

Once the magic helper transference begins to fray, we become subject to more negative projections.

The academic in the ivory tower

The position of "outsider," which is essential to our ability to make new connections, can also lead to unfavorable projections. We are often considered by managers or union activists as someone who is free from any of the consequences of action, who is paid to think about life and the world but who escapes its constraints, who has "tenure" and can ignore customers and even bosses. In the meantime, the manager or union leader must struggle with the demands of the "real world." They have "skin in the game," while we do not. This view that we are floating outside reality, that we are somehow not part of any real action—which is partially true—can, in the minds of some actors, disqualify our ability to understand the organization we are studying. How can a researcher who has not experienced the demands of the real world understand how a business or union functions? The people that we deal with do not necessarily doubt the validity of our work as far as producing knowledge, but doubt that this knowledge can be applied to "real" action. "Academic" has negative connotations here—it means "irrelevant." They see academic work, at best, as belonging to the world of schools and universities they once attended, or which their children now attend. They ask: Is the researcher really ready to "roll up his sleeves and slog away," to use the actual words of one manager describing to one of us what it meant to accept the assignment.

The usurper

At times managers (or even union officials) react to us with an almost reflexive fear that we are trying to take their place. This is a defensive reaction for any successful bureaucrat: fighting off those who want one's own position, while positioning oneself to move into someone else's. These are essential skills in that environment. The idea that we would want to move into an organizational position is far from rational, but it enables some people to make sense of our otherwise incomprehensible role. Once when Ramirez asked some general questions about the strategic direction of a division head, the latter asked his subordinates—after Ramirez had left—"Who does he think he is? Does he think he is running this place?" Tixier was similarly looked at with suspicion by union research staff who assumed that he must be trying to take over their function.

It is sometimes difficult for us to resist trying to "take over" organizational roles at particular moments and to "script" actors to move them forward. Often we see what appear to be wrong decisions by managers or union officials, and we may find ourselves pushing too hard to get them to do it right. Yielding to this temptation feeds the fantasy of usurpation and prevents the development of the responsible actors themselves.

The double agent
In a situation of high mistrust, such as many union–management relationships, it hardly seems possible that someone could understand and share the ideals of conflicting parties, as we claim to do. Thus, some people feel our role must be reduced to one side or the other; and since they know we are not a "member" of their side, they assume we must be secretly on the other. They fear we are a pipeline revealing their plans to the other party. This projection, to the extent it operates, completely undercuts our possible effectiveness by closing down dialogue or sharing of information.

We are, moreover, sometimes pushed to take sides as a kind of test of good faith. At AT&T and Lucent, when the union struck the company, both sides pushed the consultant to agree with their moral outrage about the behavior of the other. At FS, the top management tried to enlist the consultants to implement its plan to move the 50 or so senior managers of FS in a direction it hoped would become irreversible.

The go-between
An only slightly less harmful projection is when we are seen as go–betweens carrying "messages" to the other side, or to others higher in the organization. This is an easy trap for us to fall into, as it can seem that we are simply trying to increase understanding among actors. It also gives us a sense of power to be entrusted with important messages that can shape policy. Heckscher was drawn toward this role at Lucent when McGinn looked him earnestly in the eye and said, "You tell the union that there are absolutely no plans to get rid of manufacturing—that is a stupid inference"; it was in a way flattering to have a CEO give him such an important role, and difficult to reject this mission and to explain that he did not represent the union.

The problem with this projection is that the messages are almost never truthful: they are part of the game of bluff and power endemic to bureaucracies and stakeholder relations. Thus instead of getting an accurate picture and conducting honest discussions with the parties that help them develop their views, we can allow ourselves to be sucked into existing games. We will never know whether McGinn was deliberately misleading the union, but if Heckscher had taken on the role and carried the message as requested, his credibility with the union would have been severely damaged when the company later changed its policy.

Counter-transferences

The lack of definition and clarity of the interactive role, as we have said, provokes deep anxiety. We can never be sure if we are "liked" by the parties, never be sure if we are really accomplishing anything, never be sure that we will not be tossed out. There are strong temptations, therefore, to get involved in *counter*-transferences: that is, to fall into roles that are better understood and more clearly valued within the existing system. We can slide easily into expected roles that are in the end unproductive.

Going native

To understand the human milieu that we are studying, we identify with the people in question in order to understand the situation from the inside. It becomes hard to empathize and sympathize without accepting either the identity or emotional attitude of the people we work with. This produces a sort of unpleasant and not easily maintained "identity stretching." In the union environment, as well as in the situation of FS leaders, in which a group or an individual has a political agenda, the actors try to justify the vision and mission they have given themselves.

In this light, we can become the distinguished guest of management; the king's counselor. In the union movement case, we can become, at the least, a justification of the union's movement for social justice. The union environment can also fulfill our need for justification, of being part of a movement for social justice. But if this happens, we become engulfed into the environment that we are studying. This can spark defensive reactions which lead us to stop listening to anything which would cause us to distance ourselves from the tribe. We become "passive" or half asleep in the face of an anxiety-producing situation. When one works for management, the assignment given to the researcher is often ambivalent: "Help us understand what is at stake, but at the same time justify our assumptions and decisions. Justify our frustration with the union (or the market, or the line manager's incompetence)." While the actors may be different, the fantasy is the same: that one bonds with, and becomes part of, the party in question.

It is essential, though very difficult, to avoid being drawn into the moral universe of one party or another. Our "place to stand" is always outside the interests of any one party: we represent the effort to promote dialogue, shared vision, and joint action. We may criticize one or both parties from this standpoint, but we cannot be drawn into *their* definitions of the problem and become a "member" of any existing group. It can be emotionally difficult to maintain this necessary distance.

The "creator of the universe"
This is the equivalent on the consultant side of the "magical helper" projection; it is potentially at work in any consulting or research assignment. It is at the same time the most potentially motivating and potentially most dangerous fantasy. It has a specific place in clinical initiatives where the research starts from a difficulty or dysfunction in the human field studied—a dysfunction that led to the request for help in the first place. We have the feeling that from the moment we have interpreted the questions faced by those who requested our services, and once these people accept our interpretations by using them to reformulate the problems that they are encountering, we become oracles or prophets. We invent the universe, or at least their universe. This means that we no longer make a clear distinction between ourselves and the universe we are studying, or in which we are working. We become the creative narcissist; the universe we are studying becomes the extension of our actions. We feel that without us, they would not be themselves.

When Maccoby began work with AT&T and CWA, he had the fantasy of transforming what was then the largest company in the world and making it "the" model for union–management cooperation and participative management. There was enough support for this fantasy so that it was not crazy, just unrealistic. Articles in the press lauded WPoF as a model for industrial relations and leaders from management and union were invited to speak at international meetings. At the opening meeting the then Secretary of Labor, Robert Reich, affirmed that this would be the model for making a unionized company competitive and management introduced Maccoby as the architect. In the same way, Ramirez was part of a consulting team working for Italy's most admired public sector manager. Helping him in this role was to be involved in creating a new Italian public sector, being part of a crusade against what at the time was called Eurosclerosis.

The fantasy of the "creator of the universe" is certainly one of the most common fantasies in the field of sociology. Most social scientists, as we noted in Chapter 1, insist that it is essential to guard against it: But in our work the two cannot be kept separate: we have to learn to use the "creator of the universe" fantasy as a way of motivating ourselves and others, while simultaneously recognizing its "untruthfulness" and trying to move beyond it.[7]

To a certain extent, this fantasy of "creator" is a positive motivator. Why else would we try such "impossible tasks"? Why would we write this book? However, this fantasy can be kept productive only if we analyze it, share it and maintain a certain sense of humor about its pretentiousness.

The expert
We have emphasized the difference between the expert consulting role and the interactive one; although we choose the latter, that does not mean that we are not constantly tempted by the former, which is much easier to get a handle on. We do have expertise about organizational change based on long experience and study, and our initial engagement is almost always based on that expertise. We have to use it to some extent to establish our position. At the frequent moments

when we become unsure of what we are supposed to be doing or how we are perceived, it becomes hard to resist the urge to pontificate, to trot out our knowledge of many other companies, to cite studies, to write reports.

When we do this, however, we can generally observe the trap. The clients are typically delighted by what we have done, because we have acted in an expected way. Tension is released; and for that very reason the difficult task of building relations tends to be dropped. The party who has "acquired" our expertise uses it to create an answer to the problem which he then expects the other parties to accept. Then they all find reasons to reject it because it represents a threat to their own positions.

For example, in designing the overall shape of labor–management forums it would be easiest for us to come in and say, "We have studied Ford and Volvo and Péchiney, and this is how it should be done." It is quite possible that an HR director would accept this from us and use his position to impose this system. He would soon find that the union would have very different ideas about what the good models are; not only that, but supervisors and middle managers would, openly or covertly, resist because it does not fit their understanding of the world. The nature of the bureaucratic system is that all members need to be seen as an expert in their own functions—this is the basis of their legitimacy; thus an outside expert whom they do not themselves control is a direct threat.

In these circumstances the organization typically erects a Scylla and Charybdis of defenses that quickly marginalize the expert: on the one hand, "That can't be done"; on the other hand, "We're already doing that." Between those two defenses there is rarely room to slip through a new idea; however much the actors may profess respect for the expert's knowledge and even go through the motions of adopting the recommendations, they quickly assimilate such recommendations to their own interests or put them up on the shelf with other impressive but useless documents.

Resolving the transference

Our work has involved fending off or working through these various projections, avoiding being drawn into one or another temptation to "fit" people's expectations, in order to preserve the outsider's ability to move among parts of the system and to maintain an independence that helps all parties to reflect critically on themselves. Unlike the psychoanalyst, however, we cannot control the transference by interpreting it and contrasting the patient's fantasy with reality. There are too many actors, and events move at too rapid a pace. All sides pressure us to legitimize their positions *vis-à-vis* the others. Faced with this, we fall easily into defensive counter-transferences. Our work functions through empathy, understanding, and identification with clients and stakeholders; it is only a small step from there to errors such as, on one side, trying to "take over" and act for them; on the other, simply adopting their views and values.

The ambiguities in the working relationship between us and the members of the organization causes us anxiety. However, as the ethnopsychoanalyst George Devereaux writes, we gain understanding by using, not blotting out our emotions. Often we are feeling the same anxiety that those we work with are feeling. And by questioning our own thoughts and attitudes we help others to accept the anxiety of venturing into the unknown. Transference and counter-transference provide emotions and fantasies that the intervener must continually decode, facilitating understanding of the group and relationship with its members.[8]

These questions are especially important to those of us who want to make society more democratic. Why are we dissatisfied by things as they are? Why does intra-organizational functioning appear to be so undemocratic in democratic societies? What are the ideals that direct our actions? Why do we believe that countervailing power, a balance between corporate power and unions, is desirable? How well do our ideals actually work out? Can they be shared by those we work with? Or can they be shared enough so that the differences do not negate a common project? (We discuss these crucial questions in Chapters 11 and 12.)

While some of the actors express hopes or fantasies about how we can improve their situation, we must keep in mind that we as consultants are invading and disrupting a world in which other actors have roles and relationships which serve their interests, and further their ideals, whatever these may be. It is natural that some actors will welcome us and project onto us unrealistic powers to help them, while others will look for ways to devalue or undermine us—or at least our role. In order to keep our bearings, maintaining the constructive tension of "otherness," we need first of all to recognize the limitations of our work, limitations which will be used in many different ways beyond our control.

The power of projection can be very destructive to the client. In many cases interventions by experts leaves the direct client feeling very satisfied because his position in the organization has been bolstered by his association with such respected knowledge. But the impact internally is frequently regressive: it increases dependency and reinforces with the bureaucratic pattern of defending turf rather than increasing cooperation. The consultant report becomes just another weapon in ongoing battles. By contrast, by standing back from the projections of the organization we refuse to collude in these battles; thus we can build new understanding and new relations.

We avoid being sucked into these positions by recognizing the fantasies we provoke and, where possible, interpreting them—that is, telling people that we think they are projecting something onto us that is not real, or defining a position different from the one they expect. It is quite possible at some points to say, with a certain amount of humor, "You are treating me like a magician; I don't have any magic"; or "My job isn't to carry messages." This can force a rethinking of who we are and a better understanding of the fact that our role is to not have a defined role within the system.

It is also important that we talk to colleagues about what we are doing in order to have someone who can point out our own fantasies, so that they do not become secret plots that distort the scientific and professional tasks. In so doing, we have the right and obligation to keep in mind our own legitimate career interests and the integrity of the institutions that we represent. Our writing this book has in fact been a good vehicle for thinking about the ways in which our countertransferences can distort our work.

The working out of the transference in a long-term interactive intervention typically involves a long process of shifting expectations, from looking to us for answers to using us as sounding boards to doing without us entirely. In this process we cannot simply deny or block transferences: we have to meet people's expectations to some extent in order to establish a connection to people in the organization. At crucial moments, however, we need to challenge the images people have of us in order to preserve our independence and our ability to play our role.

For example, when Heckscher was asked to develop training materials for the Workplace of the Future effort in a business unit at AT&T, he began with a dialogue among the management and union leaders about their core principles and goals. He in effect catalyzed their own development of the training, organizing and producing the outcomes of the discussions. The leaders themselves conducted the initial training sessions and contributed their reflections to the further refinement of the materials. Throughout all of this, however, he was in a battle with the HR director, who wanted him to write up a glossy manual and deliver it to her, so she could then control its use in the organization: as she put it, "I want you to drop a binder on my desk and ask, 'How many do you want?' " In the end he sparked a showdown with her to preserve the broader dialogue and development process; the conflict mobilized other leaders and clarified their commitment to the interactive process.

Our experience is that our relation to the organization goes through three main stages:

1. At the start, while some of our clients know our strengths and weaknesses, there is a tendency to see us as magic helpers who are bringing a solution to organizational problems that seemed insoluble. For example, Maccoby was introduced at the start of WPoF as its architect. This was a combination of truth, transference and to some degree a way of setting Maccoby up to be a scapegoat, in case the process failed. Once it became successful, Maccoby's name disappeared from speeches and published reports, and union and management leaders were the ones who described the process at public meetings and even testimony before a government commission.

2. In the second stage, we become interactive participants in the process. We become members of planning committees, co-designers, facilitators, teachers, speaking partners, and researchers. We are seen as working for the future organization. The FS intervention is a good example.

3. And in the third stage, we are no longer needed. As in successful psychoanalysis, the clients come to feel they have done it themselves. In contrast,

where the client idealizes the analyst, or interactive consultant, this is a sign of an unresolved transference and a continuing dependency.

This stage can be very hard for us to deal with. We find that we are no longer called on to help, no longer invited to crucial meetings; it can feel like abandonment or lack of gratitude, and we may feel that the clients are making mistakes without us. In some cases, however, we have succeeded in making the transition, developing collegial relationships with some of the leaders we've worked with, and collaborating with them on other projects outside the company.

These stages do not always follow in sequence in large organizations: when key actors change, it becomes difficult to maintain long-term relations and perceptions of us can remain somewhat fluid. Sometimes, we may again become magic helpers to new leaders.

Although research or consulting situations provoke an exchange of fantasies, such exchanges are not generally mentioned in reports. Researchers explain or describe their interpretations, but they rarely describe the process and even less their personal experiences during the research. But the consequences of these fantasy exchanges can be significant. Indeed, these fantasy exchanges can result in "acting-out." For example, the "creator of the universe" fantasy can result in a desire to take the place of the managers or union leaders in the name of a higher knowledge, or knowledge serving a nobler cause than it has been serving. To be more specific, in this fantasy we want to take the place of the manager, because we have "reason" on our side. Of course, this feeling of having reason on our side is, above all, very often a rationalization of a desire for power. Perhaps this accounts for so many consultants accepting management positions with the organizations that had up to then been their customers.

The tension provoked by these exchanges of fantasies, and the interests that underlie them, sometimes produce feelings in us that distract us from our goals. We need constantly to be attentive to our own emotions; if we fail to manage them we run the danger of being swept along by our own anxieties.

Such issues are seldom if ever discussed, because they call into question the assumed neutrality of the researcher or consultant. This neutrality is supposed to direct us to specific procedures or rules that attempt, in fact, to keep our psyches out of the picture. These procedures or codes, however, never resolve the fundamental issue of the attitudes that direct our inferences and behavior. Faced with the multiple questions that relating research to action can raise, it seems to us that the answer lies in developing relationships with teachers and colleagues to analyze transferential and counter-transferential aspects of our work, which are inescapable and cannot honestly be written off—literally or figuratively—from our interventions.

In effect, we believe the answer does not, and can not, lie in defining additional rules to attempt to ensure the neutrality of the intervener (researcher, or consultant). Social science, by becoming more interventionist in human work-place issues, must give itself the kinds of processes and relationships that aren't provided by the traditional processes of the world of science (theses, scientific articles, books, tutorials). These traditional approaches do not consider the human side of intervention; they are only concerned with the methods of creating knowledge.

Our view is that to develop themselves as practitioners in society, applied sociology and anthropology must invent procedures that more strongly link knowledge production, intervention effects, and the attitude of the intervener—who for the moment can only be defined incongruously by associating words which are, at least in the present, from different universes that have not yet been reconciled: "researcher-practitioner," "action-researcher." In our own case, we have found that Freud's observations on transference have been the most helpful.

THE CONSULTANT'S VALUES: SOURCE OF STRENGTH AND WEAKNESS

Our approach lacks the protections of the detached researcher. Working at the fault lines of society can cause us to become, in a way, schizophrenic. We are constantly moving from identification with, to distancing from, actors who express different, if not opposite, rationales that are rooted in their values, institutional structures and constituencies.

As we observe practices and formulate ideas about them, our own viewpoint about society, our own ideals inevitably come into play. We cannot detach ourselves from our values, but we must recognize, identify and analyze them. Usually the actors already know them because of our writings and speeches. While this process goes on, the actors question us about our own ideals. Unlike the psychoanalyst, we cannot turn these questions into an analysis of the transference. ("Why do you suppose I think that?") If we are pro-union, the activists want to know why we are not activists. If we work with human resource managers, why don't we adopt the managerial point of view, that unions are outdated? If we align with a business orientation, why are we working in the public sector? If we respect the public good aspect of public utilities—as in the case in AT&T, EDF, and FS—why are we bringing in the business perspective? What are our goals, our project, what utopia is animating our work? We have often felt a conflict between remaining detached and objective within the organization and expressing our views in public debates.

We have been open and explicit about our value orientations in our work. We could not really hide them if we wanted to: they are visible in our writings for anyone to look at. But more important, values can play a crucial role in establishing our relation to the parties—though they are also very easily turned as weapons against us.

Shared values are a critical component of trust. As we work closely with leaders in decisions that put at risk not only their own careers but also the futures of many other people, they want to feel confident that we share their basic orientation, and that we will be loyal to their interests as they move through conflict. The path is uncertain enough for them without fearing that advisors will have divided loyalties or will try to lead them in directions they do not want to go. Most consultants are closely aligned in values with their clients—it is a prerequisite of the job: management consultants are clearly oriented to improving shareholder value, and union consultants are clearly oriented to increasing union power and effectiveness. Any suspicion otherwise dooms the relationship. At the same time, it is rarely necessary to discuss values explicitly, because in single-stakeholder relationships they are a given, a background, signaled by behaviors but not a subject of conversation.

But those who work with multiple stakeholders are in a different position: a major part of the role is our ability to *bridge* value-systems. We need to communicate to *different* actors that we are "on their side," that we share their values and will stick with them. This is a difficult trick when they see themselves as opposed.

We cannot succeed by merely trying to appeal simultaneously to competing sets of values; that would make us appear two-faced and untrustworthy to both sides. Values unite members of groups but are divisive between groups, as we see from religious wars the world over. Most managers want to know that we are not going to distract them from the core task of increasing shareholder value; unions tend to be suspicious because we are critical of some of their most cherished traditions. Tixier and Maccoby have at various times found themselves on the "outs" with crucial unions for this reason, and all of us have experienced frosty receptions from managers who are afraid we are going to try to take them down "soft" paths.

Our role therefore requires that we represent a set of values *different from* that of any party, and that we persuade them that these values are *consistent* with their traditional ones. We "stand" in effect in the future, representing most of all the possibility of a viable prospect for all the actors. We avoid being drawn into particular games and conflicts in the present by offering ways for them to jointly explore their plausible futures—by offering help in ensuring viability. We have also taken a stand for substantive values that transcend those of particular actors. Ramirez often stresses the notion of "plus-sum" solutions and the value of deploying heretofore under-utilized resources more productively. Maccoby and Tixier have claimed to represent both human and economic values and have argued that they are not only compatible but mutually reinforcing. Heckscher has positioned himself at Lucent as representing the possibility for dialogue. Ramirez has represented the value of more responsive and interactive organizational strategies. All of these claims place us outside of, but also inclusive of, the different perspectives with which we work.

We walk an uncertain, even dangerous, path in making this claim. We claim that our values *include* those of all the other parties; but from their point of view we appear fully committed to none. Those of us who have worked closely with unions have gained at least a partial status as "on their side." Yet the fact that we also work with management means that they are always suspicious, and all of us have been at times rejected by unions because we represent an independent perspective.[9] And meanwhile, our closeness to unions raises suspicions among many managers.

This is one reason that we depend on the vision of key leaders: we need "intermediaries" who are fully members of the organization yet who understand and are attracted to the more inclusive values that we represent. They can then use their influence within their organizations to educate and develop others. Through this rather slow and uncertain process we can begin to build a shared vision among the parties that can overcome historical divides.

On the management side we have always found leaders who themselves would like to see their work as part of a larger social picture beyond profit maximization, but who rarely have the chance to express this side of themselves. Roussely at EDF has been attracted by the inclusive value of "sustainable development." Maccoby, for instance, won the support of one manager when he told him—after a wide-ranging conversation—"What you want to do is to put the soul back in this company." Those who are drawn by such visions often have an unusual degree of motivation for change and the ability to stay the course through many discouragements and difficulties.

These efforts have created a cadre of people who play in a sense a role of "missionaries" within the organizations, carrying the values of collaboration, dialogue, involvement, full use of resources, and bringing them "inside" the organization.[10] But the danger still remains that they, even though insiders, will be seen as a marginal group by the rest of the organization. In the Saturn company today the original "99" who were involved in the design of the company are today seen in part with reverence and respect, in part as dinosaurs whose values are no longer relevant to the increasingly competitive environment.[11]

The work of interactive education and the development of values does not stop, in other words, with the consultants; it is a continuing challenge. The power of values and missionary zeal is vital in motivating change and establishing bonds of trust, but constant attention must be paid to connecting them to different stakeholders inside and outside the organization, showing their relation to the various identities and tasks, and building bridges among those who see themselves as representing different "religions" in the web of relations.

CONCLUSION

Interactive interveners, paradoxically, must avoid being drawn into many of the interactions that the client seeks. The value of outside consultants is in representing values and perspectives that are *not* fully part of the system; they cannot be seen as a member or representative of any one party. Thus there is a constant tug-of-war in which people in many different roles try to "place" the consultant in understandable terms; if they are unable to slot him into existing political configurations as an agent (secret or open) of some actor, they push him out into roles that do not really connect to the organization at all (magic helper, mere academic).

A few leaders understand the value of an independent outsider, not beholden to anyone in particular. Some of them have asked us to be speaking partners and to take part in key decision-making meetings as sounding boards and coaches. It is often hard for them to be fully open with people inside; they can speak more freely with us. We have mirrored their feelings and attitudes and helped them understand their dilemmas. We have helped to strengthen their vision. We have also been able to challenge their views, especially if we were able to use interviews and surveys to gain knowledge the leader is unable to get by himself. They have asked us at times to take a role of organizational conscience, to help clarify shared values and also to take strong note of deviations from them. In these roles organizational leaders, rather than trying to slot us into existing patterns, consciously use the "outside" quality of the consultant as a strength.

As an organization matures and completes a change process, the need for this kind of outside perspective is likely to decline. The moment that most demands interactive intervention is that of relational transition, where new connections must be made and old ones unmade (though this "moment" can last, as in the AT&T case, a very long time.) At such times the ability to cross boundaries and to confound existing expectations is valuable in helping an organization to look at itself and consider new configurations. But by definition it is not a role that can be stabilized and become part of the organizational structures and routines: the interactive consultant is a troubadour of visions, carrying them across the boundaries of existing groups, constantly in motion.

THE EMERGING STAKEHOLDER REGIME

10

Assessing the Interventions:
Achievements and Limitations

A brief assessment of these interventions is that the systems we have worked with have evolved a long way—but not far enough.

1. At AT&T, Workplace of the Future (WPoF) at its height in the mid-1990s had significantly increased employee participation and brought the union to the table with both strategic and operational managers. The operational managers involved had learned to use participation to increase trust and make their communications more credible. In some cases participation had resulted in measurable productivity gains, with a process that also protected the employees from losing employment, even when their jobs disappeared. Participants had learned a great deal about each other and adopted new concepts, e.g. balancing customer, employee, and owner interests, that facilitated decision making. Members of senior management estimate that savings were in the two billion dollar range. But WPoF was not sustained after Maccoby left, especially with the strains between union and management over organizing new entities. Even without these strains, it is doubtful that WPoF would survive in a company where leadership was continually changing and new managers lacked any experience of working with unions in innovative ways. It took a great deal of coaching of both managers and union officials to get it going in the first place, and without support from the top and without investment in education, inertia on both sides pulled the union–management relationship back into a traditional mode.

2. In Ferrovie dello Stato (FS), the speed of change that the organization could—or would—muster was pushed to the limit in the face of contextual (EU-driven liberalization) changes perceived to be ever more demanding. The intervention prompted considerable rethinking of the role of a railroad in society, and the foundation was laid for changes that are still moving slowly forward under continuing pressure from the EU. But internal and external resistance at the time were sufficient to block most change, and the fall of Necci brought it to at least a temporary standstill. The strategic

analysis has proved valid over time, but the implementation of the analysis continues to be rocky.

3. Lucent moved very rapidly from a quasi-monopoly status into a fierce and wide-open game in an industry that went from dramatic boom to resounding bust within a matter of months. The intervention focused on creating a new level of union–management exchange and a shared understanding of the impact of the market. The parties have managed as of this writing to get through this dizzying sequence of events with very little open conflict and with far more than the usual amount of information-sharing. They have doubtless learned a good deal from the intensive and unprecedented discussions that have pushed at the boundaries of trust and skill. But both the unions and the company are dealing with this in terms of staggering through a crisis; none of the parties has made much progress in rethinking what a long-term union–management relationship might be in this competitive world. The work of adapting the system to a knowledge economy has barely begun, and a collapse remains a real possibility.

4. At EDF, after twelve years, the social system at different levels of the company moved a certain way along the path from a monopoly to a global competitive player. The company and the unions succeeded in constructing a "political exchange" in which the unions participated in the definition of the firm's strategy, in exchange for the acceptance of change. But the agreements remain founded on basic assumptions—in particular employment stability—which may not be sustainable when the market becomes completely open. The game is to hope that the company will be transformed sufficiently to hold its place with other powerful players.

The process that Tixier encouraged can be summarized as the construction of a cognitive frame about the effects of the market and how to deal with it. From the beginning he realized that the industrial system of EDF itself could not be changed, at least in the short term; this would need a decision of the highest court for administrative law. Within this framework, it was possible to help orient the system to the new challenges of the market and its internal consequences. This intervention helped the existing system to adapt, but without a full acceptance of the probable scope of future change.

Given the interactive nature of our interventions, we cannot clearly attribute any successes or failures to anything we have done: it is a matter of what our clients have done *with* it. Many efforts that seemed successful at one time later developed problems, such as the WPoF effort at AT&T; others that seemed to fail later revived, such as the strategic direction at FS. Nor can we ever be sure, given our disavowal of expert advice, whether our actions were "the" cause of any given result. All we can say is that *the efforts in which we were involved* succeeded or failed in tackling certain problems. We can map these problems, and measure success, in terms of the issues sketched in Chapter 2.

OVERCOMING ADVERSARIAL HISTORIES

In most of our work a triggering problem has been the desire to improve an existing union–management relationship—usually because it was seen as too conflictual. That is the first category of intervention problem, and the systems we have worked with have made considerable progress at this level.

The resistance to real dialogue was deep in all the countries in which we worked, and it could mutate into many forms. It was often very difficult even to get the parties to accept the need to talk to the other. At EDF, for example, the HR manager in 1993 proposed a strategy of confrontation with the CGT, which was considered irretrievably retrograde. Tixier presented the results of his research on the system of industrial relations, showing the ineffectiveness of such strategy given the role and the functionality of the union in the enterprise. The HR manager accepted these arguments, which led him to adopt a new strategy of quietly trying to go around the union. This worked no better than the frontal strategy. It is not until this second strategy was shown to be ineffective that the enterprise engaged in a real effort to improve its social relations.

In this phase the parties did not move beyond the narrow limits of the traditional compromises. The difference from the past was that they were able to communicate much better; the amount of information exchange and of dialogue were dramatically greater. The parties thus became more able to work things out without misunderstandings and without falling into spirals of mistrust.

ORGANIZATIONAL CHANGE: TRANSFORMING BUREAUCRACY, INCREASING INVOLVEMENT

A second level of the problem has been helping organizations move from bureaucratic-Taylorist management to more team-based and participative organizational systems. This was the underlying issue when Maccoby was called in by AT&T. It involves far more of the system and requires a much larger set of changes than merely improving union–management relations. In dealing with leadership relations it is pretty clear from the start who are the main players and what the problems are; when one tries to increase participation, the key players shift constantly, and obstacles can arise in many unexpected places.

The QWL initiative at AT&T was meant to break with the bureaucratic logic because it was based on the premise that workers know more about their work than management does. This was, of course, the idea that Frederick Taylor had combated so successfully in the early twentieth century; after that management systems were based on the notion that scientific knowledge held by managers was superior to the knowledge of workers. QWL stood this on its head and was, therefore, deeply disruptive of long-established attitudes and routines. It upset the chain of command: suggestions went from worker teams directly to higher levels of management, leaving supervisors feeling powerless. It required new leadership styles, based on listening and persuasion rather than command and control. WPoF extended QWL by creating task forces that sometimes involved multiple levels of workers and management, and sometimes crossed the boundaries of work units.

Given the obstacles, these efforts went very far indeed. While it was hard to get an exact census of activity, at its height employee surveys indicated that 40 percent of employees were involved in WPoF-style participative teams. Training in problem-solving and team dynamics had been given to thousands of teams by a network of hundreds of facilitators. The surveys also found that those who were involved in the teams were significantly more satisfied with a wide variety of dimensions of their work. Many documented cases showed large and measurable productivity gains or cost savings. Unlike many HR-driven programs, WPoF affected a wide swath of operational managers. "WPoF" became a cultural reference-point that gave legitimacy to participative efforts of all kinds in the struggle to break the bureaucratic relations and habits of the past. Though the evidence is impressionistic, it seems that this was among the most successful participative transformations in large companies; the QWL programs in the auto companies, for example, have not retained the force that WPoF has as a model even today in AT&T and Lucent. It is notable that WPoF was most effective in parts of AT&T that had moved toward the knowledge-solutions mode of production such as service technicians who do not follow a Tayloristic script but must solve problems together with customer technicians.

The WPoF process acquired a significant life of its own, expanding beyond the scope originally laid down for it in the contract or in our own conception. In research conducted after several years we found a whole set of teams which, rather than trying to solve problems themselves as the model envisaged, had formed themselves as hubs catalyzing and coordinating temporary teams focused on particular issues and with changing memberships. This had the great advantage of involving a far larger segment of the workforce, focusing the greatest expertise and motivation on each problem, and creating a gradually increasing circle of understanding and commitment to the process. These teams showed outstanding results in terms both of business measures (productivity and cost savings) and of general enthusiasm about WPoF. This sort of self-generating "mutation" is almost the ideal of how an interactive intervention should work.

We have also participated in significant change in the unions, especially the CFDT in France and the CWA in the US. The American labor movement has tended to be suspicious of "participation," first because it threatens to bypass the union and build direct connections between workers and management; and second because it can weaken the central contractual framework that is the core of union power. Most unions in the 1980s were either openly opposed to QWL efforts or grudgingly neutral. But during that period the CWA became increasingly convinced of the value of "before-the-fact" involvement in decision-making. This required major changes in the union at all levels: local leaders needed to overcome their concerns that wider participation would undermine their influence, and to learn to draw strength from the increased involvement of members; they needed a difficult set of new skills—analyzing business plans, talking to management about strategy, and so on; they needed to work out roles for facilitators and team leaders; and so on. In 1992 the CWA's President asked Maccoby to lead a group of executive board members—including those who were in favor and opposed to union participation—on a study trip of examples in various telecom companies in the US. Following this the executive board passed a resolution supporting authentic participation, and directed union staff to help develop the skills needed by union participants.

Over the decade these skills and attitudes penetrated widely through the union, so that even some of the most militant local leaders saw value in broadening their tactics. Productivity was generally seen for the first time as a good thing rather than a bad thing—a way to strengthen the business, and thereby build jobs, rather than as a management attack on workers.

NAVIGATING MAJOR BUSINESS DISCONTINUITIES: RENEGOTIATING THE TERMS OF THE RELATIONSHIP

A somewhat different set of problems arises when the strategic picture in a company changes so dramatically that the old agreements and compromises become untenable. Each of our cases involved major changes in the business logic[1]: at FS as it lost its status as a state ministry; at AT&T as it moved into the deregulated environment and focused on new products and lines of business; at Lucent as it faced a cash-flow crunch that pushed it towards the divestiture of manufacturing; at EDF and FS as the competitive pressures mounted and the regulatory environment of the EC changed. Here the problem is not just to improve the way the parties manage their ongoing relationship; it is rather to reconstruct the relationship on a different foundation.

In one respect this situation simplifies things: the strategic importance of the relationship becomes unmistakable. Thus, it is easier to win management commitment to engaging the union. We no longer need to make the argument about the need to deal with unions; the potential for harm is too obvious to be ignored. But in other ways it is of course a much bigger problem. The first type of change described above leaves the "basic agreement" in place; but this second kind requires its renegotiation. At that point there is no longer a shared framework constraining the parties, and the danger of open and uncontrolled conflict emerges once again.

All of our cases were of course characterized by this kind of disruption: they moved from largely monopolistic environments to highly competitive ones, and pressure on wages and benefits sharply increased. Unions were asked to make "concessions," which is to say revisiting the basic framework of the historical relationship. This is ordinarily a recipe for a strike.

Our measure of success in this situation is whether the parties were able to restructure their relationship without a major breakdown and while maintaining the basic parity of the parties. One kind of failure would be mutually destructive warfare, such as that which killed Eastern Airlines during the 1980s. Another kind would be a sharp weakening or elimination of the union, which has been a common outcome in these cases; and a third would be a corresponding weakening of the company, which is not usually so evident but is certainly possible.

Most of our clients have been able so far to navigate this passage—with an emphasis, however, on the "so far," because all are unstable; and the one that was most clearly successful faced the least radical external pressure. Among the cases that have faced the most severe discontinuities the result is mixed:

- Ferrovie dello Stato faced a fundamental shift in identity. From one perspective, the intervention succeeded because many of the strategic visions identified by Normann and Ramirez have re-emerged in the current FS reality; in that sense they were "seers." But they largely failed in helping to make the transition easier for the parties because they were blocked from engaging internal political forces. The intervention may have had the more modest role of bringing implicit assumptions and beliefs into the open for discussion. This is more valuable in complex organizations than cynics may want to think.
- Lucent and AT&T were caught in an intense buzzsaw of competition. The unions were pushed into painful concessions. Yet, even here, the process was conducted through a high degree of involvement of the unions; at Lucent they discussed terms with potential buyers before the sale. Nevertheless, as we write in August of 2002 AT&T and its unions are back in a state of warfare, and the Lucent processes are fragile.

These partial successes were in turn tied to deeper changes in the relationship. WPoF moved the parties into discussions of strategy, which was new for them. The unions learned a great deal about how to analyze strategic questions and process changes and how to talk to managers in their own language.

LIMITATIONS IN THE TRANSFORMATION OF THE UNION–MANAGEMENT RELATIONSHIP

Even as the parties managed to rebuild their relationships in periods of rapid change, crucial limitations remained. First, although the parties learned to understand their interdependencies in a much deeper way, they still remained hostile. Maccoby and Heckscher tried, for example, to develop a view of "union value-added" which would get everyone to look at the unions as contributors to the business; this did not succeed. Most managers continued to feel that they were dealing with the union only because they had to—they would still prefer not to; many resented the time it took to meet regularly with union representatives on planning boards.

While some union representatives were more than willing to participate and study management issues, others felt overwhelmed by the work. Managers wanted union representatives to attend their planning meetings, and in a number of cases, there was pressure for them to take on a quasi-management role.

Even at its peak, WPoF did not fit the vision Maccoby and Heckscher had for it. There were a number of reasons for this:

1. Operational management lacked power. Top management could step in with decisions that frayed trust, such as deciding about downsizing or buying a new business. In these cases, operational leaders were often not consulted.
2. Although top management was supposed to meet regularly with top union officials, these meetings took place only once or twice a year and strategic issues were seldom discussed. Top management typically kept its deliberations within a very small group and its decisions were sometimes made to impress Wall Street analysts. This sometimes backfired as when AT&T announced large cuts in the workforce only to backtrack later.
3. To a considerable extent the bureaucratic logic survived, allowing the unions to confuse increased co-production and co-evolution with opportunities for bargaining. It is exactly the fear of this that had led FS management to turn down a matrix organization structure as a viable option. Many meetings became bargaining sessions under another guise, rather than open discussions of strategic options. Once the process began to fail, some key union leaders who had supported WPoF were beaten for election by candidates who argued that they had been naive to ever trust management.
4. A major difficulty was in overcoming the disparity between the strategic level and the level of daily work. In other words, it is difficult for actors to have a vision of the "big picture" within which they move.

Maccoby has often used a diagram to suggest to the parties the steps toward improved relations (see Figure 10.1).

All cases moved substantially towards a problem-solving framework, with continuing discussions between bargaining sessions aiming to work out difficulties before they turned into confrontations. All of them moved into the domain of participation but none became stable and comfortable there. At AT&T, two or three business units fully adopted the WPoF aim of bringing the union leadership into strategic discussions, but most business units avoided full engagement; and at the very top level the discussions were more in the nature of information-sharing than participation. At Lucent the intense crisis atmosphere gave the unions a good deal of leverage and influence, but they were not accepted as regular participants in decision-making. At EDF Roussely has only begun to open a broader dialogue about issues going beyond the solving of contractual impasses.

No case has developed meaningful *partnership* in the strong sense. By this term we mean that the parties would view each other as providing positive value, so that they actually need each other to accomplish their goals, and are committed

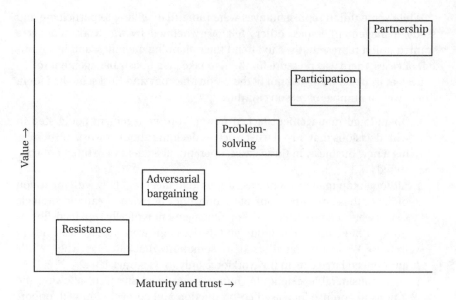

Fig. 10.1. Steps toward improved relations.

to help each other succeed. The unions of course know that they "need" management to succeed, since their members depend on the jobs that the company provides. But none of these managements have ever become convinced that the union could actually add value, and while they recognize the need to work with the union, they do not want to see it grow and become stronger within the firm. They would be happy to see it succeed with their competition.

THE LIMITS OF UNION–MANAGEMENT PARTNERSHIP: FUNDAMENTAL OBSTACLES

Our blockage at the level of true "partnership" demands further reflection. This notion has been central in our interventions and in much of the labor–management field of the past two decades, though it has covered a wide variety of efforts, from co-management at Saturn or Volkswagen to much more limited consultation. What have we learned about these "partnership" processes?

We have found that it is possible to considerably expand the domain of understanding and agreement. The partial success of the efforts is based very largely on a managed discovery of similarity between the parties. Typically there are powerful moments at which union and management leaders become aware that they share values, extending into their private lives: they begin to talk about their families and their own hopes, finding widely shared perspectives. They also begin to articulate the ways in which the meeting of business needs benefits the union and its members, and vice versa.

On both sides this expansion involves a shift in the framing of values: they see more clearly the other's values as a means to their own, and they reach a deeper understanding of their interdependency. On the union side, most have long been willing to acknowledge that the company's success is necessary to achieving their own goals of better wages and working conditions, but few have taken this as far as trying to understand how they really affect the business. The joint efforts teach them a great deal about the dynamics of business success.

But, over time, a more basic and less encouraging learning has emerged: the process appears to be fundamentally fragile and vulnerable. Success remains a temporary exception rather than the foundation for building momentum towards trust. Over twenty years of work in the Bell system—AT&T and several of its spinoffs—trust has sometimes grown for periods of as much as five or six years, but it has consistently been knocked back down again by strategic or leadership shifts. As of late 2002 AT&T, which had invested so much in joint efforts from the shopfloor to the boardroom, was locked in a pitched and highly rancorous battle with its major union over organizing; WPoF efforts were no longer active. Lucent, meanwhile, was struggling to maintain some semblance of calm, and both unions were declaring the process moribund. We are, moreover, unaware of any case in which this sort of stakeholder effort has remained stable through substantial environmental changes.[2] EDF's agreements after twelve years of work are similarly fragile, particularly in view of the increase in competition on the near horizon.

For management the process is complementary and equally difficult. In the best cases they begin to frame a view in which the success of their stakeholders is a vital element in the success of the business. This often requires doing things which, from a narrow business point of view, are "wrong"; because doing the "right" thing would lead to various kinds of failure and reactions from other stakeholders. A recent example: United Airlines' acquisition of US Airways in the spring of 2000 made eminent sense from the point of view of route structure and finance, but the reaction from pilots who feared downgrading almost doomed the company. Thus, a wise management must frequently "bite its tongue" and take into account perspectives which in the normal course of events it would discount.[3]

How do we reconcile these two major findings: the general limitations and failures of the dialogue process, and its sometimes impressive successes in building understanding and cooperation? The answer is that *dialogue is an incomplete solution*. The process of sharing perspectives, through which the parties understand their interdependence, creates energy and success at various stages of partnership efforts, and goes a long way towards building a cooperative relationship. But they do not get all the way there. Despite the expansion of understanding, there are major forces that *systematically*—and, barring great good luck, inevitably—cause breakdowns.

Some of these difficulties are particular to nations or companies. France, for example, poses the particular problem of fragmented unionism. Five major federations with extremely diverse histories and ideological traditions—including the (formerly) Communist CGT, the CFDT with its origins in Christian humanism, the FO seeking to introduce American-style pragmatic bargaining—compete for members in each workplace.[4] The division among unions creates major obstacles for intervention. It is unusual to have the confidence of all the parties: Tixier had to act at EDF without the full confidence of certain actors, especially the CGT. Indeed, the system encourages games in which unions take contrary stances merely to establish their militant credentials or their independence, without regard to the merits of the situation. Company leaders most of the time play on these characteristics of the French system to give themselves room to maneuver in relation to unions, playing one union against another even if that results, in certain cases, in a great fragility of social relations. Thus, the agreement of 1999 at EDF, which was signed by all of the five unions present in the enterprise, was truly exceptional.

The Italian case highlights another problem, visible also in France to some degree: the intertwined relations between company executives and politicians. In the public sector, until very recently, political preferences and allegiances held sway over appointments. Thus, the real forces behind organizational changes—as in the FS case—are often hidden, having more to do with political maneuvering than the economic health of the company. This has begun to change in recent years due to reforms in corporate governance and to the rise of foreign competition and foreign ownership. Failing firms, in particular, like Fiat in 2002, have seen the old ways change.

Beyond these national differences, however, some problems are universal and fundamental across our cases and, to our knowledge, across the industrialized nations in most industries.

The primacy of collective bargaining contracts

The collective bargaining contract is fundamental to the structure and nature of unions and the entire labor relations system, not only in these cases but in every country that we know of. Contracts work by stabilizing relations for a period of time—usually three years—and by establishing clear rules for the relationship during that time. They also tend to be centralized, especially in the industrial sector, in order to maximize the unions' power, to assure equity among the members, and to prevent management from playing different groups off against each other.

This approach to relations clashes with the need for rapid responsiveness that has become a mantra among the managers in these companies. The centrality of the contract severely limits what can be "worked out" on an ongoing basis. Even as far back as the QWL effort of the late 1970s at AT&T, the union's primary concern was that the workers not discuss issues that had been settled in the contract. Although Jim Irvine, the vice president of CWA for AT&T (and Lucent) believed that WPoF could create a "living contract" and succeeded to some degree with work rules that were issues, especially wages and benefits, but also job classifications that could be settled only in the traditional bargaining. Today, as Lucent seeks to reduce its size and shift its focus, discussions with the unions tend to focus not on how to meet everyone's interests but on how to avoid violating contract clauses. From the management perspective, these discussions seem endless and essentially off the point: the ship is burning and the unions are arguing about who has the responsibility for handling the hoses. For the unions, however, these discussions define what they are: if they give up contractual rights during a crisis they may never get them back. As pressure builds the parties frequently move farther apart rather than working more closely together.

There are, of course, some instances where unions have made enormous concessions to save companies—taking huge pay cuts, suspending work rules, and so on. In exchange they usually get increased decision-making rights. The record of such "crisis-driven" partnerships is not very encouraging, however. Eastern Airlines seemed a shining example in the early 1980s: pay cuts were exchanged for union seats on the board of directors, and all parties sang in harmony. But the fragility of the compromise became apparent soon afterwards, and the acrimony built rapidly toward a disastrous end for the company. United Airlines has more recently gone through a similar cycle, though it is not yet over as we write.

Centralization creates related problems. The managers in these companies believe deeply in the need for local variation. Sometimes they argue this is based on the need for responsiveness to local customers. They also point out that workers cannot be involved in decision-making—a good goal from everyone's perspective—unless they can change work rules to meet their particular needs. This is indeed a major reason why American unions have been resistant to worker participation efforts: they fear that management will weaken the guarantees of the contract on issues like overtime and seniority by "allowing" workers to take different paths and thus weakening the overall unity of the membership.

Thus, efforts to fundamentally modify the nature of the relationship in a less centralized and less rule-based direction have had rocky histories. The Saturn auto plant in the US is one of the most dramatic illustrations, with major modifications in the national contract permitting both greater flexibility and greater union involvement in decision-making. But the national union—the United Auto Workers—has been very uncomfortable with this breach in the contract and has refused to allow it to be repeated in any other plant; and many workers within the plant keep returning to the clarity and security of the contract, creating tensions with their own leaders, whenever conflict arises with management. Nor is the other side any easier: General Motors management is uncomfortable with the power-sharing side and has also been unwilling to generalize the effort.[5]

Resistance from excluded parties

The partnership model usually brings together two parties—unions and management; but other groups can affect the success of this relationship.

Some of these are obvious external forces. Shareholders, for example: if it were not for their demands it would be a great deal easier for management and unions to find acceptable compromises. Customers, too, have a disturbing way of expecting lower prices and higher quality which precludes many "win–win" union–management solutions. More subtle are "hidden stakeholders": parties who are formally included within the main stakeholder groups but have independent interests. This problem more frequently becomes visible on the union side. Unions are limited in their ability to make commitments by the fact that local presidents answer more to their members than to their national leaders. Thus, it is very frequent for national leadership to seek a compromise that benefits the union or membership as a whole, but is blocked by one or more locals who feel they would lose out.

On the management side the resistances of the hidden stakeholders are usually less visible but no less effective. Almost every company we have dealt with in any capacity has complained about the blocking power of the "frozen middle": managers of departments or functions whose support is needed but who see no benefit to themselves in cooperation or change. Some FS managers privately told the consultants that they knew top management came and went, and that fully committing to any one top administration's agenda was suicidal if one wanted to stay in one's career. In the same way, some of the top administrators complained about what they termed the lack of "cooperation" and "managerial quality." Both groups are of course right—from their own point of view. Reconciling these is difficult, and getting harder, as managerial tenure periods become ever shorter.

At EDF middle managers had good reasons for resistance: the development of a market focus devalued their skills and prestige, which had been based on controlling local resources. The mantle of leadership passed from these local barons to those who headed international divisions and those who were on the front lines facing market pressures.

A particularly important group for the labor–management challenge is first-level supervisors. In one instance during the WPoF effort their objections came to the surface with extraordinary vehemence: in a private meeting they expressed rage at being asked to cooperate with difficult union leaders while their own accountability for performance was unchanged. They did not feel able to raise this objection directly to their superiors, which is why it so often remains hidden, but it was clear that their feelings made it very difficult to achieve a climate of trust.[6]

The legal/institutional framework of stakeholder relations

The last two points—the primacy of the collective bargaining contract and the exclusion of other important stakeholders—brings us beyond the firm, to the level of the basic framework of relations among stakeholders. In most industrialized countries—certainly in the three we have worked with—the entire system of laws and customs has developed around a basic tripartite notion, often called "neo-corporatism",[7] with government, unions, and companies working out differences through negotiation. To be sure, there are important differences: in the French public sector, the government plays a much more direct role than in the US case; French law encourages multiple unions, while the US requires exclusive representation in most instances. But beyond these differences, core features are shared in all cases:

1. Unions represent workers, management represents shareholders.
2. The government acts as a general representative of all other social goods aside from the interests of shareholders and union members.
3. The legal structure encourages the negotiation and enforcement of formal and (usually) centralized contracts between unions and management.
4. Parties other than unions have different and far more limited legal status.

These basic characteristics flow from both formalized law and administration and from the way the institutions have developed. In the US there was historically a great struggle over the legal status of collective bargaining contracts, ending with their being enshrined as the cornerstone of labor relations, enforceable by courts. Many US courts have found that worker participation programs are actually illegal because they violate the assumption in law of union independence and the primacy of contract.

Many institutional habits and structures also reinforce the centralized contractual nature of the relationships. Union leaders reach their positions by being effective contract negotiators and contract administrators; efforts to move towards business partnerships call on different skills and generally leave them feeling uncertain. Management has in the past developed a separate function of "labor relations" to deal with unions—but not other stakeholders; it is almost always distant from the core strategic decision-making processes of the firm, and is specialized in the arcane procedures of grievance and contract negotiation. Government agencies are built to monitor contracts and encourage arbitration. Thus, in addition to the formal structure, a large number of interests grow up reinforcing the dominant neo-corporatist pattern.

We saw a particularly clear example of the impact of the neo-corporatist paradigm at Lucent. There the parties struggled to work out a new level of dialogue, bringing the unions into strategic discussions about divestitures and other financial matters from which they had always been excluded in the past. But a sudden and late intervention by a governmental body (the National Labor Relations Board) threw this process into disarray and gave the initiative to the more "traditional" actors who favored adversarial bargaining. Whether they were "right" or not, the point is that this episode shows that the existing system is reinforced in many ways, so that even an intervention that successfully restructures the relationship between union and management leaders may be destroyed by missiles incoming from other directions.

The exclusion of other parties is also reinforced by the larger system. The US is the only country where middle managers are actually prevented by law from organizing unions[8]; but in our other cases as well they remain largely unrepresented. The US, conversely, has far stronger organizations of other types—ethnic associations, women, local communities, and so on—than does France, but in the absence of any coordinated framework for them they remain scattered and immature, capable of only brief bursts of effective activity. In the absence of any system for determining who speaks legitimately for what group, management naturally tries to ignore these pressures as much as possible or, when pressured, to shape and select friendly interlocutors; there is neither incentive nor structure for really engaging the interests of these other parties.

CONCLUSION: THE LIMITS OF CURRENT INTERVENTIONS?

We have participated in modifying the perspective that our interlocutors take on their practice, but we have not succeeded in building a new model of labor relations. We have helped our interlocutors to better grasp the nature of the changes that affect their organizations. In a certain sense we have played the role of a guide or *passeur* between the boundaries of a prior model of relations which was weakening and the emergence of a new rationality based on a common search for value. But these interventions have not given rise to a new model that can be stabilized.

We can identify two different boundaries that our clients "bumped" against in these periods of change. The traditional system in all cases was, and largely remained, *internally bureaucratic* and *externally neo-corporatist*. This means that the internal systems are hierarchical and rule-based, with each part focusing on a specific piece assigned from above; and external relations are structured primarily around government regulations and union negotiations.

In our work the pressures of increased competitiveness and the development of a knowledge-solutions economy have challenged this traditional system. Bureaucracy and corporatism have proved rigid, slow, and clumsy; they require long processes of working through centralized rules and procedures, whereas the management increasingly seeks rapid and decentralized adaptiveness. Thus, the organizations we have worked with have pushed at the boundaries.

- They have tried to increase participation and reduce bureaucratic control, and at AT&T in particular they created a vast new infrastructure of teams dealing with workplace issues. Yet, the balance of power remained with the bureaucracy; participation remained encapsulated, and when the pressure of the intervention was relaxed bureaucratic controls began to reassert their dominance. The decline in job security at all levels supports the rationality and effectiveness of a "duck and wait and see" attitude of many subordinates.
- They have tried to improve the dialogue with stakeholders in order to better work together to solve problems; and in the case of unions at AT&T, Lucent, and EDF, the parties learned to work out very difficult problems and to dialogue about issues that had traditionally been off limits. But they did not reach a stable relationship capable of dealing with the challenges of a knowledge-solutions economy, and they remained deadlocked around the fundamental issues of employment security and merit. With other important stakeholders the dialogue never developed effectively at all.

Though we cannot predict the future, it appears in all these cases that competitive pressure is still building and will require further transformations. EDF has only begun to open itself to the market and will soon face a major increase in competition; FS is also being pulled reluctantly towards greater openness; AT&T and Lucent are in the midst of the storm and having a hard time keeping their heads above water.

The barriers we face now are only partly under the control of the organizations we work with; to a great extent they are grounded in larger social institutions. The scope of these issues, going beyond the rebuilding of existing relationships, makes it perhaps impossible to navigate the transitions demanded of these organizations through dialogue. We do not have the means to bring all the right parties to the dialogue, and the existing parties do not have all the capacities they need to make the changes. It often seems that it may not be possible to bring about these changes without major conflict. This brings us, in a final chapter and at the forward edge of our work, to consider what we can usefully say about the future of industrial relations so as to guide us beyond the limits of what has been achieved so far.

11

The Current Impasse

At this point in our journey, we have reached one boundary and become aware of a larger territory to be explored. Our work began as an attempt to revive and improve the functioning of the existing stakeholder system. Step by step we have been pushed toward the idea that the central task is the construction of a new one.

Though our interventions have followed very different paths in these varied countries and companies, all of them have shared a central dynamic. Whether in the French electric industry, the Italian Railroads, or American telecommunications, the parties have found it difficult to *sustain* the agreements and visions that they had worked so hard to build; competitive pressures and social change repeatedly undermine the solutions and put things back into question. Thus we have come to believe from our practice that the fundamental issues lie beyond the capacity of *these* actors to resolve, even in the best cases.

The common problem of economic change has, in short, overwhelmed the differences among the systems we have worked in. This is consistent with the idea, developed by many economists and social analysts, that the leading economies are together undergoing a fundamental shift from "industrial" to "post-industrial" society. As Daniel Bell elaborated the idea as long ago as 1973, the fundamental move toward a knowledge-solutions form of production brings with it transformations in almost every social institution: in values, in class structures, in work relations. This theory helps a great deal in explaining our experience of *systemic discontinuity* lasting one or several decades in the companies we have worked with.[1]

Our hypothesis is that the general increase in competition observed in many economic sectors, including the ones in which we have worked, has undermined the neo-corporatist industrial relations system[2] and requires the transition to a different regime of "post-industrial relations."

THE POST-INDUSTRIAL SHIFT

The concept of a single systemic economic change stands in tension with analyses that focus on differences in "models" of capitalism and socio-political systems.

Many analyses have focused on the differences between national and regional forms of capitalism and industrial relations systems: between the strongly free-market approach of the US; the social-democratic, consensus-based system of northern Europe; the politically charged, conflictual system of southern Europe (including France); and the company-dominated paternalistic system of Japan.[3] Currently there is a tendency for each of these to look to the others for answers: American unionists wish their country was like Germany, German businessmen wish their country was like America; some relatively young French unions are mod-eling themselves on the US form of collective bargaining, while US militants wish they could generate the level of collective energy they see in France.

When we began comparing our own experiences, we, too, expected the cross-national differences to illuminate each other. Certainly the particularities of national systems affected our work: political linkages between enterprises and the state, and divisions among unions, were particularly important problems in both Italy and France, and less central in the US. Yet all of them seemed at the end of the day to be overwhelmed by similar economic forces.

In effect, existing national systems are similar in that they are alternative ways of dealing with a particular economic phase—the *industrial* phase in which economies move from an agricultural base to the dominance of mass consumer goods. One can roughly line up these alternatives along a single spectrum (Figure 11.1).[4]

From a little distance the array depicted in Figure 11.1, wide as it seems to the participants, can be seen to cover a narrow range of possibilities. All of them are essentially neo-corporatist, in the sense sketched in the last chapter: they attempt to stabilize competing interests through a negotiated relationship between unions and corporations, with government as both a mediating and regulatory force. The US is generally seen as highly economist and pro-business, yet in the 1950s the stable relation of the New Deal government, the AFL-CIO labor federa-tion, and big business interests led to a generally accepted balance that was not fundamentally different from that of, say, Sweden on the other extreme.

Currently all of these models, from one end to the other, are experiencing delegitimizing pressures. Public support for unions and for government regula-tion is in decline across the board. As the post-industrial sectors of knowledge

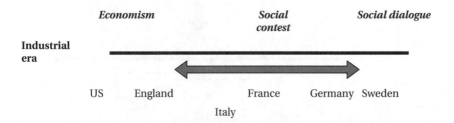

Fig. 11.1. Range of alternatives in the industrial era.

and solutions-based organizations grow, demands grow for more "dynamic" and "flexible" business strategies and an attack on "bureaucratic" rule-based relations. The centralized contracts and stable organizations of the neo-corporatist era are seen no longer as guarantors of needed stability and commitment, but rather as impediments to change. Managers and governments have increasingly taken aggressive stances toward unions, forcing rollbacks in work rules and trying to avoid unionization wherever possible. Unions are largely on the defensive, trying to hold on to what they have gained; this only increases the sense of conflict and widens the gap with management.

The data trend is in the same direction throughout the industrialized world. At the broad quantitative level, union membership dropped between 1979 and 2001—in the US from 25 percent to less than 15 percent, in the European Union from 44 percent to 32 percent.[5] In every country poll data suggest a weakening of union commitment among younger workers; in no country has organizing penetrated very far into new economic sectors. In every country the welfare state has been under increasing pressure, regardless of whether the government is nominally social-democratic or conservative. In the end, the most thorough recent studies of the labor and political situation in Europe conclude—usually reluctantly—that the overall system has reached an impasse that is likely to result in a continued decline of the central neo-corporatist institutions.[6]

The way forward apparently cannot be found among the array of current options: *none* of the existing models resolves the fundamental pressures they all face, because they all are struggling with a second dimension—the *post-industrial* shift (Figure 11.2).

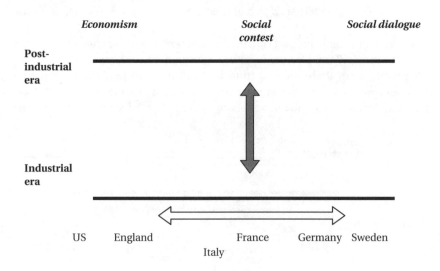

Fig. 11.2. The post-industrial shift.

In effect we began by thinking about relationships on the horizontal axis—increasing collaboration and dialogue—but have ended by realizing that we are working on the vertical: the problem is to facilitate a transformation in the system, from the organization of work through the definition and coordination of stakeholders. The "vertical" dimension has manifested itself, in each of the four cases (as well as many other projects we have worked on), in terms of:

- Increasing pressure in every country for the opening of markets (liberalization) at the expense of long-standing regulations, government-managed pricing and supply or demand mechanisms, and labor agreements.
- A weakening and delegitimation of unions and of government regulations at the national level, as we have seen.
- A move in corporate strategy toward focusing on knowledge and service value-added; productive efficiency, quality, reliability, and engineering excellence have become expected baseline capabilities rather than strategic differentiators.
- A great increase in the pace and continuity of reorganizations and strategic re-focusings.
- A shift in workplace organization toward more empowerment of frontline knowledge workers—with more teamwork, involvement, and participation in order to draw on employee knowledge and initiative.
- Increased outsourcing, joint ventures, alliances and other innovative co-productive arrangements that blur formerly clear organizational boundaries.

All of these create enormous obstacles to stable and trusting relationships between the unions and companies with which we work.

STAKEHOLDER REGIMES IN THE PAST: THE NEO-CORPORATIST COMPROMISE

The neo-corporatist system of stakeholder relations is a way of balancing conflicting interests during one major historical phase. In modern times interest groups have periodically fought for their points of view, especially during periods of great social change; this can result in social crises with significant violence and uncontrolled conflict. Much of Europe experienced these, for example, in major ways around the period of 1848, and later in the post-First World War period; in the US the greatest such crisis was probably the battles of the 1930s.[7] These battles are typically fought until a kind of stasis is reached where everyone feels that more fighting is not going to accomplish anything. At that point they give rise to what we are calling "stakeholder regimes."

Stakeholder regimes are sets of institutions and rules accepted by all about how differences will be fought out. They transform unregulated conflict into *regulated* conflict: an orderly system of negotiation with boundaries that both sides are unwilling to test further. They are necessarily compromises, based on a balance of power among whatever groups have been able to establish their position. They are not seen as ideal by any party but are seen by all as better than continuing the uncontrolled battles. They are necessarily impermanent, because they are based on an empirical balance of forces: if those forces or the constellation of interests shift significantly, then one party or another may decide that it is worth going back to the battlefield for a new test of strength outside the framework of rules. New parties, not included when the prior regime was set up, may also gain in strength and decided that they want to force their way into the game.

The neo-corporatist regime is based on the concept that stakeholder relations should be stabilized through centralized bargaining and formal contracts among a few large organizations: business (representing shareholders), unions (representing employees), and government (representing everyone else: communities, customers, etc.). Though some countries are more centralized than others, and the nature and scope of negotiations differs, those basic points are nearly universal in industrialized societies. In the US neo-corporatism was created during the Depression, when the Wagner Act validated unions and collective bargaining and when government began to play an active regulatory role. In France the prevalence of open conflict and turmoil continued longer than in most other countries—into the 1950s—and the process of stabilization was consequently more painful and incomplete, with more internecine battles; but the outlines are not fundamentally different.[8]

This system has worked very successfully to create agreements among conflicting social interests in a relatively peaceful way. We tend to forget that less than 70 years ago most Western societies were still very vulnerable to major internal upheavals. Once the role of unions was stabilized, and government became an active representative of other interests, conflicts became much more limited and problems were generally "worked out." All parties, including management (even if reluctantly), tended to accept this way of organizing relations and for at least 30 years, between the end of the Second World War and the early 1970s, it served as a shared framework within which everyone operated.

A key element of this order has bureaucratic structure and tight control at the shopfloor level, a system in which decision-making came from above and never from below. Frederick Taylor, the father of "Scientific Management," believed that "Any 'improvement' [a worker] makes upon the orders given to him is fatal to his success." The response of industrial unions—again, after considerable conflict—was to give up the old goal of direct participation and to seek instead stability and predictability, preventing management from taking arbitrary actions by tying everything in a web of rules.

Meanwhile, at the higher strategic levels, employment stability became the norm in large companies everywhere, based on the desire for a stable and reliable labor force. This became part of the overall "deal" that stabilized the stakeholder system: unions and worker rights converged with the need of companies around the need for security. In Europe many countries went much further than the US in enshrining employment security as a legal right, with strong government regulations making layoffs difficult. In Scandinavia and Germany this has been further bolstered by the system of "codetermination," which gives labor some rights to information and veto on issues that affect employment levels. France's system has less codetermination overall, but EDF was set up with a strong system of "paritarisme" that made the unions equal partners with management and the government in many aspects of the business.

Employment security was further bolstered (even in the US, where legal rights were weaker) by a widespread culture of corporate paternalism. In the most successful corporations of the high industrial age—General Motors, Dupont, Mitsubishi, Stora, Royal-Dutch Shell, Nestlé, IBM—a sense of shared destiny and fellowship were crucial in oiling the gears of these ponderous bureaucracies, providing motivation for people at all levels to find better ways than the rules could detail to get things done. The companies took on the responsibility to provide security and support in return for obedience and effort. Again the picture is essentially universal. In France, the same idea was captured in the term "entreprise-cité"—the "enterprise-community"—in which all employee needs could be met and in which reciprocal obligation was the rule.[9]

Many studies have showed that this combination of corporate paternalism and neo-corporatist stakeholder representation worked well. In the 1950s a set of Harvard Business School professors found that unions served as an effective disciplining force to prevent management from favoritism and other forms of arbitrariness;[10] later many studies have shown the positive effects of unions on productivity (in classic industrial settings).[11]

The unraveling of this balanced system had little to do directly with unions or labor relations policies. It was driven primarily by an economic and technological shift, starting in the 1950s but gathering steam only in the 1970s, that reduced the economic importance of mass production and emphasized the value of knowledge and the importance of workers being motivated to use their knowledge. More recently it has been accelerated by the breakdown of economic oligopolies and monopolies which has put further pressure on organizations to change. Management, pressured by these shifts and also sensing an opening, has widely and aggressively pursued deregulation and limitations on unions. Governments have widely divested themselves of their business holdings and deregulated key industries, while the globalization of commerce has broken up nationally based oligopolies. These pressures have been felt keenly in all the cases and nations described in this book.

LOOKING TO THE FUTURE: ARE STAKEHOLDERS NECESSARY?

Our interventions, then, which started by trying to improve stakeholder relationships, have become a matter of reconstructing the regime. But that problem reopens the prior question: why is it necessary for businesses to deal with out-side stakeholder groups at all?

We have seen that as we move into a "post-industrial" era, the institutions cre-ated out of the conflicts of a century ago no longer reflect very well the existing balance of forces. Governments, unions, and corporate paternalism seem out of touch with the concerns of many workers and other stakeholders. One conclu-sion that could be drawn is that we do not need stakeholder systems any more—that whatever the situation in the past, the time has now come for pure market individualism. Business leaders widely believe they know better than the inter-est-groups whose conservatism, narrow focus and lack of knowledge hinders the process of change. This view is also bolstered by a strong theory: neo-classical economics, which has no place for dialogue or stakeholder involvement.

We are claiming, by contrast, that in order to make a successful transition to a post-industrial order companies (including those we work with) cannot act alone, but must find ways to engage stakeholders in dialogue. Many others have made this claim, but there is no body of theory with the prestige of economics behind them.

Our experience leads us to believe that it is as important now as it ever was for businesses to pay attention to stakeholder concerns and to find a way to deal with them before they turn into uncontrolled conflicts. The success of the businesses we describe in this book depends on a strong social environment: they depend, for example, not only on government capital investment like the Internet, but also on schools that develop the skills essential for these industries. This is a *pragmatic* argument in the sense that it depends on the particular problems at hand: certain demands become significant sources of conflict at particular moments in history. More broadly, the success of business strategies and of the economy depend in part on the health of the entire social system—its responsiveness to the interests and values of the bulk of citizens; and this health in turn depends on effective mechanisms for managing disagreements and preventing them from escalating into uncontrolled conflicts. Though nature of the issues and the stakeholders has changed, the need for *some* kind of stakeholder regime has not.

Why effective business strategy requires stakeholder involvement, even (or especially) in the new economy

Strategic demands for co-production

One reason that stakeholder involvement is important is that it is essential to the success of business strategy in a knowledge-solutions economy. This may seem paradoxical: leaders often think of involvement as at best a moral duty but an impediment to clear business direction. The era of liberalization has brought strategy to the fore at the expense of relationships: at AT&T, EDF, Lucent, and Ferrovie dello Stato, deregulation has moved strategic choice to center stage as never before in their histories. The CEOs of these companies have often acted as though strategic imagination can fly above the dull world of organizational politics and relationships, but they soon find—as Armstrong, McGinn, and Necci all did in our cases—that the latter can quickly bring them to earth. They have discovered that strategy has to be *implemented*; and implementation requires the nurturing of relationships.

In fact, the paradox is that the strategic demands of a knowledge-solutions world require *greater* attention, not less, to relationships with stakeholders inside and outside the firm. In the emerging economy, unlike the industrial model of production vertically integrated within single firms, competitive advantage comes from working with many groups outside the boundaries of the firm; this cannot succeed in an atmosphere of mistrust and conflict. In brief, from the perspective of corporate strategy, stakeholders need to be viewed as co-producers of value, and co-production needs to involve stakeholders as partners.

Forces pushing businesses toward collaboration include:

- *Knowledge management*: It is now a cliché that the economy depends more than before on the production of knowledge rather than goods; even the value of goods depends more heavily on the knowledge packed into them. But the creation of knowledge is the cooperative activity *par excellence*. To solve a complex problem one must bring together people who understand various facets of it, and they must somehow find a way to bring those different viewpoints together into the best possible combination. In a simpler day the hierarchical superior could know enough to gather input and make the synthesis; now increasingly bosses know no more than their subordinates about any given issue. In this situation commands and incentives are feeble and usually counterproductive instruments; people have to form genuine teams in which they want to work things out, and they have to be able to reach consensus which reflects each vital specialized type of knowledge.

- *Speed*: The speed of change in technology and customer preferences reinforces the need for openness to partnership. When Citibank, for example, wants to move into the arena of e-business, it cannot wait to develop its own software for online accounting. If it is going to get to market fast enough to meet its competitors, it has to find some company already making the software and link to them to put out a product. Again, this puts the company in the position of needing to build relations of trust.

- *Asset liquidity*: The micro-chip and related technologies have made it possible to carry out this kind of collaboration by making it much easier to unbundle and recombine existing bundles of assets, activities, and actors. This in turn makes for much more interactive environments, as everyone seeks out the best partners and allies for each given project and task.[12]

A startling indicator of the fundamental economic shift, at least in the US, has been uncovered by Margaret Blair's data on the proportion of total corporate capital tied up in fixed assets (plant, property, and equipment). As of 1978, these "illiquid" investments accounted for 83 percent of corporate capital; by 1998, the figure had dropped to 31 percent. This is dramatic evidence of the growing economic importance of intangible and relatively fluid factors such as knowledge and relationships.[13]

Interdependence with stakeholders is thus a logical consequence of a shift in the form of value creation, from *production* to *co-production*. The current move is toward more choice and less stability.

A number of strategic analysts, Ramirez among them, have examined the co-production relation between customers and firms. Whereas in the past customers were seen simply as "consumers" at the end of the production chain, today they need increasingly to be viewed as one part of the value chain. Firms need to interact constantly with customers and with other firms in order to create the tailored solutions that are possible in a knowledge- and service-based economy.[14]

But this analysis has not yet been extended to other co-producers—or stakeholders. In a highly interdependent and solutions-oriented economy, the co-production relation involves not only customers but also employees (and the organizations representing the employees) and groups such as between firms and stakeholders such as environmental, political, or consumer rights organizations.[15]

If companies are to rely more heavily on allies and partners, they have to be more responsive to them. Conceptually brilliant strategy is not enough without a set of co-productive relationships to support and implement it. One indicator is the poor record of mergers: though they are always justified by elaborate and sophisticated strategic analyses of market penetration and cost synergies, they usually fail to produce the expected value—in fact, measured by stock price, they seem to destroy value.[16] Most of those involved will agree that the problem lies in the cultural clashes and internal politics that undermine internal cooperation after the merger has taken place. And this is only the most visible and measurable manifestation of the much larger problem of cultural ineffectiveness and resistance that dogs companies with increasing frequency.

Businesses are, in short, dependent on the good will of many parties—some internal to the firm (knowledge specialists, middle managers), some external (customers, allies and partners, pressure groups). For many of these, especially employees and partners, active cooperation is more important than ever; for others, the issue is more preventing active opposition. Thus there is a whole set of vital relationships that are essentially ignored in the theories of markets and hierarchies, and which have been disrupted by the liberalization moves of the past few decades.

The changing nature of work

The transformation of the knowledge-solutions economy drives changes not only in strategy but also in the organization and nature of work: successful businesses in this arena can no longer organize through simple hierarchy and authority, but must also pay attention to relations. At AT&T, Lucent and EDF we observe that the shift to a knowledge-solutions form of production eliminates many traditional "routine" jobs and transforms those that remain, increasing their conceptual demands.

The traditional job in the industrialized/bureaucratic order was largely transactional—each employee, especially those at lower levels, was supposed to "stick to" a specific job and perform a routine and tightly controlled set of tasks. In the emerging economy the value of routine performance declines, often to be absorbed into automated technology. In its place two major categories are growing. One is knowledge work: there employees are expected to contribute innovation and invention. The other is around service: as consumers become more sophisticated and offerings become more complex, many service-focused jobs require more responsiveness and the ability to solve problems. The most complex tasks of all combine both knowledge and service demands: these are the highly demanding "solution-creating" types of jobs which ask that employees understand customer demands and create new offerings to meet them.

These changes of work became visible and gathered momentum during the 1970s, when managers at all levels began to recognize that the ability to draw on employee knowledge was a competitive advantage. They therefore began with experiments in "participation." At first the move was extremely hesitant and slow; management sought to open up a little involvement without losing the control inherent in the bureaucratic order. But over time, as both the limits of these partial solutions and the potential benefits of true involvement have become more apparent, the experiments have become more far-reaching. They constitute a fundamental challenge to the familiar bureaucratic order, and their full implications have not yet been developed.

For example, the automation of operator services means the customer does more of the work, punching in numbers—so thousands of operators are no longer needed. As AT&T and other companies make use of the internet, customers can now find information and transact business without the intermediation of salespeople or consultants.

Penny, an AT&T service technician, exemplifies the transformation of work in the current economy. When Maccoby interviewed her in 1994 she held an occupational position, represented by the union—yet she controlled a fifty-million dollar corporate account. The customer did not want to deal with managers; they invited Penny to their corporate meetings. When asked if she was able to service all the telecommunication needs of her customer, Penny said she felt competent about voice questions, but when there were data problems, she asked for help—not from her superiors, but from her co-worker, Ann.

Employees like Penny put pressure on both management and unions. Their attitudes and expectations are very different from the older "bureaucratic" mindset. They expect management to support them and give them responsibility and chances for meaningful contributions. They expect unions to allow them to work flexibly and not hold them to rigid work rules. Furthermore, seniority rules can get in the way of their career development. These employees see themselves as empowered not by management or union protections but by their relation to the customer. At AT&T's Solutions company, where technicians work interactively in a "co-production" relation with customers, the executives fought to keep out the union in part, at least, because they were concerned that major customers, particularly in financial services, did not want unionized workers on their premises who might try to organize workers.

The difficulty of these changes for management is obvious: how to maintain accountability and control while encouraging empowerment and participation. This involves skills different from those of traditional managers, and also a new set of organizational systems—training, team-building, and so on. For unions the problems are less obvious but no less fundamental. The strategy of industrial unionism was based on the centralized contract: creating a single clear "platform" which could be easily enforced and which became the basis for constant extension at each round of bargaining. In the core industries of the old order— auto, steel, and mining—there has been tremendous pressure to move away from centralized and uniform contracts and to allow more local variation. The unions see this as threatening to their power by enabling management "whipsawing" of one plant against another; but few unions have been able to resist the pressure.

At EDF the skilled workers like Penny belong to CFDT, the union most interested in cooperating in the workplace. These skilled workers feel secure about their jobs. The less skilled workers who are most afraid that their jobs will be eliminated by automation belong to CGT, which has been up until recently uncooperative.

Co-production and stakeholder involvement: evidence from our cases
The need to work interactively with many groups—rather than through the arms'-length mechanism of the market or the controlling mechanism of hierarchy—is more than theory: we see it played out vividly in each of our four core cases:

(1) At Ferrovie dello Stato (FS), the intervention focused on understanding the strategic challenges; so we have an especially clear picture of how EU-required competition demanded changed forms of interaction with a wide array of stakeholders. FS was accustomed to some of these, such as the State and the trade unions; others, such as EU policy makers or other European railways, it discovered or re-discovered. As the context changed, however, the overall architecture of relations as had existed was challenged. Some important modifications were obtained. The number of employees was decreased by some 100,000, and the several hundred union negotiations reduced to about 30. But the existing system of relations fought hard against change, and old work rules and traditions continued to hobble the strategists' vision of a dramatic shift in focus.

(2) Electricité de France (EDF) faced many of the same challenges. Until the 1980s customers were rarely seen as significant: they were viewed as users of a public service. At the end of the 1970s work conflicts led to blackouts; shopkeepers and small business leaders showed their displeasure by hurling

eggs and tomatoes at the generators. Faced with this aroused customer base, the unions agreed never to cut power again, and a thorough soul-searching and policy review was undertaken with the aim of improving service. This had some beneficial results during the 1980s. The next event, starting in the 1980s, was a challenge to the monopoly, as large industrial customers gained the capability of buying power from other providers. Gradually EDF had to face an environment with much more active and differentiated stakeholders. In addition to different customer bases, local communities became concerned in the 1970s about the growth of nuclear power plants; the company had to find ways to win their support as well.

(3) AT&T, at the start of our interventions in the late 1970s, was still a monopoly. It sought to improve morale and relations, but within the traditional framework of the paternalistic system. Employees were the first stakeholder group to develop post-industrial issues, launching demonstrations in the late 1970s aimed at relieving "job pressures" caused by tight control. Around the same time customers began to seek more than "basic black" telephones and "plain old telephone service." As the company was broken into smaller pieces, the customer demands proliferated. Furthermore, decisions that had previously been made internally, such as the subsidization of local telephone service from long-distance revenue, were suddenly "uncovered" by market pressures and thrown into the political arena. The 1980s and 1990s were a long period of furious stakeholder claims and counterclaims, working through the courts and the legislators, about which aspects of phone service were public rights and which were customer choices. AT&T was often hampered by its clumsiness in dealing with these conflicting claims. At the present time, AT&T sees its future in providing business with full voice and data solutions. This requires partnering with both the customer and other providers.

(4) At Lucent the issue has become clear as it has moved, like most of its competitors, from a product-based toward a solutions-based strategy. Western Electric and Bell Labs, the original pieces of Lucent, were internally driven organizations. Neither stopped very often to ask what the customers wanted; both put engineering criteria—manufacturing quality, cost, and elegance—at the top of their priorities. It became clear within a few years of the company's birth, however, that the traditional strategy would not work: the best products made in the best way would not provide the margins demanded by the industry. What was needed was the ability to provide solutions to complex problems brought to them by the customers, and services that kept the solutions functioning and in tune with the demands. This brought to the fore new relationships. Internally, installers and maintenance workers—who had been an afterthought in the old system—suddenly became a dominant force in the success of the company. Externally, the company needed to be able to respond to changing value creating logics by constantly finding new allies who could provide skills

and products that it lacked for given problems. When the internal focus of the company led to serious misestimation of the optical switch markets, Lucent entered a period of severe crisis. The fact that the unions, because of their members' close relation to customers, had been largely right on the issue helped make the point that the company needed to enter into dialogue with more parties, rather than assuming that it could direct its business through traditional bureaucratic commands.

Stakeholders and democratic values

We have focused our stakeholder argument on the needs of business, because in the recent era which has shaped our understandings, it is counter-intuitive to claim that a business will do better by engaging stakeholders than by carrying the flag of change on its own. But this is only one part of the picture: it is also import- ant to emphasize that stakeholders are needed because they are a foundation of democracy, as a way of representing values *other* than those of business growth. It is sometimes easy to forget that economic values are not the only ones, that all these societies have long traditions emphasizing liberty, equality of opportunity, and patriotic commitment. While these values sometimes coincide with business growth, they can conflict; and at those times societies must have ways to resolve the conflict and make choices. Over time mechanisms have been created, from conflict and political debate, to incorporate the core groups and values of each period—culminating in the most recent period with the neo-corporatist structure we have described.

Some managers and political theorists adopt, implicitly or explicitly, the con- trary notion that business leaders can, and even should, represent all values and find the fairest solutions—that they can take responsibility for the needs of their employees and the well-being of communities as well as of stockholders. This view, which we have elsewhere called "managerialism,"[17] has been attractive to rulers at all times: they can claim to rise above the particular interests of their subjects and to represent the greater good.

If managerialism really worked, it would be much simpler than a true stake- holder model. We have seen throughout this book how messy and difficult the lat- ter can be, and how easily it can lead to mutually destructive circles of mistrust. Reconciling differences within the head of a single leader is certainly easier than fighting it out in the unpredictable arena of politics. But the fact is that manager- ialism, like all forms of paternalism, does *not* work to effectively reconcile diverse values. The modern state is in fact based on the experience that kings, for all their claims to benevolence, failed to represent the people, and the people wanted to take a direct hand in matters. And there is continual evidence in our own work that management, even at its best, has great difficulty in really understanding the per- spectives of blue-collar workers or other stakeholders—even other groups within management—and overestimates its own capacity to reconcile differences. This is, very simply, a human limitation, and no way has been found to overcome it other than through confrontation among diverse viewpoints fighting it out on an equal plane.

Peter Drucker, the senior guru of management thinkers over the last half-century, states the case with characteristic force:

The important fact about "enlightened despotism"—also the one fact that 'enlightened despots' always forget—is that while it appears as enlightenment to those in power, it is despotism pure and simple to those under it. (Drucker, 1969: p. 69)

Thus as interveners we believe in the importance of developing an effective framework of stakeholder representation not only because it is needed for business success—though there is strong evidence for the truth of this counterintuitive argument—but also because it is necessary for a healthy society and for the advancement of the core values of human development and liberty.

OBSTACLES TO INTERACTIVITY: THE PROBLEM OF TRANSFORMING STAKEHOLDER REGIMES

If we accept, then, that more rather than less cooperation and interaction with stakeholders is needed to secure governability, the question remains: How? The fact that dialogue is *needed* is not enough to ensure that it can happen. In fact, historically every major economic transition has been marked by serious conflict before new stakeholder relations are established. The construction of a successful system is difficult: this is the core of both our achievements and our limitations as interveners. Effective stakeholder dialogue builds constructive tensions that can produce benefits for all parties, even though each party *thinks* it could do better on its own. But when it does not work, it can quickly degenerate into mutual destruction or gridlock.[18]

The problems are particularly serious during periods of major change. This is because stakeholder systems in such periods are by their nature prone to the ills of conservatism, narrowness, and instability.

Existing stakeholder agreements and actors: conservatism and resistance to change

Any stakeholder regime is based on compromises among different points of view. It aims to increase understanding and to build agreements, but the underlying differences in values remain: the parties see the world from different perspectives. Thus agreements inevitably have a kind of concrete character, as solutions to particular problems. But then, because the parties do not want to keep fighting over and over again, these agreements reached for very particular reasons tend to become accepted as permanent bedrock, assumptions that are not put into question for fear of starting the fights all over again. Further negotiations tend to work at the margins, probing the frontiers rather than revisiting the foundations. The shared history of the parties becomes a stabilizing framework limiting open conflict.

In the case of the labor–management compromise, there were fierce battles throughout the 1930s and 1940s over the boundaries of management prerogatives and worker rights. The outcome was different in various settings. In the US, for instance, unions largely managed to win limits on work speed and overtime; in Northern Europe unions largely ceded the shopfloor but were more successful in asserting demands at the strategic level. In each case the issues that were the center of these historical fights have become sacred and immutable; changes in these agreements are seen as threatening the very identities of the parties.

Once the basic agreements get worked out, the parties gain an increasing interest in keeping the core as it is, merely pushing at the boundaries. Unions today, as we have noted, are often explicit about this: they want to build on past gains, past contracts, past relationships. Paradoxically enough, unions—particularly industrial unions—want corporations to be protected because they have come to depend on them as the dispensers not only of economic security but also of social identity; they favor the paternalism created in the 1950s. The same is true, though less visibly, of middle managers: most are willing to work harder and make sacrifices for the company's success, but they do not accept the qualitative shift asked of them—the move away from lifetime security, the demands for flexibility and entrepreneurship.[19] The shared history of implicit and explicit agreements, which in the prior era helped keep things running smoothly and productively, now becomes an obstacle to change.

The weaker actors become particularly "locked in" because they have the most to lose by reopening the agreements. They have fought in the past to gain a voice, a foothold of influence, and they are always afraid of losing it. They see change not as an opportunity to explore new possibilities but as threats to their role. Labor unions in the countries we have worked in are almost universally caught in this conservative dynamic. They have been through their period of establishing, in bitter and often bloody fights, their right to sit at the table as management's interlocutor. For the last 50 years or so they have held that position, battling step by step for gains in wages and working conditions. The legacy of the past and management's unwillingness to reopen old battles—which sometimes become embodied in stabilizing legislation—are the unions' sources of security. So when faced with a radically altered situation like Reaganite or Thatcherite government policy, in which management *does* ask that everything be reopened in the name of market flexibility, they are profoundly threatened.

These are enormous problems for the unions we have worked with, and it is far from clear after two decades of effort that they are capable of adapting to the new form of production. The list of blockages is long, and applies almost without distinction across the industrialized world. Unions have remained fundamentally ambivalent and ineffective in dealing with the widespread move toward employee participation and teams. They have been almost entirely unable to appeal to the growing cadre of part-time, independent, contract, and other types of workers outside the pattern of full-time secure jobs. They have nowhere penetrated deeply into new economic sectors of microchip and biochemical production, or into knowledge work such as consulting and research. They have been unable to build lasting alliances with the emerging set of "new" stakeholder groups with political influence: ethnic and gender groups, single-issue organizations ranging from environment to abortion to community associations and consumer advocates.[20]

The problem of globalization has only more recently become a focus of union attention, but there is already evidence of the same kind of fundamental difficulty in adapting to larger changes. Many labor groups have begun to speak of the need for increased solidarity across national borders, but (again with a few exceptions) they have made little progress. The traditional strategy of unionism is based on bringing together all workers in an industry in order to "take labor out of competition"; unified strikes across the industry are the main weapon. As one crosses national borders this kind of unity becomes well-nigh impossible to maintain. The obstacles to coordinated action are many.

- Individual unions are built on many dimensions to encircle and protect particular territories. The most powerful initial reaction everywhere is to try to build protective barriers around national markets, thus hanging on to the power base of the past. This strategy only alienates them from unions in other countries.
- Unions depend ultimately on the solidarity of their members, especially on their willingness to make sacrifices for the collective good during strikes and job actions. That kind of social solidarity is almost impossible to extend across national borders. Auto workers at Ford in the US may get emotional about their American brothers and sisters at Chrysler or GM, but they have trouble identifying with Ford workers in Malaysia.[21]
- There is a basic split—in wages, health and safety conditions, job security, and working conditions—between the developed and developing nations which undermines unified action. Those labor bodies in developed societies that have begun to act on globalization tend to seek labor protections in international trade treaties. But unions in the developing world usually oppose these protections because their members' security is based on their willingness to accept lower wages and less restrictive working conditions than their "Western" brethren.

These problems are deeply rooted in many aspects of union structure and culture. Efforts to overcome them have been isolated and successes few.

Certain problems are also more specific to particular countries. US unions, though relatively well-organized, are weak in their ability to analyze and mobilize around strategic issues; French unions are weak in their ability to work together even within the national scene; Italian unions are highly fractured. These obstacles are less salient in Scandinavia and Germany, where the long experience of codetermination has built much more capacity.

The four basic obstacles we have sketched, however—conflict between the traditional centralized contract and the new demands for decentralized employee participation; the conflict between demands for labor-market flexibility and unions' overwhelming commitment to job security; tensions with emergent stakeholder groups; and inability to transcend national solidarities—characterize unions in all the countries where we have worked, including those in Scandinavia.[22] Whatever differences exist between national systems, none are in a position to respond to the demands of a post-industrial society merely by extending and refining their existing approaches. Some sort of discontinuous and dramatic shift is required.

Emerging stakeholder groups: narrowness and instability

Periods of change also produce another dynamic that can be even more destructive: *new* interests emerge, not represented within the old system, crucial to the emerging order and demanding recognition of their issues. But such groups naturally have trouble at first in formulating their interests broadly, as a contibution to the whole; they can only push hard for what *they* value and need. Thus they necessarily seem narrow in relation to the established order. Moreover, they are starting from the beginning, lacking the stabilizing framework of past compromises. Thus they drift into the dynamic of push and counter-push, spiraling into outright battles when the parties need to test each other's strength.

The US environmental movement is a good case of such narrowness. A mature movement would be one that would participate in building a society that would foster economic production and worker prosperity at the same time as protecting the environment. There are a few flickers of such a vision in proposals for "sustainable development," but these have not translated yet into organizations and systems that can work toward that end.[23] For the most part, environmental groups focus ferociously on their one concern. The inability to form alliances with unions is partly due to union traditions, as we just saw, but part of the responsibility also falls on the single-mindedness of environmental advocates who too often dismiss business and worker concerns. There have been many attempts to build stable "mutual-gains" systems of negotiation among these groups, local communities, and businesses; while some have had initial success, few to our knowledge have produced stable frameworks for ongoing relations; they often disintegrate quickly into mistrust.

The problem is exacerbated by the competition for legitimacy among the emerging groups. There is not just one environmental federation to deal with, but many with different strategies and approaches, with new ones appearing all the time. The same is true for other cases: local communities, ethnic minorities, or consumer groups rarely speak with one voice even within each category, to say nothing of across categories. Even if business wants to initiate a stakeholder dialogue—even if they bring us in as interveners to help them do so—it is difficult at this stage to identify a set of interlocutors with the legitimacy to reach stable agreements.[24]

These obstacles are different in kind from those we identified around the "old" stakeholders. The latter come from the stability of a long-established system and are supported by many interconnected dimensions of habits, skills, values, and solidarities. The problems of the "new" stakeholders, by contrast, are the result of a *lack* of systemic connections; they represent growing pains of an unformed system. We can observe this trajectory historically. Unions today are locked into the neo-corporatist order, as we have seen; but in the 1930s they showed the same "immaturity" as many emerging groups today. They took a wide variety of positions, some extremely radical, others extremely particularistic. They were organizationally weak, often unable to make agreements that their members would stick to. They fought with each other over jurisdiction and strategy. In the US it took government intervention in the form of the Wagner Act of 1935 to overcome internecine battles, and it took years before the basic patterns of collective bargaining and grievance handling, and arbitration were widely institutionalized. Today unions (and some other established groups) are on the other side of the fence, battling to protect their position long established in the old order, while at the same time emerging groups are seeking to gain a voice in the new.

From the point of view of management and other advocates of liberalization *all* of these groups, old and new, get in the way of needed change. Their response has generally been to deny the relevance of stakeholder groups entirely. They would clearly like unions to disappear; those among them who think about values (rather than simple self-interest) believe that without unions they would be able to create a new world of entrepreneurship that would be better for employees than the stuck-in-the-mud, seniority-based, merit-denying systems held onto by unions. They feel the zeal of the revolutionaries—these "conservatives" are radical, and they feel the revolutionary's contempt for those who stand in their way. From the perspective of the existing stakeholder groups, of course, things look quite different: management appears as heartless, cold, inhumane mercenaries at the service of anonymous investors, and they themselves are the guardians of larger values of community and caring.

THE CURRENT IMPASSE

The current situation has undone the overlap in interests that made possible the neo-corporatist compromise. Managers saw an advantage in loyalty and stability; they were willing to accept the costs of implicit lifetime careers, high internal training costs, good benefits—even the costs of unionization or of government regulation—in order to guarantee stable and reliable workforces and predictable markets. Thus, though they might grumble at the cost and try to reduce it, they were willing to enter into deals—explicit and implicit—based on a trade of loyalty for security. This left a "win–win" space in which consultants like us could maneuver to create cooperation and involvement.

Today managers are for the most part no longer willing to make that tradeoff. Hard and soft factors conspire against it: the cold eye of global financial markets scrutinizes the costs involved, and the revolutionary values of entrepreneurial individualism fire their imaginations. The space for compromise has largely disappeared. This is the core lesson of the troubles we have run into in our work: we are often successful in building healthy relationships when there is an overlap of values, but we have found ourselves being pushed beyond the limits of that overlap.

As interveners, therefore, our problem is that we can no longer call on enough shared commitment to construct stable agreements. As the neo-corporatist compromise breaks down, the danger of unmanageable conflict grows. At least two types of "out-of-control" disputes can be seen developing today. The less dramatic, though very important, is the explosive growth of litigation, driven by new stakeholder types such as women, minorities, the disabled, and environmentalists. Whereas collective bargaining was bounded and played with clear rules, this new form of attack on corporate prerogatives seems unpredictable and often more deeply threatening; most HR managers are more worried about being sued than about strikes or organizing drives. The government is struggling to define a new role for itself in managing the emergent claims, but so far has succeeded largely in making things more confusing and inconsistent. In an American world where someone who accidentally spills hot coffee on herself can win millions of dollars from a large corporation—but someone fired on personal whims generally has no recourse—the governmental role seems increasingly uncoordinated.

The second and even more uncontrolled manifestation of the breakdown of the neo-corporatist framework is, of course, the battle against globalizing organizations, such as multinationals or the World Bank and the IMF, which has recently produced violent conflicts in post-industrial societies. This is in fact a confluence of the two kinds of stakeholder breakdown. The old groups—especially labor unions—are battling to protect the national frameworks within which they were able for half a century to negotiate successful contracts. For them the change toward globalization is almost unequivocally bad because it destroys the basis of their power. But other groups like environmentalists and third-world countries are not opposed to globalization, and many actively support it; they are simply demanding recognition of their issues within it. It is a volatile mix, with practically no grounds for agreement or stabilizing framework, and it seems to be spiraling toward greater conflict rather than reconciliation.

When stakeholder regimes work they contribute simultaneously to business success, to economic productivity, and to other societal values represented through the democratic process. The breakdown of the regime threatens to produce a lose–lose cycle in which all of these are undermined.

12

Toward Post-industrial Relations

Following through on the action orientation of this book, our final problem is: What can we do to help in the creation of a new stakeholder regime for a post-industrial society?

Stakeholder regimes are defined by three basic considerations: the participating actors, the rules for their interactions and decisions, and the common ground joining them and which they seek to enhance. In the neo-corporatist order, participants were restricted to unions, management, and government; decisions were a mix of centralized collective bargaining and government regulation; the common ground was the pattern of stable corporate employment. Now many other participants are pressing their claims, while the legitimacy of unions and government—and in many parts of the world, large companies—is under attack. Collective bargaining and regulation as decision-methods are also increasingly heavily criticized. And corporations feel they can no longer take on the paternalist burdens of employment security and extensive benefits.

The challenge to the neo-corporatist order is to include a wider range of groups; to rely less on rules fixed for a period of time and be more open to continuous negotiation and dialogue; and to be more flexible in dealing with individual variations and changing circumstances. How could such an alternative be constructed? To pose this question is to see how far we are from success. It also shows the importance which a "strategic" value co-production approach can have to recast labor–management relations in a post-industrial context.

ACTORS: EMERGING STAKEHOLDER GROUPS

It is impossible to decide *a priori* what actors should be involved in dialogue. Freeman, who first proposed the stakeholder approach in management, defined stakeholders as "any group or individual who can affect, or is affected by, the achievement of a corporation's purpose" (1984: vi). If one took that view seriously, it would lead straight to a mess. Should middle managers be included?

If so, should they be treated as a single group or as multiple sub-groups, and how would one justify a choice? What about minorities and women, religious groups, political associations? Should blacks and Latinos each have their own representation? Catholics? Black women? Black Catholic women? And local communities: should there be a voice for every town, state, and nation the company operates in? How about environmental groups? Consumer groups? And for any of these which is involved, how would legitimate representatives be chosen from among the myriad possible claimants?

Such problems may lead one to despair of the possibility of a rational approach. Yet historically stakeholder regimes have actually been constructed, and we can learn from those examples something about how it is done. The lesson in brief is that they have been constructed not by theoretical analysis of who "should" be part of them, but rather by conflicts in which some parties successfully pushed their way into the decision-making system.

Stakeholders attain their place in a system by showing enough disruptive power to convince businesses that they cannot be ignored, and by appealing to broad social values that attract political support. The modern labor movement is based on both these foundations. They attained their privileged position as accepted stakeholders first by demonstrating, in bitter and sometimes bloody battles, that management could not destroy them. Then they also convinced the public that they contributed to the general good. Here the key arguments were that unions boosted economic growth by raising purchasing power, and that they furthered widely-accepted notions of workplace rights.[1]

The question for the post-industrial phase, then, is: What groups may be able to attain the power and legitimacy to elbow their way into the system? The question is as hard to answer now as it would have been, in 1900, to guess what type of labor movement would evolve and which organizations would gain power. We can observe that some parties have already built a track record that gives them some stability and stable voice in corporate decision-making. A few key women's organizations in the US, such as NOW, are regular interlocutors around many workplace issues; the consumer movement has become something that businesses do not forget, though its organizations are not as developed; environmental groups are beginning to have a significant impact in most industrialized countries, though they remain organizationally even more fragmented and unstable than consumer associations.

None of these actors is now fully established, widely accepted, or integrated into a reliable system of decision-making of the type that collective bargaining became at its height. But those three at least have "pushed" a fair way and seem like likely candidates, when the dust settles, for a regularized role. Many large businesses, for example Shell and EDF, especially in the arena of environmentalism and "sustainable development"; Mitsubishi, in the diversity arena, have begun to explore the notion that they would do better to have regularized relations with key groups than to try to fight battles on many fronts. The final choice of actors will depend not on analysis but on concrete outcomes of conflicts.

PROCESS: INTERACTIVE DECISION-MAKING

Two dominant, and quite different, but highly complementary decision-making processes shape the neo-corporatist order: collective bargaining and government regulation. The former is an adversarial contest founded on a balance of power, with discussions based heavily on concealment, posturing, and bluffing. The latter is generally a bureaucratic process of gathering information into a hierarchy and issuing binding rules, with no genuine stakeholder discussion at all.

Both these processes have been criticized on an increasingly widespread basis for producing narrowly rule-based resolutions. Rather than developing ongoing consensus, they achieve—albeit by different means—concrete compromises embodied in highly detailed contracts and substantive rights. Until the 1970s these codes were seen as reassuringly stable and protective; since then they have increasingly been seen as restrictive, holding back individual initiative and blocking responsiveness to change.[2] In the US the criticism developed early and has become politically dominant; in Europe the trend is more recent and still controversial, but directionally similar.

The intensity of the changes that enterprises are undergoing today brings the rules of process to the foreground. Rather than "locking in" rules for the division of wealth, the problem is to develop processes of intersubjective understanding between the different stakeholders, defining the meta-rules that govern the interaction of the parties—principles of action for resolving the problems which they face.[3]

The last two or three decades have been a period of intensive experimentation and invention of processes aimed at achieving consensus through continuing dialogue, with the parties treated as equals. Though the roots can be traced far back, one can see around 1980 a takeoff in efforts to create direct dialogues and to "work out" consensus, as opposed to the older methods of adversarial bargaining and regulation.[4] When the newer methods work, they lead to shared principles and visions rather than detailed rule books, and it is these principles that frame continuing collaboration. Thus they overcome the exclusiveness and rigidity that have been so criticized in neo-corporatism.

Unfortunately, we should hasten to add, consensus-based methods do not always work—not by a long shot. We have used many of these approaches and techniques, but there is still more art than routine to applying them. We believe, as we have outlined in Chapters 7–9, that most of these dialogic approaches have been weakened by a tendency to excessive rationalism which leaves out critical dynamics of identity and transference; and that by adding these we do somewhat better in difficult cases. Yet we have not found that *any* method of dialogue can, in the difficult transitions we have focused on, create agreement and harmony. The path is a more indirect one.

What the advances in methods of dialogue *do* tell us is that there is more of an opportunity than in the past to create flexible and ongoing discussions among multiple groups. Though we cannot move to it in a straight line, the outlines are emerging of a new stakeholder system—less stable but more resilient, with decision-making based on these approaches, which can therefore include more parties and respond to change more rapidly than the neo-corporatist order.

THE DEVELOPMENT OF STAKEHOLDER REGIMES

We have suggested that the transition between stakeholder systems is not a straight-line matter: one cannot go from the old to an improved new order without intervening turbulence.

There are a number of possible routes. Most managers these days would like to move to a system without stakeholders, or at least passive or even co-opted stakeholders with only an advisory function, which would seem to make their lives a great deal easier. We have argued, however, that the growing assertiveness of many new stakeholder groups, and the increasing dependence of business on the active support of knowledge workers, makes this "managerialist" approach an unstable—and therefore an unviable—one. At best businesses will move back onto the turbulent route of trying to work out relationships with the social groups on which they depend; at worst this approach, by trying to deny other forces, will prevent the creation of relationships and lead into a spiral of unregulated conflict.

The seemingly ideal route (the top arrow in Figure 12.1, below), moving directly and rationally from the old tripartite system to a more inclusive and flexible one, is blocked by several obstacles. First, old stakeholders resist yielding their privileged position in the existing order and fear that they may have to redefine fundamental aspects of their identities and values. It seems likely, for example, that in a knowledge economy that requires continuing education and career development, unions will need to deal with basic changes to their "sacred" and universal principles of seniority and job security.[5] Whether they can do so without disintegrating is still an open question.

Second, new stakeholders need to mature. As we have suggested, before new groups gain a stable position in a new system of regulation they either need to begin narrowly, pushing an agenda based purely on a particular interest; or, if their ideology is broad, it outstrips their organizational capabilities, producing instability, factionalism, and frequent lack of realism. The capacity to mobilize a membership while gaining needed support from the wider society, and putting it all together in an organization that works, is one that must be built slowly.

Third, discussion and decision-making processes remain to be constructed. The parties need to create reliable forums of some kind in which they can meet and work through disagreements. The existing rules of bargaining at the enterprise and national levels need considerable modification to allow greater flexibility and inclusion.

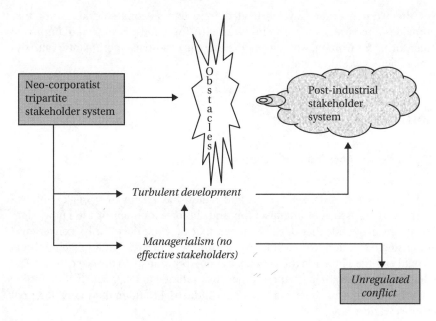

Fig. 12.1. Paths toward a new stakeholder regime.

A final obstacle to smooth transition is that management and social sciences are not up to the task of *designing* a system that can simply be "applied," as a new design might be applied in architecture. People need to learn, adjust, and try things out; and when the change is large and complex this can be long and difficult. In this case there is much we do not know about building consensus, and about where it is and is not really feasible. In theory it often seems that dialogue is an ideal method of decision-making, but it is in practice, where it has many shortcomings, that it will need to be worked out by trial, with lots of error.[6]

Since the direct path of rational design is so blocked, there is only one workable route forward: that of turbulent development, in which these processes of change and learning proceed unevenly and with much conflict as the parties try to establish new roles and relationships.[7]

There are a few cases that suggest how over time this development can happen. The modern women's movement, for example, has come a long way as a stakeholder force. Thirty years ago it was marked by the same narrowness of focus that the environmental movement often exhibits today, and businesses largely reacted with similarly constricted vision. But in the intervening time some of the main women's institutions, such as NOW, have gained greatly in stability and legitimacy and have become regular partners with large corporations in trying to improve relations with their female employees. Starting from opposed visions—pure meritocracy on the business side, strong affirmative action on that of the women—they have struggled toward a negotiated framework that provides increased support and flexibility for child-rearing, and improved mentoring for women, while strengthening the essentially meritocratic values of the business world.[8]

BUILDING THE FUTURE

The variety of post-industrial routes

While every industrialized nation and region has begun to struggle with the same general issues of liberalization and the development of the knowledge-solutions economy, that does not mean that they are necessarily "converging" on a single solution. One would expect, on the contrary, that a range of orders would emerge, similar to the varieties of neo-corporatism in the last century. The diagram put forward in Chapter 11 must be modified to reflect the fact that there is not one arrow moving toward the post-industrial frontier, but many potential routes (Figure 12.2).

And indeed a number of different approaches have begun to emerge. On one end, the US's ideology has stressed free markets—yet regulatory controls and interest-group pressures have often emerged in new forms. On the other, the strong resistance in France and Germany to changes in their established institutions, and a determined attempt to work out new agreements that encourage

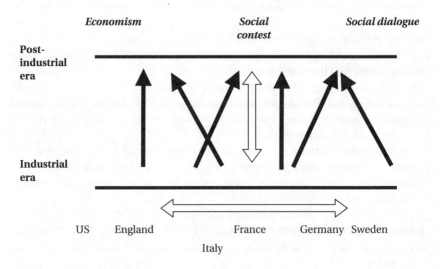

Fig. 12.2. Post-industrial choices.

new levels of competitiveness without changing the basic framework. This array constitutes, as it were, a range of experiments that can help us better understand the effects of different routes.

(1) Sweden, for example, an area outside the direct scope of this book, but one where several of us have worked, has traditionally been seen as an exemplar of low entrepreneurship/high regulation. Yet in the past decade there had been a substantial shift toward an embracing of mobility and dynamic change. Although large companies like Volvo, Ericsson and ABB still dominate Swedish industry, government policy has begun to encourage start-ups by loosening regulations and offering entrepreneurs capital rather than unemployment salaries. Over 80 percent of Swedish employees belong to unions and union leaders represent their members on company boards. There is a continual stakeholder dialogue about combining profitability with a fair distribution of profits and protection of the environment. However, union participation in management of the type achieved in WPoF is still rare. When Maccoby met with company leaders at a meeting organized by the employers' organization in 2000, the employers saw unions as basically reactive and adversarial, although accepting of needs to improve profits as long as the workers got their share and redundant workers were protected by the national safety net. In his work with Swedbank, Maccoby was able to get management to develop a version of WPoF called "the handshake," and the union leader for the bank was brought into the top management decision-making process.

(2) The US, conversely, is not moving unambiguously to the slot of high entrepreneurship/low regulation. Although the trade union movement has severely declined, there has been a corresponding rise—unmatched in other Western countries—in rights for individuals and minorities: ethnic groups, women, gays, religions, and many other categories have gained legal protection over the last three decades. Many associations, pressure groups, affinity groups, support groups have developed to lobby for these rights and encourage people to assert them. Thus as companies have celebrated the reduced danger of strikes, they have been surprised to face an increased danger of lawsuits.

(3) Italy suggests the possibility of a less centralized model. Its economy is based more on family-owned businesses than other industrialized countries; some have argued that this gives Italy greater adaptiveness in a period of rapid change. Parts of Italy also show the power of what Putnam has termed "high social capital," in the form of strong local communities and decentralized stakeholder engagements.[9]

(4) France has rejected fundamental reforms in the role of the state, in pensions, and in labor flexibility; the dramatic conflicts of 1995 have paralyzed successive governments. The question now is whether, given the rising strength of the extreme right manifested in the election of 2002, the nation

can find the basis for compromises with the forces of globalization. The center-right government that came to power in 2002 has begun more serious attempts at social dialogue than its predecessors.

(5) At the European Community level, efforts have gathered steam towards clearer definition and regulation of social responsibility. A white paper issued in 2002 has put the issue once again on the front burner, casting Europe very much in the role of seeking an alternative to the American market approach.

The vision of a possible post-industrial stakeholder order thus remains very indistinct: the possibilities are numerous. It is quite possible that it will include elements that have historically been seen as incompatible: high mobility and change, strong employee associations, a governmental role as convener and guardian of principles—combining elements of Scandinavian, French, US, and Italian patterns. The current problem, in other words, is not the implementation of a model, but the discovery or invention of a path that will resolve the tensions created by the decline of the neo-corporatist regime.[10]

Intervention as exploration and experimentation

If the transition experienced by the organizations we work with is as complex as what we have just described, involving the de-construction of old stakeholders, the construction of new ones, and the invention of modes of interaction, then the role of an intervener is also more complex than getting everyone to sit down and talk rationally. It is clearly impossible to avoid conflict. The new order can only be constructed through conflict that establishes the strength of the claimant stakeholders and "forces" management to pay attention to them. It may, however, be possible to make this transition easier by helping parties to learn more from the battles and to develop more quickly through reflection, thus making conflicts less brutal and avoiding the dangers of mutually destructive spirals of mistrust.

The work of intervention in such a situation moves even further from an expert role. In most of our work up to the present we have had to some degree a clearer vision of the future than our clients: we have been more familiar with other models, more experienced in creating strategies or labor–management dialogue. Though there is never a predetermined "right answer," and the client has to develop its own direction and capacities, we bring some sense of what skills are needed. But as we move out onto the edge of social transition that we have explored in this chapter, our vision is not much clearer than our clients'. We have at best a "fuzzy vision" largely based on our values as well as our analysis of social development; all we can do is to find leaders who share the vision and who would like help as they explore possible paths.

The nature of this sort of change, where models are non-existent, is necessarily one of experimentation: organizations have to try things and reflect efficiently on the results so as to guide further action. The consultant in this situation is nothing more than a colleague who brings certain perspectives and disciplinary skills. Scientists gain tremendously by opening their preliminary findings to scrutiny in conferences and journals, but actors in stakeholder relations, such as managers or unions, cannot be so open; they still need to preserve their negotiating space. A consultant in this situation can act in a sense as an outside "reviewer" to help review the lessons of ongoing efforts and to generate new ideas.[11]

We have said that the problem of reconstructing stakeholder systems has three facets: the reorientation of existing stakeholders; the development of new stakeholders; and the creation of mechanisms for these parties to relate to each other and reach stable agreements. There is a role in each of these for outside interveners as follows.

(1) There is still much to be done with the stakeholder groups that anchored the neo-corporatist order—unions, companies, and government. Each of these needs to gain a vantage point for seeing the transformations going on around it—to face the fact that the old order is crumbling and to consider alternative courses of action.

The first task is to help them to *broaden* their view of their interests. The old stakeholder order forced management, for example, to take into account the interests of unions; but it did not force them to consider the interests of environmental or consumer or women's groups. The latter are in the process of trying to "push" their way into the decision-making process. Management's first reaction is typically to resist these incursions. But such resistance only increases the chance for more severe conflict. It is helpful to all parties if management thinks this through, using the "co-production" logic sketched above, and recognizing real interdependencies—what groups it needs in order to succeed, and what groups could block its progress. If companies, based on such an analysis, deal proactively rather than reactively to the emergent interests, there is a far greater chance of an effective "working through" of conflict rather than a destructive spiral of mistrust.

Similarly, unions have tended to focus on their traditional definitions of their task: preserving member jobs, protecting seniority, raising wages. They have been forced onto the defensive by growing evidence that many members and potential members are no longer focused on those issues, and that raising wages can in some situations be harmful rather than helpful. Again, it is a painful but necessary process for unions to broaden their perspective so that they can push for those goals when appropriate, but can also take other paths: encouraging training for job mobility, recognizing individual performance, accepting lower direct compensation when the situation demands it.

Outside interveners can help the parties to analyze their interdependencies—what groups have real power to affect them. Based on that, they can help to build bridges to those other parties and to increase the level of understanding. Finally, they can help focus all the parties on the issue of how to build a system that will reflect the differences in interest in the least damaging way—not by reducing conflict, but by channeling it into regularized discussions and negotiations which reduce the risk of uncontrolled conflict.

(2) Emerging stakeholder groups, as discussed above, are necessarily "immature" in organization and strategy. They often act before they have the organizational capacity to sustain the action; they may miss strategic opportunities; they may focus on too narrow a set of issues; they may fail to establish connections to potential allies. Interveners can help in the development of new stakeholders so that they can play an effective role in the new stakeholder regime.

(3) Finally, the mechanisms for bringing the stakeholders together still need to be invented. Collective bargaining and political regulation, the main mechanisms of the neo-corporatist order, took many years to build and institutionalize. We are scarcely at the beginning of understanding how to set up constructive ways of resolving the conflicts in the emerging order. If we are to shorten the learning curve and avoid unnecessary disruption, it is necessary to convene conversations about the future that involve a wider stakeholder swath: national government, the educational system, other employee associations, local communities, peak associations of employers and labor. From this conversation the emergent vision should become clearer, and it will also be clearer who can participate effectively in building it.

As we have faced the limitations of our own work (analyzed in Chapter 10), we have each in our own way begun to explore these paths at the frontier of a new stakeholder order. Tixier and Ramirez have been working mostly with existing stakeholders—unions and management—to broaden their view of their interests, to recognize interdependencies, and to think ahead about how to manage them. Heckscher has helped start a "new stakeholder" group representing types of employees not fully included in the traditional system. And Maccoby, in some of his work, has begun to explore frameworks for bringing together new configurations of stakeholders for problems that do not "fit" the old order.

Stakeholder scenario-based strategic planning at Shell
One development that could further a new stakeholder order is the growing awareness of some corporations of the need to be proactive in dealing with outside groups. The notion that corporate strategy depends on collaboration with stakeholder groups has become increasingly compelling as managers see the huge costs of public relations disasters like the Exxon Valdez spill or the charges of racism at Texaco. In recent years a few multinationals that have to deal with many constituencies, such as human rights groups and environmentalists, have developed specialized departments to constructively engage with such stakeholders.

Ramirez has taken a position working as "Visiting Professor Of Scenarios And Corporate Strategy" in Shell International's "Global Business Environment" unit in London, for 2 years (2000–2002). This position has allowed him to engage with issues of stakeholder relations in the context of plausible futures for Shell. While in order to obtain "licenses to operate" in 140 countries Shell has had a long track record of fairly satisfactory relations with diverse stakeholders, it was awakened from complacency by the public outrage, orchestrated by Greenpeace, over its proposed Brent Spar (North Sea) platform sinking. This occurred almost at the same time as a second set of allegations regarding its supposed role in the assassination of a human rights militant by the Nigerian government. These events pushed its senior management to explicitly question the assumptions it has had on how to engage with stakeholders, and all associated engagement policies from top to bottom. Shell's then Chairman, after considering the dilemmas involved, decided to dedicate serious resources to engaging with such interest groups.[12] Its commitment to contribute to sustainable development—and to allow itself to be tested and contested according to this criterion—has become deeply embedded in all types of procedures and operational and decision practices within the Group.

Shell's current set of initiatives were initiated in reaction to outside pressure; but the reaction strengthened, updated, and reviewed a policy which went in the direction which this book espouses. It has gradually crystallized into a view that a core part of the corporate strategy must be being a trust-worthy proactive partner in the dialogue with environmental and other stakeholder groups. Thus it converges with the strategic approach which Tixier is beginning to explore with the CEO of EDF.

EDF: working toward a vision of sustainable development

Tixier's work has begun to stretch beyond the focus on internal union–management relations. Starting in 2001 he began to serve primarily as a speaking partner to the CEO, Roussely, around building a comprehensive approach to stakeholder relations, including involving new groups beyond traditional labor unions. That initiative is, interestingly, converging with Ramirez' work at Shell around the concept of "sustainable development."

In conversations with Roussely, Tixier has been involved in crystallizing a stakeholder-based strategy with a broad scope. It includes some familiar elements, including a deep strategic dialogue with unions and wider workforce involvement. The most significant added element includes stakeholders beyond the firm—like Shell, focusing especially on the strategy of sustainable development (see Chapter 6). Roussely's strategy is to try to make deals with national and local communities in which the enterprise is embedded. The North American model of free markets has lost a great deal of its attraction after crises experienced in deregulated markets such as California. EDF's strategy is to position itself as a firm that respects a range of interests. It has adopted policies that try to preserve local employment levels, or to encourage alternative employment, as well as preserving the environment. Within France another important part of the company's strategy is to have a very high level of customer satisfaction. EDF is in fact the most highly rated public enterprise.

It must be recognized that such a strategy is more feasible in a situation like EDF's where direct competition is still muted and the major business problem is to increase market share: scarcely 30 percent of the electricity market has been opened to competition in France. This percentage will increase in the next few years; but even when EDF's capital becomes more available on public markets, the bulk will remain in public hands.[13] This muting of the market is also characteristic of many infrastructural industries like power or transportation.

The system of dialogue at EDF continues to focus on new union–management agreements and includes the traditional system of top-level discussions established after the Second World War. But the vision has now broadened to include more direct input from the work force and also more attention to stakeholders outside the firm.

Building worker representation outside traditional unionism
Heckscher has worked on another dimension of the change process—the development of new stakeholders, in particular a group called Working Today, founded in 1998 to represent the interests of mobile workers. Industrial unions are limited by the fact that they are anchored in particular employers: they are set up to preserve jobs, not to help people move between jobs. For a significant part of the work force, however, the key need is the ability to manage careers across employers. This includes many temporary workers at the low end who have always lacked security; but it also includes an increasing number of workers who embrace mobility by choice, as freelancers and part-timers who value flexibility and opportunities for self-development.

All of these contingents, both voluntary and involuntary, lack societal support for their mobility: most of our institutions are set up on the assumption that workers will stick with one company. In the US the most glaring issue is health care. Working Today has made its first priority the setting up of flexible and affordable health care insurance that people can carry and rely on across jobs. This has required a very long process of bending and massaging regulations that are designed to be employer-based in order to base them in associations.

The original aim of Working Today was a more familiar one of building a mass movement to resist employer layoffs. As a member of the original board Heckscher played a role in rethinking this vision; it gradually evolved toward a rather different one of embracing mobility and helping people deal with it effectively. It also adopted a strategy of bringing together existing employee associations, as opposed to trying to build a mass membership directly; with associations such as Asian Women in Media, Solid Rock Christian Center, the Translators and Interpreters Guild, and Women Employed, it quickly attained a reach of over 75,000 affiliated members, serving as a "hub" providing information, services, and the power of numbers.

The vision of helping mobile employees is still far ahead of the reality: many parts of the vision exist in rudimentary form or not yet at all. Working Today could in time become a coordinator of lifelong learning for its members; it could provide information about prospective employers and data that can help people in negotiating better conditions; it could offer services in addition to health care, including pensions and access to investment advice. It could also serve to set standards of employment in industries where it is well established, by using the power of publicity and lobbying to pressure the worst employers to come up to the general level. It could coordinate the knowledge market, developing service exchange networks among freelancers and facilitating knowledge exchange. And it could support many local associations with advice and contacts to overcome their frequent isolation and build broader and more effective strategies.

Working Today in this vision could help to address the needs of many groups that are left out of the neo-corporatist stakeholder framework, and it could help with the development of a large existing body of associations that remain organizationally weak and unsure of their direction. It aims to develop the power to represent workers effectively without relying on centralized rule-based contracts. These innovations, if they succeed, could contribute to the eventual development of a new stakeholder regime.

Building a network of stakeholders to shape the health care system
One strand of Maccoby's work, moving beyond the domain of single corporations, has tried to build new stakeholder forums considering major policy issues. Starting in 1986, Maccoby began working on the issue of health care in the US. He became facilitator of the bipartisan National Leadership Commission on Health Care Reform which resulted in a report that called for universal health insurance, improved quality of care and administrative reform to cut costs. When the Clinton administration took over, the Commission was working with the Democratic and Republican leadership in the Senate. The failure of the Clinton initiative led to the formation of a National Leadership Coalition on Health Care, with over 100 companies, unions, religious groups and non-profits.

Maccoby helped this group to set an agenda and then organized a study of some of the best examples of leadership of health care organizations. His goal has been to understand what leaders need to do to improve quality and productivity. A major problem is the variability of treatment of the same health problems. This causes increased costs and contributes to medical errors. Maccoby's report "Leadership for Health Care in the Age of Learning" (2001) analyzes the need for health care management to move from a craft form of production to the co-production model appropriate to knowledge-solutions work. Since physicians are trained in the craft mode, leaders must face resistance and overcome it with education, dialogue and incentives.

CONCLUSION

Economic change may break apart established relationships, but it does not do away with the need for relationships. Adam Smith was among the first to note the dangers that economic development can pose for morality and community. Those that think that increased wealth alone can cure all conflicts have been proven wrong time and again. The great periods of economic advance have always brought in their wake unrest and conflict as groups seek to reconstruct social bonds, to re-establish non-economic values, and to redefine the identities that unite them.

The present moment is only the most recent iteration of a centuries-old cycle in which economic liberalization first drives like an errant locomotive through the structures of negotiation and interaction among social groups, leaving chaos in its wake. Our view, however, is that the next stages of the process are not inevitable—there are choices. If the various stakeholders—those losing power, those gaining it, those redefining themselves—focus narrowly on their own beliefs and reactions, the result can only be a vicious circle of mistrust and uncontrolled, possibly violent, conflict. If, however, the parties maintain processes of external dialogue and internal reflection, then the course of the transformation may move somewhat more smoothly toward better use of resources and greater equity.

In the space between those alternatives there is room for intervention, for *doing*. Most activists focus on generating power behind their own points of view; but the interventions described in this book involve a different kind of activism, one that tries to create dialogue and relations among those points of view. Our experiences in no way suggest that conflicts can be eliminated, but they do suggest that groups can, with some help, learn from their conflicts instead of repeating them, and that they can through this learning build systems in which the differences can be worked through instead of producing mutually destructive conflicts and increasing depths of anger. This is the belief that has kept us going as we have gradually recognized the magnitude of the challenge involved in shaping post-industrial relations.

NOTES

CHAPTER 1

1. On "co-production," see Normann and Ramirez (1994) and Ramirez and Wallin (2000). We develop the concept further in Chapter 11.
2. In a more technical sense we began by trying to improve the functioning of relational systems but have concluded that they need to be changed in their core principles: thus we are shifting from "within-stage" to "between-stage" intervention, or linear to non-linear. Khalil (1996) is among the more useful technical discussions of the difference.
3. See Weber (1919/1946a, b). In the former he says: "To take a practical political stand is one thing, and to analyze political structures and party positions is another." We suggest that to reflect systematically on the experience of taking a practical political stand is yet another.
4. We recognize that we are simplifying physics here, which is why we add the adjective "classical." In a sense Heisenberg introduced the same problem into physics that we are pointing to in the social realm, but it is far more constantly evident and important for the latter.
5. This criticism is not about unintended consequences. Interveners can of course make the error of an incomplete analysis, as economists are prone to do in ignoring political and cultural factors. But the point here is that *even if* the analysis were complete and perfect, the process of "putting it into action" is anything but a "straight-line" proposition because the person putting it into action has to interact with other people.
6. See also Gilmore, Thomas; Krantz, Jim; and Ramirez (1986, p. 160): "The notion of disturbing a system as the best way to understand it."
7. The "Action research" tradition, well-developed in Scandinavia, takes a similar approach. It is somewhat more grounded in an value-based view that knowledge *should* be democratizing; and it is somewhat less focused on the question of change, or rather tends to treat change more as an unpredictable outcome of shared research. See, for example, Naschold *et al.* (1993).
8. Heckscher's academic advisers in his doctoral work included Talcott Parsons and Lawrence Kohlberg; Tixier's included Michel Crozier and Renaud Sainsaulieu.
9. Ramirez and Tixier interviewed managers at AT&T and Lucent, and officials of the CWA union. Heckscher and Maccoby interviewed managers at EDF and union leaders at CFDT. Maccoby visited Ferrovie dello Stato. Heckscher talked to some of Tixier's contacts in the CGT and CFDT unions.

CHAPTER 2

1. At FS there was one significant attempt to work with middle management, but Necci's behavior only showed the top's lack of commitment to systemic change.

CHAPTER 3

1. AT&T probably made a costly mistake in separating long distance from local services. Charles Brown, then CEO, had grown up in Long Lines which was established in 1883 to connect local exchanges between Boston, NYC, Philadelphia and Washington, DC and between NYC and Albany. It became a company with a strong culture. However, technology was blurring the distinction between local and long distance. It would have been better for AT&T to follow the Swedish model of separating manufacturing from all-distance operations. Today, long distance has become a commodity and has no future for AT&T competing with operational companies offering all distance telephony, including wireless. The government offered to leave the Bell System intact if Brown agreed to spin off Western Electric and much of the Bell Labs (what eventually became Lucent). But Brown had his own vision of being the only global one-stop-shop company for research and development and saw AT&T challenging IBM in computers. This was a fateful decision.
2. In this regard, Florida Power and Light won the Japanese Deming award for quality processes in the late 1980s. Companies throughout the US sent managers to their Quality Institute. However, the costs of service mushroomed because service workers followed the "quality process" exactly. They put away their own practices based on experience of dealing with different types of situations found in Florida, for example, swamps, skyscrapers, and suburbs.
3. The concepts of ideal future and interactive planning were taken from Ackoff (1981).

CHAPTER 4

1. We owe this succinct analysis to Cesare Vaciago, a previous managing director of the Italian Railways.
2. The figures are all from Spirito (1994).
3. Necci, L. & Normann, R. (eds) 1994: p. 261.
4. Spirito, idem.
5. see Normann (1984) for the intellectual basis of this approach.
6. Ramirez described the scenarios methodology in *Futures* in 1996.
7. On the 15 of February 1994, Ramirez left his full-time position in SMG to accept becoming an associate professor of management at HEC, France's leading business school. His contract allowed for one day per week of external activities, which he dedicated to consulting—largely with FS.
8. See Amado and Ambrose (2001).
9. One of the people interviewed in the preparation of this chapter noted that while Necci had indeed successfully "activated mechanisms from private investors," he had also been lucky upon coming into FS. Apparently, FS was one of the very few places in the Italian public sphere in which budgets that had previously been voted, had not yet been spent. And the sums involved were considerable. Necci's skills in navigating the system, which he had previously acquired in Eni, proved helpful in unblocking the already voted sums.
10. The documents were: "ASA: Mobilita media-lunga Vercorrenza" (middle and long distance mobility); "ASA: Mobilita metropolitana e regionale" (metropolitan and regional mobility); "ASA: Real Estate development Document for the strategic plan, draft." It relates to the future of Metropolis, a company created by Necci to manage all real-estate-related FS assets; "ASA: Logistica Integrata. Documento di piano strategico 1995–2004: Discussion draft" (multi-modal freight); one for the network; and an overall "Conto economico per business: Hypothesis for rendering costs more efficient."
11. Ramirez and Wallin (2000).
12. One of Ramirez's doctoral students, Flavio Vasconcellos, would later (1996–97) do a study of FS for his doctoral dissertation, and determine that such a structure was excluded on the grounds that it would prevent the accountability which management officially sought to implement! Instead, the ASA's would give way to divisionalization, with clear bottom line result accountability.

CHAPTER 6

1. The general opinion is less negative regarding the most decentralized structures (the under CMP?) that allowed a link between industry reform and the most immediate and concrete work issues.
2. The second most popular union, the CFDT, generally obtains about 23% of the vote; Force Ouvrière (FO) gets around 13%, and the mid-level management union between 5% and 7%, while the CFTC gets another 5%.
3. Tixier was then directing the public interest group on industrial change (GIP), a research laboratory financed by large industries and under the control of the National Center for Scientific Research (CNRS). His team included Laurent Duclos and Nelly Mauchamp.
4. On the origins of the agreement and its tribulations, see Laurent Duclos, "L'accord emploi comme instrument de gestion des relations professionnelles," *Cahiers des Relations Professionnelles*, no. 12, May 1998, pp. 57–58.
5. The three others were the CFTC, the CGT–FO, and the CFE–CGC. GDF (Gaz de France) was a co-signatory on the management side.
6. In some bodies, the majority signatory union—either the CFDT or the FO—demanded to have a higher number of representatives at the negotiating table than other unions.
7. Cf. *Liaisons Sociales*, attached to no. 12367, Tuesday February 25, 1997. FO was also opposed to the development of collective experiments in reducing work hours. Theoretically, these were supposed to rely on voluntary participation, but they could become the occasion, according to FO, for "intolerable pressure."
8. The agreement's target was more ambitious than the contract since it called for 15,000 hirings.
9. The Economy and Finance Minister, Dominique Strauss-Kahn, even wanted to come and congratulate the negotiators publicly but they refused because it would make the industry appear a sort of appendix to the state. He could only declare on television that it was a "good agreement."
10. The content of the anticipated measures also differed from the previous one. It allowed a passage to 35 h for all personnel without loss of salary, though pay rises were moderated. The working hours of office staff (over which the previous agreement had not been very innovative) was dealt with explicitly. And it extended the previous arrangements with respect to planned retirement. It stated that departures should be "compensated for by overall hirings within the company as a whole."
11. The right of opposition could be exercised before the courts when the union wanted to void an agreement. In order to do this, it had to have at least 50% of the votes in staff elections.
12. "Oui, mais . . . à la concurrence Européenne," Interview with Denis Cohen by Hervé Nathan, *Libération*, February 17, 1999.
13. "Previously we had the reputation of privileging force and of taking to the streets. The fact that the CGT now engages in negotiations has contributed a lot to unfreezing the EDF's situation . . . Unionism means struggle but also negotiation, and we are rediscovering something that had been forgotten." Interview with Denis Cohen, *Libération, op. cit.*
14. "La CFDT se félicite de l'unité syndical retrouvée chez EDF–GDF," Interview with Bruno Léchevin by Dominique Gallois, *Le Monde*, January 26, 1999.

CHAPTER 7

1. There are no widely accepted maps to the field of intervention. Chin & Benne (1985) distinguish three types: *Rational–empirical* strategies—using logic, research, expertise to drive change; *normative–reeducative* strategies—developing new skills in group interaction, fostering growth and development, etc.; and *power–coercive* strategies. The approach we sketch here does not fall into any of these buckets: it has elements of the first two but goes beyond them in its attention to sociodynamic aspects and in its systemic focus.

For an extremely good overview of what we are calling the interactive approach to management consulting, see Weisbord (1987).

2. Kaplan & Norton (1992).

3. Of course the distinction between the expert and interactive approaches is drawn here in an "ideal-type" way which exaggerates their separation. There are many "gray areas." Most expert consultants do think about the dynamics of the client organization and conduct dialogues at least with the leadership to try to adapt their ideas to those conditions. On the other hand, most interactive consultants have some "bag of tricks" that they frequently pull out.

4. Roethlisberger & Dickson (1939); Lewin (1951); McGregor (1960).

It is worth re-emphasizing that the distinction between expert and interactive approaches is not absolute. Many "experts" in practice do a lot of "sounding out" of their clients as they develop recommendations; many interactive methods involve prepackaged "processes" for dialogue. We ourselves bring expert knowledge of organizational systems and labor-management relations to the task; we do not stay with the "pure" facilitative role that eschews all content. The two approaches are fundamentally different in theory, but as is often the case real life tends to draw them closer together.

5. Trist & Murray (1990).

6. Davis & Cherns (1975).

7. Ackoff (1981).

8. Schön was an important helper for Ramirez in his doctoral work on organizational aesthetics (Ramirez 1987, 1991) and prefaced Normann and Ramirez's book (1994). Heckscher worked with Argyris at the Harvard Business School, as well as with both Walton and McKersie; Maccoby has long been colleagues with Schön, Normann, Walton, and Crozier. Churchman and Crozier were both doctoral advisers for Ramirez.

See Ackoff (1981); Schön (1984) Argyris (1970), (1985), and (1990); Argyris & Schön (1978); Walton & McKersie (1965); Crozier (1964).

9. One good criticism of the top-down approach is Beer *et al.* (1990). The pioneers of the focus on dealing with rapid change in an interactive mode were probably Emery & Trist (1965).

10. There are of course some types of intervention that might be called "facilitative" that do bring out non-rational issues, including the 1960s "T-group" approaches that go to the extreme on this side. But these have become much less popular in recent years, and the pendulum has swung heavily to the notion of facilitation as the organizing of rational/business analysis in a group—which is why we focus on it here.

11. So many writers have explored or touched on aspects of the interactive approach that we cannot attempt a systematic list. In addition to those cited above, however, we should mention John Forester's work, drawing on Jurgen Habermas' philosophy of communication, which is perhaps the most systematic effort to conceptualize dialogue as a force for change (Forester (1999); Habermas (1984), (1991)). Mike Beer and colleagues' particularly thorough approach to dialogue in large corporations is also of great interest (see Beer & Rogers (1997)). A recent strand has been the development of dialogues in large systems of thousands of people (Dannemiller Tyson Associates (2000)). From our perspective, however, all of these underestimate the power of "sociodynamic" forces from the past, as discussed in the next section.

12. We use the word "sociodynamic" to highlight the analogy to psychodynamics, but it is not primarily about individuals: individual pathologies can affect organizational functioning, but we are concerned here with the persistence of *organizational* patterns.

13. A major debate in the strategy literature can be interpreted in these terms. Hamel & Prahalad (1990) argue that the key capacity of corporations is, in effect, their ability to forget the past; but others emphasize on the contrary the development of core competencies. Empirical studies have favored the latter: for example, Roggi's (1999) evidence from the UK finds that "the results . . . are consistent with the notion of firms disclosing core competence along path dependency." (On path dependency, see Comfort 1997).

14. This sociodynamic side of organization is touched on by a number of fields, especially anthropology and the more qualitative studies of culture. Long ago Mills (1951) & Whyte (1956) noted the pressures for conformity that spread through large corporations, rejecting

diversity and suppressing conflict; Kanter (1977) is a keen observer of the way embedded attitudes and routines locked in discrimination against women; Jackall (1988) has shown the patterns that lead to short-term thinking and avoidance of responsibility. This remains, however, a very scattered field and has produced few generalizations helpful to interveners.

15. On social character, see Maccoby (1976, 2003). A good analysis of the disjunction between traditional character and new business cultures is Leinberger & Tucker (1991).

16. We are not making a theoretical criticism of Marxism here, but we are noting that in practice it is often seized upon not for its theoretical correctness but because it justifies a desire to overthrow the boss rooted in issues of self-respect.

17. For more elaboration of the sociodynamics of dominant-subordinate groups, see Hall & Heckscher (2002).

18. See Heckscher (1995).

19. See The New York Times, Thursday, May 31, 2001: "Pride and Practicalities Loom Behind Failed Lucent 'Merger' " by Seth Schiesel.

20. On the debate concerning the difficulty of changing identities, see Gioia *et al.* (2000).

  The few sustained reflections on how to change these deep identity aspects of organizations have stressed one important theme: the need to link the future to the past—helping the participants to see the direction they are moving as in crucial ways continuous with their past experiences rather than a rejection of them. But writers disagree on how much room there is for reinterpreting the past.

21. Emile Durkheim (1947) was one of the first to discuss the creation of value systems in times of crisis. In such situations identity becomes profoundly destabilizing. When systems of social status break down people begin to refer to smaller "tribal" reference-groups and to hold to these limited identities with fierce determination; they will destroy outsiders who threaten them and even destroy themselves if it seems they cannot hang on to their self-respect.

  There are many paradoxes in the operation of identity. For example, some unionists have a "militant" identity—they define themselves as fighters, and their relation to management as one of deep distrust. On the surface this seems radical rather than conservative. But the underlying conservatism is visible in the fact that they cannot give up this identity even when it would be in their interests to do so: they are "locked into" a militant mode, and they continuously recreate the conditions for it by interpreting management as malevolent and acting in ways that make management more likely to be malevolent. The converse pattern is even more common on the management side.

  Many writers on trust suggest that trust is fragile and that it is always easier to fall back into mistrust. This doesn't make sense, however: if it were true human society would be impossible. The view of trust as grounded in an identity-based relationship helps correct the proposition: What is difficult is to move away from the *established level* of trust. It is just as difficult to decrease trust as to increase it: we see constantly in our work how even in the most difficult circumstances, union and management leaders who have established a certain relation try to come back to it, and will work enormously hard to avoid it degenerating.

22. See Nonoka (1988).

  The "systemic" scope has some relation to "systems thinking" as advocated by Senge (1990); Ackoff (1981); or Churchman (1979), but (as with many concepts in this book) takes a different angle on it. We are not focusing on the way in which actors in the system "should" think, although that is important; we are focusing here on the way in which *interveners* need to think in terms of structuring their actions.

23. James (1907). Richard Normann makes a similar distinction in the management realm: he argues that leaders of change must understand and integrate both the "WoB" and the "WoM," the "World of Business" and the "World of Management."

24. Decision-making also involves cognitive analysis, of course, as well as non-rational factors. Our role has been less on the analytics (with the exception of Ramirez and Normann), more on the "politics" of change.

CHAPTER 8

1. We are aware that the plural of "forum" is "fora," but we feel that correctness in this case is also pedantic.
2. A highly developed form of participant research is the "profiling" method used by Michael Beer & Russ Eisenstat. See Beer and Rogers, (1997). They generally put together a team of prestigious managers to conduct research throughout the company and to report to the top team, thus catalyzing a multi-day review of the organizational systems.
3. Argyris (1991).
4. Fisher & Ury (1981). The real origin of the approach goes back 15 years before that, to the concept of integrative bargaining of Walton & McKersie (1965).
5. Necci & Normann (1994). For a methodological discussion, see Ramirez (1996)
6. Many articles and books have been written on "scenario planning" (see Ringland (1988); van der Heijden (1996); Schwartz (1991)). Ramirez has described his approach at greater length in Ramirez (1996).
7. The notion of an "ideal future" was first developed by Ackoff (1981).
8. The original 7S model was developed by Peters & Waterman (1982). There are various versions of the "Ss," and Maccoby changed his list a bit as he went along, but the basic framework is constant.
9. The "gap survey" simply asks people to assess on a scale of 1 to 5 how *important* each element is to achieving the ideal future and how *well* it is currently practiced.
10. On the Xerox culture change effort, see Autier and Ryan (1998); and Schlesinger *et al.* (1991). The consultants' own version, which differs a good deal from these, is Kearns and Nadler (1992).
11. See Tixier (1992); Heckscher (1995).
12. Personal communication.
13. Bahr (1998): p. 226.
14. On the problem of the alienation between union leadership and the local base, see, for example, Tixier (1992).

CHAPTER 9

1. At times this "speaking partner" role carries a price: when this relationship is accentuated it reduces one's power to cut across other boundaries and to "float" through the organization making new connections: everyone starts to see you as an agent of that actor.

    Nevertheless, this is an interactive role in two senses. First, our value as speaking partners comes from the fact that we are outside the web of organizational relationships: leaders can speak freely to us in a way they cannot speak to any of their subordinates, peers, or superiors because we are not in the political game. Second, we do not play the expert: we write no reports and develop no elaborated analyses. We seek to reflect the leader's thinking, sometimes developing clarifying concepts or typologies that crystallize things. We bring our own experience and knowledge to the interaction, but we do not produce expert advice that can be attributed to us and used in the process of implementation.
2. Argyris (1991).
3. This position as an "outsider" is analogous to that of a psychoanalyst, whose "leverage" comes from being outside the patient's sphere of relations. It is because the analyst does not "counter-transfer"—that is, respond to the patient's invitations to enter into a real-world relationship—that he can help the patient to overcome old patterns and establish new ways of relating. This analogy should not be treated literally—we are dealing with organizations instead of individuals; but in just the same way it is our refusal to become enmeshed in existing organizational politics that gives us some ground to stand in trying to change them.

4. Tixier has used larger teams to conduct research projects in certain specific phases of his intervention, but he has carried the relational part— helping people to hear, interpret, and use the research—on his own.

5. See Krantz and Gilmore (1991).

6. Wooldridge and Micklethwait (1996).

7. On the paradoxical relation of truth and action, see Weber (1946/1918).

8. The ethnopsychoanalyst Georges Devereux has elaborated this identity dynamic in *De l'angoisse à la méthode* (1980). This author, who worked with African tribes, suggests that the position of interacting with and studying a social group that is strange to the observer provokes anxiety in the researcher which is a kind of signal of the differences that he experiences; this provokes identity confusion in him, and it is by working through this confusion that he comes to understand the identity of the other. We should also note the affinity with Weber's concept of *Verstehen* (empathy) as central to sociological method.

9. Sometimes the issue is not even between unions and management: it is difficult to win the trust of competing unions with differing values. Tixier, for example, has never been trusted by the CGT as much as by the CFDT.

10. The current CEO of SBC, one of the most successful of the "Baby Bells," was once a QWL coordinator within AT&T. This experience has clearly shaped the fact that SBC has one of the best union relations in the industry.

11. This assessment is based on Heckscher's interviews and workshops at Saturn since 1989.

CHAPTER 10

1. On the concept of "business logic," see Normann & Ramirez (1994).

2. The last qualifier is important. Partnerships can remain quite stable in stable economic environments: the Shell plant in Sarnia, Canada, has continued with a remarkable level of peace since 1978, and European examples may go back even further. But when competitive pressures heat up, the partnerships almost inevitably break down in rancor.

3. A particularly well-researched and persuasive argument for the strategic importance of engaging stakeholders is Kotter & Heskett (1992).

4. See Amadieu (2001).

5. On the problems of generalizing the Saturn model, see Rubinstein & Kochan (2001). There are other isolated cases in these countries of a different kind of relationship. In Canada (very similar to the US in its basic labor relations system) there is a Shell plant in Sarnia that has operated for over twenty years with an extremely short contract that leaves out most of the normal details. The Xerox plant in Rochester and the Harley–Davidson plant have had some positive results. But these special cases have never drawn much of a following.

6. In Europe, unlike the US, managers may be unionized—but almost always in different unions from workers; the problem of exclusion is merely displaced into a problem of division.

7. Here and in the next chapters we adopt a view that neo-corporatism is the common form of stakeholder relations across the industrialized world. Though there is no general agreement on terminology, "corporatism," especially in the French context, refers to a role for professions or trades in the state; "neo-corporatist" is more usually used to refer to the tripartite labor–management–government system (Tixier 1996b; Schmitter 1983).

Some major reviews of the field agree with our usage in characterizing essentially all industrialized systems as (neo-)corporatist (Williamson 1985; Schmitter 1983). Others would exclude the US or other nations from the neo-corporatist category. Our view is that this depends on the definition and the use one wants to make of the concept; for our purposes, defined in terms of the role of collective bargaining and government regulation, the concept applies across the board, including the US.

8. Strictly speaking, managers in the US are allowed to join unions but, unlike blue-collar workers, are not protected from retaliation. The effect is the same as a simple prohibition.

CHAPTER 11

1. Bell (1973). The post-industrial theme has been taken up by many others; we have been particularly influenced by Piore *et al.* (1984). Applied to corporate organization, a frequent term for this systemic divide has "post-Fordism": see, for example, Sabel (1981). For a more recent, solid overview see also Best (1990).

2. On the concept of corporatism, see above Chapter 11, footnote 6.

3. A large literature on economic varieties of capitalism can be roughly divided into two themes: (1) those that emphasize the difference between high-trust, collaborative regimes like Germany and Japan, and low-trust free-market regimes like the US (Jeffrys, 1995; Albert, 1991; Hollingsworth, 1997b); and (2) those that emphasize the transition from industrial to post-industrial regimes (Coriat, 1997; Piore and Sabel, 1984; Best, 1990). In our terms these respectively focus on "horizontal," synchronic differences, and "vertical," diachronic development.

4. The literature on types of capitalist *stakeholder regimes* (distinct from, though related to, discussion of capitalist *economic* forms—see footnote 3) is rich and varied. We do not really mean here to propose a full-blown alternative to Esping-Anderson's (1990) widely used typology of liberal, social-democratic, and conservative regimes, or to others of the sort. Our picture could as easily be drawn as a triangle: it would fit closely with Hyman's (2001) triangle of society, class, and markets (with society = social dialogue; class = social contest; economy = economism). The simple straight-line here is simply the clearest way of highlighting the fundamental point we are making: that all the differences are secondary to the larger difference between industrial and post-industrial regimes.

5. Boeri *et al.* (2001: p. 15). The exceptional case is the Nordic countries, where labor membership has risen in the last few decades; but both qualitative and quantitative studies suggest that the apparent strength is due to union management of unemployment and pension funds, masking the underlying loss of commitment to labor and the welfare state. Boeri *et al.* (2001) do a very thorough econometric and social analysis of the Nordic "Ghent system"; they conclude that although it has many attractive features it is probably not a solution to the general problem of union decline.

6. The two studies we refer to are by Hyman (2001) and Boeri *et al.* (2001). Hyman's qualitative study of different labor approaches focuses on Italy, Germany, and the UK; but in his last chapter he concludes, as we do, that all of these are variants of social democracy and all face the same fundamental problems. Boeri *et al.*, after a stunningly careful and wide-ranging review of evidence from across Europe, conclude that the forces causing the decline of unions are unlikely to be reversed by any currently visible solution. A third major review, by Waddington *et al.* (2000), is a bit more cautious but outlines in a similar way a set of key problems facing labor movements in all the EU nations. Western (1995) is also in the same line.

7. There were other periods of major stakeholder battles even in the short history of the US. The Civil War was in this sense a fight in which the North tried to change the rules of the game to fit new economic realities. There were major struggles as the working class began to emerge in the 1880s; these did not lead to a new regime because the working-class institutions were largely defeated. Further struggles before the First World War led to a regime in which craft unionism had a key role, with little government regulation.

8. See Tixier (1996b).

9. On the community of loyalty, see Heckscher (1995: ch. 2). Though many people treat the Japanese tradition of lifetime employment as a special case, it was in fact the implicit norm in large corporations throughout the industrialized world (the only difference, perhaps, being that the Japanese extended it more to blue-collar as well as white-collar employees).

10. Slichter *et al.* (1960).

11. For summaries of these, see Freeman and Medoff (1984) and Towers (1996).

12. Ramirez and Normann (1994) and Ramirez (1999).

13. The figures given refer to the PP&E as a percentage of market value of debt plus equity in the non-financial corporate sector (Blair & Kochan 2000: 1).

14. Ramirez (1999).
15. The framework of "co-production" should also be applied to stakeholder groups themselves, including the relation to their own members as well as with people outside their membership. The notion of co-production relations has roots in economic and social theory dating back at least three centuries. It is an evolution beyond the notion of value as coming from the activities that brought it into being, as in Adam Smith and Marx. It is closer to Simmel (1977: 82) in treating value as residing in the actions and interactions that the acquired resource supports (see Ramirez, 1999).
16. For example, " . . . the median decline in the equity value of $5 billion-plus stock buyouts of U.S. companies is an eye-popping 23.8 percent, according to an analysis by Salomon Smith Barney." N. Deogun and S. Lipin, 2000. "Takeover Stocks' Premiums Are Starting to Fizzle Out." *Wall Street Journal Online*, October 16, 2000.
17. Heckscher (1988: ch. 4).
18. Coleman (1997) is one of the few attempts to examine the role of stakeholders in transitional situations. He notes the conservative effects of what we are calling "old" stakeholders, but also their importance in stabilizing the system so that the "new" demands do not become merely chaotic.
19. See Heckscher (1995).
20. This paragraph, though telegraphic, is based on considerable evidence of problems that unions face not just in one country or another, but across the board. For further discussion of the difficulty of union relations with emerging stakeholder groups, see Heckscher and Palmer (1993); on their inability to define a strategy toward worker participation, see Heckscher, Charles (1988: ch. 8). Concerning unions' problems in appealing to contract workers, younger workers, and those in new industries, see Boeri *et al.* (2001), *passim.*; Waddington and Hoffman (2000: 30ff).
21. The United Auto Workers of Canada are in some ways an exception: they have cooperated relatively closely with the US Auto Workers' union. Nevertheless, considerable tension still remains because the US union fears that the Canadian one will undercut its wage packages by exploiting the currency differences between the countries.
22. Once again our own experience confirms broader econometric and social studies. The comprehensive review by Boeri *et al.* (2001), for example, demonstrates that a "seniority bias" and focus on job security has distorted union policies throughout Europe and weakened their appeal to many younger workers and those in newer industries.
23. See Hawken *et al.* (2000).
24. There are, of course, companies who are trying to establish relations with "new" stakeholders—see the discussion of Shell below. But these represent not stable system of relationships, but rather than first steps in the construction of such a system.

CHAPTER 12

1. In earlier phases, the labor movement leaned more heavily on one or the other of these two pillars; it was not until the 1930s that power and public acceptance came together. Craft unions at times became quite powerful without appealing to a wider public beyond their memberships; and many mass movements of syndicalism or socialism made grand social claims without establishing the solid organizational strength to make them stick. The most stable parts of the labor movement were narrowly economist, and the wider political goals were embodied in fragile coalitions and ephemeral organizations. In the US this phase lasted for many years, from about the 1880s to the 1930s. The eight-hour day was one early campaign that brought everything together into a very successful claim on management, but it was not until the post-Second World War period that a movement was solidified with the ability both to bargain for member benefits and to affect larger social issues. In other countries, notably in Scandinavia, the acceptance of unions as major social actors took much less time and happened much earlier, though the trajectory was essentially similar.

2. Here we are using the language of political and stakeholder theory. In the language of strategy suggested earlier, the organizing of stakeholders today does not utilize the liquidity that is available. Stakeholders are too "bundled together", they come together as a single "policy", financed by a bundle of taxes—and deliver only according to the universally disliked "minimum common denominator" logic of such bundling.

3. The theory of intersubjective understanding has been advanced particularly by Habermas (1984), and brought into the field of intervention by John Forester (1989). Forester, however, exaggerates what is already, in Habermas' work, a bias towards cognitive understanding.

4. Two excellent histories and overviews of the "process" movement are Weisbord (1987) and Gray (1989). See also the discussion at the start of Chapter 7.

5. The universality of the focus on seniority and job security is well documented by Boeri *et al.* (2001).

6. Particularly relevant here is Argyris and Schon's (1978) argument that organizations are poorly designed for experimental learning and reflection.

7. Amado and Ambrose's (2001) reinterpretation of Winicott's "transitional change" explores this notion of turbulent and uneven transformations.

8. Of course the stakeholder role of women is still far from being as stable or effective as that of unions in the past. Many results are disappointing. Pay differentials in most countries remain high and many occupations remain very skewed in their gender mix. We do not yet know whether this is because the women's movement, and its relation to business, are still evolving, or whether it is because they have stabilized in a relatively weak position.

9. Piore and Sabel (1984) and Putnam (1993).

10. Some readers have pointed out that this view assumes the essential continuity of capitalism—which is true. The analysis is based on an assessment of forces, drawn largely from our practical experiences with the actors, and of course impossible to measure objectively. The forces for a knowledge-based capitalism seem extremely strong; there are significant forces around different *variants* of that (more centralized, more decentralized, etc); but there seem to be few forces for any major *alternative* to it. Of course, revolutions are usually unexpected—but also improbable!

11. This "experimental" conception of social change is rooted in the works of Dewey (e.g. 1938). Many recent analysts have followed the same basic path: for example, Pava's (1986) concept of "normative incrementalism."

12. Trompenaars and Turner (2001).

13. In this vein EDF has moved aggressively to buy companies throughout Europe: EMW in Germany, Montedison in Italy (in alliance with Fiat). This strategy has been much criticized because EDF seems to be manipulating the game—using capital held by the state to buy companies on the free market. The purchases of foreign companies are a way of compensating for the losses to come as the markets are opened. EDF intends to have 50% of its revenues from sources outside France by 2005.

BIBLIOGRAPHY

Ackoff, R., 1981. *Creating the Corporate Future*. New York: John Wiley & Sons.

Albert, M., 1991. *Capitalisme contre Capitalisme*. Paris: Le Seuil (Anglo-Saxon vs. Rhenish).

Albert, S., & Whetten, D., 1985. "Organizational identity." In L. L. Cummings & B. M. Staw (eds.), *Research in Organizational Behavior*, vol. 7. Greenwich, CT: JAI Press: pp. 263–95.

Amadieu, J.-F., 2001. *Le Syndicalisme En Miettes*. Paris: Le Seuil.

Amado, G., & Ambrose, A., 2001. *The Transitional Approach to Change*. Karnac Books.

Argyris, C., 1970. *Intervention Theory and Method: A Behavioral Science View*. Reading, MA: Addison-Wesley.

—— & Schon, D. A., 1978. *Organizational Learning: A Theory of Action Perspective*. Reading, MA: Addison-Wesley.

—— 1985. *Strategy, Change, & Defensive Routines*. Boston: Pitman Publishing.

—— 1990. *Overcoming Organizational Defenses*. Boston: Allyn and Bacon.

—— 1991. "Teaching smart people how to learn." *Harvard Business Review*, May–June: 5–15.

Astrachan, J. H., 1990. *Mergers, Acquisitions, and Employee Anxiety*. New York: Praeger.

Autier, F., & Ryan, J., 1998. "The document company: the social construction and enactment of strategic change." Paper presented at the 18th Strategic Management Society Annual International Conference, November 1998.

Bahr, M., 1998. *From the Telegraph to the Internet*. National Press Books.

Beer, M., & Rogers, G. C., 1997. "*Hewlett-Packard's Santa Rosa Systems Division: The Trials and Tribulations of a Legacy*." Boston: Harvard Business School Case Study N9-498-011 (rev 8-11-1997).

—— Eisenstat, R. A., & Spector, B., 1990. *The Critical Path to Corporate Renewal*. Boston, MA: Harvard Business School Press.

Bell, D., 1976. *The Coming of Post-Industrial Society: A Venture in Social Forecasting*. New York: Basic Books (orig ed. 1973).

Best, M. H., 1990. *The New Competition: Institutions of Industrial Restructuring*. Cambridge, MA: Harvard University Press.

Blair, M., & Kochan, T. (eds.), 2000. *The New Relationship: Human Capital in the American Corporation*. Washington, DC: The Brookings Institution.

Boeri, T., Brugiavini, A., & Calmfors, L. (eds.), 2001. *The Role of Unions in the Twenty-First Century*. Oxford University Press.

Brown, A. D., & Starkey, K., 2000. "Organizational identity and learning: a psychodynamic perspective." *The Academy of Management Review*, 25(1): 102–20.

Chin, R., & Benne, K. D., 1985. "General strategies for effecting change in human systems." In W. G. Bennis & K. D. Benne (eds.), *The Planning of Change.* New York: Holt, Rinehart, & Winston.

Churchman, C. W., 1979. *The Systems Approach and its Enemies.* New York: Basic Books.

Ciborra, C. (ed.), 1997. *Groupware & Teamwork: Invisible Aid or Technical Hindrance?* Wiley Series on Information Systems.

Coleman, W. D., 1997. "Associational governance in a globalizing era: weathering the storm." In Hollingsworth, J. R. & Boyer, R. (eds.), 1997. *Contemporary Capitalism: The Embeddedness of Institutions.* Cambridge: Cambridge University Press: 127–53.

Comfort, L. K., 1997. "Toward a theory of transition in complex systems." *American Behavioral Scientist,* 40(3): 375–83.

Coriat, B., 1997. "Globalization, variety, and mass production: the metamorphosis of mass production in the new competitive age." In Hollingsworth, J. R. & Boyer, R. (eds.), 1997. *Contemporary Capitalism: The Embeddedness of Institutions.* Cambridge: Cambridge University Press: 240–64.

Crozier, M., 1964. *The Bureaucratic Phenomenon.* Chicago, IL: University of Chicago Press (original French ed. 1963).

Dannemiller Tyson Associates, 2000. *Whole-Scale Change: Unleashing the Magic in Organizations.* San Francisco: Berrett-Kohler.

Davis, L. E., & Cherns, A. B. (eds.), 1975. *The Quality of Working Life.* The Free Press.

Deal, T. E., & Kennedy, A. A., 1982. *Corporate Cultures: The Rites and Rituals of Corporate Life.* Reading, MA: Addison-Wesley.

DeGrazia, S., 1948. *The Political Community: A Study of Anomie.* Chicago: The University of Chicago Press.

Devereux, G., 1980. *De l'angoisse à la méthode dans les sciences du comportement.* Paris: Flammarion.

Dewey, J., 1938. *Experience and Education.* New York: Macmillan Company.

—— 1926. *The Public and Its Problems: An Essay in Political Inquiry.* New York: Henry Holt and Company.

Dimaggio, P. J., & Powell, W. W., 1983. "The iron cage revisited: institutional isomorphism and collective rationality in organizational fields." *American Sociological Review,* 48(2): 147–60.

Drucker, P. F., 1969. *The Age of Discontinuity: Guidelines to our Changing Society.* New York: Harper Colophon.

Durkheim, E., 1947. *The Division of Labor in Society.* New York: The Free Press.

Ebbinghaus, B., 1990. "Does a European social model exist and can it survive?" In G. Huemer *et al.* (eds.), *The Role of Employer Associations and Labour Unions in the EMU.* Aldershot/Ashgate: p. 1–26.

Emery, F. E., & Trist, E. L., 1965. "The causal texture of organisational environments." *Human Relations,* 18(1): 21–32.

Esping-Andersen, G., 1990. *Three Worlds of Welfare Capitalism.* Princeton: Princeton University Press.

Fisher, R., & Ury, W., 1981. *Getting to Yes: Negotiating Agreement Without Giving in.* New York: Houghton Mifflin.

Forester, J., 1989. *Planning In the Face of Power.* Berkeley: University of California Press.

—— 1999. *The Deliberative Practitioner: Encouraging Participatory Planning Processes.* Cambridge, MA: MIT Press.

Freeman, R. B., & Medoff, J. L., 1984. *What Do Unions Do?* New York: Basic Books.

Gioia, D. A, Schultz, M., & Corley, K. G., 2001. "Organizational identity, image, and adaptive instability." *The Academy of Management Review*, 25(1): 63–81.

Gray, B., 1989. *Collaborating: Finding Common Ground for Multiparty Problems*. San Francisco: Jossey-Bass.

Habermas, J., 1984. *The Theory of Communicative Action*. Cambridge: Polity Press.

—— 1991. *Communication and the Evolution of Society*. Cambridge, UK: Polity Press (translated and with an introduction by Thomas McCarthy).

Hall, L., & Heckscher, C., 2002. "Negotiating identity." In T. Kochan and R. Locke (eds.), *Negotiations and Change: From the Workplace to Society*. Cambridge, MA: MIT Press.

Hamel, G., & Prahalad, C. K., 1990. "The Core Competence of the Corporation." *Harvard Business Review*, 6: 79–93.

Harrison, B., 1992. "Industrial Districts: Old Wine in New Bottles?" *Regional Studies*, 26, 5: 469–83.

Hawken, P., Lovins, A., & Lovins, L. H., 2000. *Natural Capitalism: Creating the Next Industrial Revolution*. Boston: Back Bay Books.

Heckscher, C., & Palmer, D., 1993. "Associational movements and employment rights: an emerging paradigm?" *Research In The Sociology of Organizations*, 12: 279–309.

—— 1995. *White-Collar Blues: Management Loyalties in an Age of Corporate Restructuring*. New York: Basic Books.

Hirschhorn, L., 1988. *The Workplace Within: Psychodynamics of Organizational Life*. Cambridge, MA: MIT Press.

—— & Barnett, C. K. (eds.), 1993. *The Psychodynamics of Organizations*. Philadelphia: Temple University Press.

Hollingsworth, J. R., 1997. "Continuities and changes in social systems of production: the cases of Japan, Germany, and the United States." In Hollingsworth, J. R. & Boyer, R. (eds.), 1997. *Contemporary Capitalism: The Embeddedness of Institutions*. Cambridge: Cambridge University Press: 265–310 (US vs Japan & Germany).

—— & Boyer, R. (eds.), 1997. *Contemporary Capitalism: The Embeddedness of Institutions*. Cambridge: Cambridge University Press.

Hyman, R., 2001. *Understanding European Trade Unionism: Between Market, Class and Society*. London: Sage Publications.

Jackall, R., 1988. *Moral Mazes: The World of Corporate Managers*. New York: Oxford University Press.

James, W., 1907. *Pragmatism, a New Name for Some Old Ways of Thinking; Popular Lectures on Philosophy*. New York: Longmans, Green, and Co.

Kanter, R. M., 1977. *Men and Women of the Corporation*. New York: Basic Books.

Kaplan, R. S., & Norton, D. P., 1992. "The balanced scorecard: measures that drive performance." *Harvard Business Review* Jan–Feb: 71–79.

Kearns, D. T., & Nadler, D. A., 1992. *Prophets in the Dark: How Xerox Reinvented Itself and Beat Back the Japanese*. New York: HarperCollins.

Kotter, J. P., & Heskett, J. L., 1992. *Corporate Culture and Performance*. New York: The Free Press.

Krantz, T., & Gilmore J., 1991. "Innovation in the public sector: dilemmas in the use of ad-hoc processes." *Journal of Policy Analysis and Management*, 10(3): 455–68.

Leinberger, P., & Tucker, B., 1991. *The New Individualists: The Generation After the Organization Man*. New York: HarperCollins.

Lewin, K., 1951. In D. Cartwright (ed) *Field Theory in Social Science: Selected Theoretical Papers*. New York: Harper & Row.

Maccoby, M., 1976. *The Gamesman: The New Corporate Leaders*. New York: Simon & Schuster.

—— 1988. *Why Work?: Motivating the New Work Force*. New York: Simon and Schuster (2nd edn., Miles River Press, 1995).

—— 1996. "Interactive dialogue as a tool for change." *Research Technology Management*, Sept–Oct: 57–59.

—— 2003. *The Productive Narcissist: The Promise and Peril of Visionary Leadership*. New York: Broadway Books (forthcoming).

Maister, D. H., 1997. *Managing the Professional Service Firm*. New York: The Free Press.

Mayo, E., 1949. *The Social Problems of an Industrial Civilization*. London: Routledge & Kegan Paul.

McGregor, D., 1960. *The Human Side of Enterprise*. New York: McGraw-Hill.

Michels, R., 1962. *Political Parties: A Sociological Study of the Oligarchical Tendencies of Modern Democracy*. New York: Free Press (original ed. *Zur Sociologie des Parteiwesens in der modernen Demokratie*, 1911).

Mills, C. W., 1951. *White Collar: The American Middle Classes*. London: Oxford University Press.

Naschold, F., Cole, R. E., Gustavsen, B., & van Beinum, H., 1933. *Constructing the New Industrial Society*. Assen: Van Gorcum/Arbetslivcentrum.

Necci, L., & Normann, R. (eds.), 1994. *Reinventare l'Italia*. Milan: Arnold Montadadori Editore.

Nonoka, I., 1988. "Toward middle-up-down management: accelerating information creation." *Sloan Management Review*, Spring: 9–18.

Normann, R., 1984. *Service Management*. Chichester: John Wiley & Sons.

—— & Ramirez, R., 1994. *Designing Interactive Strategy: From Value Chain to Value Constellation*. Chichester: John Wiley & Sons.

Pava, C., 1986. "New strategies of systems change: reclaiming nonsynoptic methods." *Human Relations*, 39(7): 615–33.

Peters, T. J. & Waterman, R. H. Jr., 1982. *In Search of Excellence: Lessons from America's Best-run Companies*. New York: Harper & Row.

Piore, M. J., & Sabel, C. F., 1984. *The Second Industrial Divide: Possibilities for Prosperity*. New York: Basic Books.

Powell, W. W., 1990. "Neither market nor hierarchy: network forms of organization." *Research in Organizational Behavior*, 12: 295–336.

Putnam, R. D., 1993. *Making Democracy Work. Civic Traditions in Modern Italy*. Princeton, NJ: Princeton University Press.

Ramirez, R., 1985. "A participative socio-technical approach to occupational health and safety." In S. Bagnara, R. Misiti, & Wintersberger (eds.), *Work and Health in the 1980's: Experiences of Direct Worker's Participation in Occupational Health*. Berlin: Allemagne.

—— 1996. "Reinventing Italy: Methodological Challenges." *Futures*, 28: 241–54.

—— 1999. "Value Co-Production: Intellectual Origins and Implications for Practice and Research." *Strategic Management Journal*, 20(1): 49–65.

—— & Normann, R., 1994. *Designing Interactive Strategy*. Chichester: John Wiley & Sons.

—— & Wallin, J., 2000. *Prime Movers: Define Your Business or have Someone Define it Against you*. Chichester: John Wiley & Sons.

Ringland, G., 1998. *Scenario Planning: Managing for the Future*. New York: John Wiley & Sons.

Roethlisberger, E. J., & Dickson, W. J., 1939. *Management & the Worker*. Cambridge, MA: Harvard University Press.

Roggi, O., 1999. "Why ambition fails post-privatisation: Evidence from the Water Industry in UK." Paper Accepted to the Strategic Management Society 19th Annual International Conference Berlin, 3–6 October 1999.

Rubinstein, S. A., & Kochan, T. A., 2001. *Learning from Saturn: Possibilities for Corporate Governance and Employee Relations*. Ithaca, New York: Cornell University Press.

Sabel, C. F., 1981. *Work and Workers in the Age of Fordism and Its Decline*. Cambridge: Cambridge University Press.

Salaman, G., 1977. "An historical discontinuity: from charisma to routinization." *Human Relations*, 30(4): 373–88 (Also in Allen, R.W. and Porter, L.W. (1983): 208–222).

Salisbury, R. H., 1979. "Why no corporatism in America?" Chapter 8 in Schmitter, Philippe C., and Lehmbruch, Gerhard, *Trends Towards Corporatist Intermediation*. Beverly Hills: Sage Publications.

Schein, E. H., 1985. *Organizational Culture and Leadership*. San Francisco: Jossey-Bass.

—— 1987. *Process Consultation: Lessons for Managers and Consultants*. Reading, MA: Addison-Wesley.

Schlesinger, L., Jick, T., Johnson, A. B., & MacIsaac, L. A., 1991. "Xerox Corporation: Leadership Through Quality (A) & (B)." Harvard Business School Case 9-490-008 (rev. 6/19/1991).

Schmitter, P. C., 1983. "Democratic theory and neocorporatist practice." *Social Research*, 50(4): 885–928.

Schön, D. A., 1984. *The Reflective Practitioner: How Professionals Think in Action*. Basic Books, September 1984.

Schwartz, P., 1991. *The Art of the Long View*. New York: Doubleday.

Senge, P., 1990. *The Fifth Discipline: The Art and Practice of the Learning Organization*. New York: Doubleday/Currency.

Slichter, S. H., Healy, J. J., & Livernash, E. R., 1960. *The Impact of Collective Bargaining on Management*. Washington: Brookings Institution.

Smith, T. S., & Stevens, G. T., 1996. "Emergence, self-organization, and social interaction: arousal-dependent structure in social systems." *Sociological Theory*, 14(2): 131–53.

Spirito, P., 1997. "History of Ferrovie dello Stato." Internal company document, Ferrovie dello Stato, Rome.

Taylor, C., 1989. *Sources of the Self: The Making of the Modern Identity*. Cambridge, MA: Harvard University Press.

Tixier, P.-E., 1992. *Mutation ou Déclin du Syndicalisme? le cas de la CFDT*. Presses Universitaires de France.

—— 1996a. "An impossible French social compromise? The firm as the basis of social regulation." Mimeo: Paris, GIP, Feb. 1996.

—— 1996b. "Les relations professionnelles: un objet d'intervention sociologique." *Revue Internationale de Psychosociologie*, 3(4): 17–30.

Towers, B., 1997. "Collective bargaining, democracy and efficiency in the British and US workplace." *Industrial Relations Journal*, 28(4): 299–308.

Trist, E., & Murray, H. (eds.), 1990. *The Social Engagement of Social Sciences*. University of Pennsylvania Press.

Trompenaars, F., & Hampden-Turner, C., 2001. *21 leaders for the 21st Century*. Capstone.

US Department of Labor, 1985. *Quality of Work Life: AT&T and CWA examine the process after three years*. Washington, DC: US Department of Labor, Bureau of Labor-Management Relations.

van der Heijden, K., 1996. *Scenarios: The Art of Strategic Conversation*. New York: John Wiley & Sons.

Vasconcelos, F. de, 1998. *La Formation des problematiques dans les organisations; une analyse des structures matricielles*. Jouy-en-Josas: Doctoral dissertation, HEC.

Waddington, J., & Hoffman, R. (eds.), 2000. *Trade Unions in Europe: Facing Challenges and Searching for Solutions*. Brussels: ETUI.

Walton, R. E., & McKersie, R. B., 1965. *A Behavioral Theory of Labor Negotiations*. New York: McGraw-Hill.

Waterman, R. H., Peters, T. J., & Phillips, J. R., 1980. "The 7S framework." In J. B. Quinn, H. Mintzberg, & R. M. James (eds.), *The Strategy Process*. New York: Prentice Hall.

Weber, M., 1946. "Politics as a vocation." In H. H. Gerth and C. Wright Mills (translated and edited), *From Max Weber: Essays in Sociology*, New York: Oxford University Press: pp. 77–128 (German ed.: "Politik als Beruf," Gesammelte Politische Schriften (Muenchen, 1921), pp. 396–450. Originally a speech at Munich University, 1918, published in 1919 by Duncker & Humblodt, Munich).

—— 1946. "Science as a vocation." English edition: In H. H. Gerth & C. W. Mills (translated and edited), *From Max Weber: Essays in Sociology*, New York: Oxford University Press: pp. 129–156 (German edition: "Wissenschaft als Beruf," Gesammelte Aufsaetze zur Wissenschaftslehre (Tübingen, 1922), pp. 524–55. Originally a speech at Munich University, 1918, published in 1919 by Duncker & Humblodt, Munich).

Weisbord, M. R., 1987. *Productive Workplaces: Organizing and Managing for Meaning, Dignity, and Community*. San Francisco: Jossey-Bass.

Whyte, W. H., Jr., 1956. *The Organization Man*. New York: Simon and Schuster.

Williamson, P. J., 1985. *Varieties of Corporatism: A Conceptual Discussion*. Cambridge: Cambridge University Press (Rev. in CS 3/87: 198).

Wooldridge, J., & Micklethwait A., 1996. *The Witch Doctors: Making Sense of the Management Gurus*.

Yankelovich, D., 1999. *The Magic of Dialogue*. New York: Simon & Schuster.

Zaleznik, A., 1993. "The mythological structure of organizations and its impact." In Hirschhorn and Barnett (eds.), 1993: ch. 11, pp. 179–89.

INDEX

ABB 205
Accenture 8, 108
accountability 190
"acculturation" process 50
Ackoff, R. 110
action research 109, 158
adversarial bargaining, traditional 66
AFL–CIO 181
  Center for Workplace Democracy 41
AFSCME (American Federation of State,
  County, and Municipal Employees) 146
Air France 86
Alitalia 46
Allen, R. 41
Alphandery, E. 91
America *see* United States
American Association for the
  Advancement of Science 27
American labor movement 168
American market approach 206
American pragmatism 110
American-style pragmatic bargaining 174
American telecommunications 180
American Transtech 35
American unions 175
analyst, role of 44
Anjorlas, G. 89
anti-capitalist ideology 117
anti-capitalist militancy 88
anti-union ideology 36
arbitration 197
Argyris, C. 110, 112, 130
Armstrong, M. 42, 187
ASAs (area strategici d'affari) 57–8, 60
Asian Women in Media 210
asset liquidity 187
AT&T 4, 8, 13, 15, 25–45, 65, 113, 116,
  119–20, 122, 130–3, 136, 139–40, 146,
  149, 151, 153, 156, 158, 161, 165,
  168–71, 173, 175, 179, 186, 188–9, 191
  Long Lines 25, 28–9, 35, 146
  manufacturing arm 67
  Quality of Worklife program *see* Quality
    of Worklife program
  research capability 67

union involvement 31–5
Workplace of the Future *see* Workplace
  of the Future
Auroux Laws of 1982 89
auto industry 33

Bahr, M. 36, 39, 43, 68–9, 75, 140
"balanced scorecard" approach to
  accountability 109
Balzer, R. 31
battlefield community 133
Bell, D. 180
Bell Labs 27–8, 32, 66–7, 120, 191
Bell Marketing System 30
Bell Operating Companies
  (RBOCs) 28
Bell System 25, 27–8, 32–3, 173
  bargaining 29
  break-up of 45
"big bang"
  approaches to intervention 124
  divestiture 78
Blair, M 187
Bloomfield Hills, Michigan 32
Bluestone, I. 27, 29
Bolivar Project 26–9, 32, 109
Borman, F. 114
Boston Consulting Group 108
brainstorming 111
Brent Spar platform sinking 209
bureaucracy
  culture 107, 118
  relationships, history of 83
  stability 80
  structure 184
  transforming 167
bureaucratic-Taylorist management 167
Burlingame, H. 26, 28, 37, 39, 42–3, 45
Bush, G. 97
business
  discontinuities, major 169–70
  logics 53
  strategy 123, 186
  success, dynamics of 173
  unit councils 129